STORY, SIGN, AND SELF

THE SOCIETY OF BIBLICAL LITERATURE
SEMEIA SUPPLEMENTS
edited by
William A. Beardslee

THE SWORD OF HIS MOUTH: FORCEFUL AND IMAGINATIVE
LANGUAGE IN SYNOPTIC SAYINGS
by Robert C. Tannehill

JESUS AS PRECURSOR
by Robert W. Funk

STUDIES IN THE STRUCTURE OF HEBREW NARRATIVE
by Robert C. Culley

STRUCTURAL ANALYSIS OF NARRATIVE
by Jean Calloud, translated by Daniel Patte

BIBLICAL STRUCTURALISM: METHOD AND SUBJECTIVITY
IN THE STUDY OF ANCIENT TEXTS
by Robert M. Polzin

STORY, SIGN, AND SELF: PHENOMENOLOGY AND
STRUCTURALISM AS LITERARY CRITICAL METHODS
by Robert Detweiler

STORY, SIGN, AND SELF
Phenomenology and Structuralism as Literary Critical Methods

by

Robert Detweiler

FORTRESS PRESS
Philadelphia, Pennsylvania

SCHOLARS PRESS
Missoula, Montana

ISBN 0-8006-1505-0

Library of Congress Catalog Card Number 76-9713

5786K77   Printed in the United States of America   1-1505

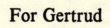
For Gertrud

ACKNOWLEDGMENTS

It is a pleasure to acknowledge the encouragement and helpful criticism of Will Beardslee in the writing of this study; of Laurence Alexander and James Dagenais, my teaching colleagues in interdisciplinary seminars; of Walter Lowe, whose help on Ricoeur was crucial; of John Leavey, whose catholic library and bibliographical directions were indispensable aids; of Walter Enloe, whose help on non-linguistic structuralism was especially valuable; and of Manon Maren-Grisebach, whose excellent survey text of literary critical methods led me to consider composing my own. I owe considerable thanks as well to June Mann, who overcame many distractions in and around my writing to produce, as usual, a fine manuscript. Part of this study was written during a summer spent in Hamburg, Germany with the support of funds from the German Academic Exchange Service and Emory University. I gratefully acknowledge that aid.

TABLE OF CONTENTS

Introduction

This study is intended to accomplish four things. I have written it first as a general overview of phenomenology and structuralism as critical methods for persons who already have a working knowledge of other contemporary literary critical approaches. Since my training as a teacher of literature has been mainly in American new criticism, and since my experience in biblical exegesis has been mostly in historical and form-critical methods, I share, I believe, a common background with a majority of American interpreters of secular and religious texts and can thus place the two Continental methods that are the subject of my study in a framework familiar to most readers.

Other overviews of phenomenology and structuralism respectively already exist, however, that are directed more or less immediately to textual interpretation, and there would be little point in merely duplicating these studies. A second aim, therefore, is to consider literary critical phenomenology and structuralism together and in interaction with each other. Although many critics may have a grounding in one of the two methods, few probably have a foundation in both, and thus my survey can serve as a stepping stone from one method to the other. Since it is my thesis, further (certainly not an original one), that phenomenology and structuralism have much of value to say to each other—indeed cannot develop their fullest potential without each other—I have provided constant points of comparison between the two and have concluded with a comparative-mediatory chapter.

A third and very important aim of my study is to provide an arena where interpreters of secular and religious texts can meet. Both phenomenology and structuralism are ideal for this purpose, since they traverse the historical-disciplinary boundaries that have helped to distinguish between secular and religious texts, and since both, in fact, have already contributed strongly to the dismantling of unnecessary and artificial barriers between the two

1

kinds of critics. I want to promote this healthy turn by giving
many examples of both methods of criticism, phenomenological
and structuralist, applied to secular and religious discourse, in
order to show how much the secular critics and biblical exegetes
have to share and exchange.

My study contains little that is original. It consists in good part
of definitions gathered in part from other persons' definitions, of
summaries of the work of leading methodologists, and of sketches
of representative books and essays. The value of this approach lies
in the strategy of juxtaposition and also, I hope, in providing
other critics with the basic information and groundwork
necessary for them to proceed more efficiently where I have left
off. Although my summaries and sketches cannot, of course,
convey the fullness of the original texts, my hope is that they will
introduce readers to kinds of materials helpful to them and thus
send them, with purpose, to the original texts. The strategy of
juxtaposition functions in the spirit of structuralism and
phenomenology—the latter at least as Paul Ricoeur has
implemented it: new realignments of things inspire new
perspectives on reality. I have also selected a number of
illustrative texts with common and similar subjects (for example,
four texts on the early chapters of Genesis, two on American
romantic writers, two on Jean Genet) in order to enhance the
reader's opportunities for comparison and contrast.

Regarding this modest study as a basis for other studies,
however, I must add that I am aware of offering what is
fundamentally *mis*-interpretation in the hermeneutical sense that
all interpretations are only approximations of a text that never
coincide with the text's full meaning. Since my sketches are
interpretations of interpretations, they perhaps intensify
"misinterpretation," yet even if this is so, I think that they can
serve as a version of Ricoeur's "heuristic fiction," of models that
are deficient in some aspects but still direct one toward new
configurations of meaning.

One of our better critics, in a recent review of a text that takes a
"logical" approach to literary theory, declared his pleasure at the

publication of such a book "At a time when the surest way to
fame as a literary theorist seems to lie in the cultivation of opaque
paradox and bizarre novelty." /1/ I suspect that phenomenology
and structuralism are included in that description or perhaps
meant to be characterized directly—and if they are, he is right.
Much in these two methods indeed projects "opaque paradox"
and some of it still seems bizarre even if it is no longer novel. To
deal with paradox, however, is not necessarily to abandon
rationality—in fact, paradox is a formal category of logic—and
to traffic in the bizarre (real or apparent) is a critical activity as old
as Aristotle.

Thus yet another reason for undertaking a study such as mine is
to help dispel the impression that phenomenology and
structuralism as literary critical methods are mainly hermetic,
eccentric, and gratuitously-complicated approaches. While it is
true that some of the Gallic critics especially have shown a
perverse flair for obfuscation and irritating the reader, I have
become convinced that behind most of the obscurity of the two
methods is the recognition that wonted logic often cannot do
justice to the infinite complexity and subtlety of language and to
the text composed of this intractable language, so that one must
enter into an imaginative struggle with language rather than
trying to discipline it through uncompromising categories.
Anyone who wishes to engage phenomenology seriously cannot
avoid Husserl's original paradox—that one can break through to
a truly radical empiricism only by suspending the presuppositions
of normal empirical inquiry—and structuralism asks for the same
sort of commitment to its project. If it seems nevertheless that the
practitioners of the two methods are merely playing complicated
games, one can only respond, with Lévi-Strauss, that we are all
constantly involved in playing games, and that the game of
Western logic seems serious because we are inside it.

This study, however, does not take a phenomenological or
structuralist approach itself. Rather, I have undertaken to
describe, in a conventional systematic manner, the theoretical
aspects of these methods and the numerous ways in which the

methods have been applied to specific texts. If the two methods are to develop a solid utility, they must interact not only with each other but also with the dominant Western tradition, and I have tried to present them in the context of that tradition. They are, of course, much more crucially a continuing part of the history of Western thought than the strategic exaggerations of Heidegger and Derrida suggest, and I am interested in communicating their accessibility rather than accenting their uniqueness.

A depressing aspect of such an encompassing study is the growing recognition of how much must be ignored. I have done nothing with prominent thinkers connected to the two methods such as Jaspers, Marcel, Dufrenne, Althusser, and Foucault. I regret excluding these and others quite arbitrarily, but one must set limits in order to remain coherent. I have also decided not to enter the "post-structuralist" debate represented by a recent issue of *Contemporary Literature,* on "Directions for Criticism: Structuralism and Its Alternatives," that attempts to relate the two approaches to more conventional criticism. /2/ Although the concerns of this debate would be natural extensions of my study, they would also take it beyond its proper confines. I have, on the other hand, used scores of primary and secondary sources, and without wishing to overwhelm with references, have tried to be scrupulous in giving credit. Where I have failed in this last, as I no doubt have, it is because in the course of preparing such a manuscript one absorbs so much material that it becomes impossible to recover all of the precise loci of information.

NOTES

/1/   Monroe C. Beardsley, review of John M. Ellis's *The Theory of Literary Criticism: A Logical Analysis*, in *Comparative Literature*, 27, No. 2 (Spring, 1976), 177-80.

/2/   *Contemporary Literature*, 17, No. 3 (Summer, 1976). Some representative essays in this issue are Edward W. Said, "Roads Taken and Not Taken in Contemporary Criticism," 327-48; Hayden White, "The Absurdist Movement in Contemporary Literary Theory," 378-403; and Ralph Freedman, "Intentionality and the Literary Object," 430-452.

Chapter I

Basic Concepts of Phenomenology and Structuralism

A. Phenomenology

Phenomenology has its roots in the Continental philosophical tradition, reaching back to Descartes, Kant, and Hegel, and has emerged in terms of reaction to each of these. Edmund Husserl, the founder of phenomenology, wished to retain the radical empiricism of Descartes without accepting Descartes' premises, the skepticism of Kant without his *a priori* categories, and the spirit of universality in Hegel without his metaphysical definition of the term "phenomenology." Kierkegaard, with his arguments against mere logical system-building in philosophy and in favor of constant individual involvement, and Nietzsche, with his attempted exposure of the whole philosophical tradition as vulnerable to nihilistic interpretaiton, were nineteenth century forerunners of Husserl, while the Viennese psychologist Franz Brentano, Husserl's teacher, provided a direct and central contribution through his concept of intentionality that Husserl translated into philosophical terms.

Husserl himself was first a mathematician and then a student of psychology before settling into philosophy as the discipline in which to locate his research on the foundations of a logic that would precede and replace the assumptions of positivism (the dominant philosophical doctrine of the early twentieth century) and of the methods of the natural sciences. In his early works, *Logische Untersuchungen* (1901) and *Ideen* (1913), he began to shape the epistemology that would inspire the approaches of the other first-generation phenomenologists Heidegger, Merleau-Ponty, and Sartre and result in a major philosophical movement of the modern age. /1/

7

Rather than continuing a historical overview (which has already been done better by others), I will turn to the basic terminology of phenomenology and in the process of defining it provide some sense of the evolution of the method. The terms, because they are part of an endeavor to overcome a wonted mode of philosophical thought, are quite difficult to define, and the attempts to render them more exact and lucid have occupied not only the earlier phenomenologists but successive generations as well. Although in the following chapters I will not refer systematically to these terms, nor to the corresponding structuralist terms, because they are not used systematically by the literary critics oriented to phenomenology and structuralism, it is necessary to have the terms in mind as the components of the philosophy out of which phenomenological and structuralist literary criticism has been formed. /2/

Maurice Natanson, a prominent American phenomenologist in his own right, offers this concise definition of our first method: "Phenomenology is an essentially descriptive examination of the noetic and noematic structure of intentional acts as grounded in transcendental subjectivity; and its concern is with a total reconstruction of consciousness, in terms of which science will achieve its rationale, art and religion their validation, and philosophy its own consummation." /3/ This heady statement already contains a number of fundamental phenomenological terms. Taking our cue here, we can enumerate them and the other central concepts that spring from the writings of the "original" four, Husserl, Heidegger, Merleau-Ponty, and Sartre: intentionality, the pre-objective world, intuition, the epoché, the reductions, the life-world, essences, *noesis* and *noema*, and the transcendental ego.

The concept of intentionality for Husserl referred to the intentionality of consciousness, a theory with its roots in Brentano's psychology that Husserl adopted, cleansed of its psychologistic elements, and expanded into a foundation of his "first philosophy." /4/ According to this theory, consciousness is neither a condition nor a faculty but an act, and as such is always object-directed, always consciousness of *something*. This is not to say that consciousness constitutes the world, as is the function of the ego in subjective idealism, but rather that consciousness always necessarily "apprehends" its objects, which simultaneously reveal themselves to consciousness; in this interaction of apprehending and revelation both consciousness and the world of objects "exist."

Heidegger expanded the concept of intentionality to refer not only to the intentionality of consciousness but to the intentionality of *Dasein*, of "being-there," a move that eventually led him to reject phenomenology itself as a hindrance to being in its task of apprehending and revealing itself. /5/ Sartre inverted Husserl's concept of intentionality into a theory of consciousness that shows itself to be a nothingness and is realized only in intentional acts. Out of this strategic shift of emphasis Sartre developed his existential phenomenology: consciousness is existence without essence, and freedom becomes a project of creation and constant re-creation. Merleau-Ponty stressed the thereness of the unified world through the reduction; he argued that intentionality itself is prompted and discovered by the knowledge that we are part of the world's thereness (we might say part of its givenness), and hence our intending of the world's constituents is possible only because we share the identity of those constituents. To intend the object is thus to intend ourselves, and the phenomenological endeavor becomes a grand process of inseparable self-and-world recognition.

The concept of the pre-objective world refers to the arena that is apprehended by the intending consciousness, that gives itself to consciousness, and that we are a part of. It is the world made accessible through the intuition and the epoché and laid bare through the reductive steps. As the world of essences beneath the world of facts, before and at the root of the scientific effort, it is prior to the reflecting and objectifying processes that separate subject and object. It is the world as it is and of which we are before we reorganize it into common-sense, logical, or empirical categories. Husserl understood this world as the world of full human awareness, but Heidegger complicated the concept of pre-objectivity by relating it to pre-reflectiveness, to the world as constituted prior to the ego's domination. /6/ Merleau-Ponty also argued that the pre-objective world exceeds the limitations of the individual ego and tried to show the implications of a "genetical phenomenology"—an effort to develop Husserl's "return to the things themselves" in terms of a fundamental theory of perception. /7/ Perception for Merleau-Ponty is rendered possible through the body's (the phenomenological body's) pre-reflective relationship to the world and its pre-reflective identity with the world.

The concept of intuition has been poorly defined by the phenomenologists. It is not any sort of mystical faculty but an attitude of utter openness combined with a persistent thinking-back, a recollection (for Husserl a *Zurückfragen*), that leads one to original perceptions of the world. /8/ These insights can be said to come through intuition because they are not mediated by everyday logic or empirical research; those are the very intellectual tools that inhibit the intuition by separating subject and object. The insights of the phenomenological intuition, situated through bodily presence in the world (Merleau-Ponty), are self-evident because they result from the unified effort of undifferentiated subject and object. Yet one arrives at such intuitive apodictic insights not "naturally" but through practicing the epoché and reductions. Phenomenological intuition is immediate experience, but that immediacy is achieved only through a disciplined "unnatural" (as we shall see) effort. Robert Magliola includes intuition in two of the steps of his Husserlian hermeneutics, and although this is confusing, since one assumes generally that the intuition is more of an attitude that infuses the hermeneutics, it does underscore the strategic significance of the intuition. /9/

The epoché, a Husserlian term rendered best in English as "suspension," is the essentially negative step that precedes the reductions. /10/ What is suspended is the natural standpoint, the common-sense acceptance of the reality of the world about us. It is a radicalization of Descartes' radical doubt because, as Husserl himself insisted, Descartes failed to distinguish the psychological from the transcendental subject in his doubting process and thus held the *cogito* to be axiomatic, whereas in Husserl's phenomenology the *cogito* is preceded by other constituents of the self. /11/ The epoché is the same as the bracketing process, a term Husserl borrowed from mathematics; the perceptions of the natural world are bracketed, indicating that they are not denied but only temporarily ignored. The resultant attitude is one that promotes "descriptive neutrality" rather than interpretation, not the neutrality of the empirical scientist, whose method is careful inductive observation of the real world based on a commitment to causality, but an attempted presuppositionless neutrality.

The suspension of natural observation and judgment effected in the epoché prepares for the reductions. Considerable divergence exists among the interpreters trying to explain the stages of reduction, and most of the difficulty arises from attempts to describe Husserl's reductive procedures. Quentin Lauer, for example, discusses six reductions that Husserl invents and employs: the psychological, eidetic, and phenomenological reductions are the first three, followed by the reduction that leads to pure subjectivity, the reduction that leads to the transcendental ego, and the reduction that leads to the pure flow of consciousness. /12/ Natanson, on the other hand, explains only the eidetic and transcendental reductions in Husserl, while Joseph Kockelmans says that "Husserl distinguishes a twofold reduction: the 'eidetic reduction' and the complex of reductive phases which he labels the 'phenomenological reduction.'" /13/ But Magliola says that Husserl employs two reductions, the first of which is the phenomenological or transcendental, and the second the eidetic. /14/ Husserl's reductive phases are, in any case, not adopted strictly by the other original phenomenologists (Heidegger, Merleau-Ponty, Sartre), although Heidegger's hermeneutical method of *Aufweisung* (showing), *Freilegung* (exposition), and *Auslegung* (explication), for example, is certainly inspired by Husserl's reductions. /15/

I find a blend of Natanson's and Kockelman's explanations the most helpful and viable. They agree that the eidetic reduction, the first of Husserl's two most important reductions, is an attempt to describe the essence of the residuum left after the epoché is complete, to describe the nature of what remains outside the brackets. The *eidos* (the essence of an object) is exposed in this procedure through systematic but imaginative testing of what can be discarded from the scrutinized object without destroying its identity. For example, a literary critic, having defined a poem apart from all conventional descriptions of the genre, would still inquire what it can yet be reduced to without losing its "poeticity." Further, then, the phenomenological or transcendental reduction brackets *this* residuum still outside the brackets to focus on the pure stream of consciousness, to transcend one's own temporal, historical ego-existence and encounter pure intentionality. In other words, our literary critic would bracket poeticity itself in order to discover himself in the act of intending intentionality. For Sartre, the phenomenological reduction produces a world-transforming nihilation that leads one to an engagement that occurs in total freedom and must re-create the world. For Merleau-Ponty, the reductions reveal not the nothingness of the world in the nihilating power of consciousness but the reverse: consciousness becomes secondary, and the world emerges as the locus, condition, and means of perception.

The life-world *(Lebenswelt)* is somewhat easier to explain. Husserl called it "the moving historical field of our lived existence." /16/ We could just as well describe it as one's personally-experienced history of consciousness. It is the world of one's immediate experience, not the world that one defines through the natural attitude or the categorizations of science but that which one constitutes through the epoché and reductive processes, the world as it gives itself to the intending consciousness. As Merleau-Ponty says, "the world, which I distinguished from myself as the totality of things or of processes linked by causal relationships, I rediscover 'in me' as the permanent horizon of all my *cogitationes* and as a dimension in relation to which I am constantly situating myself." /17/ For Merleau-Ponty, in fact, the life-world does not just appear through the intending consciousness but also includes intentionality. Yet as Kockelmans points out, many Husserl scholars do not agree with Merleau-Ponty that Husserl wished to make the life-world concept that fundamental but argue that he saw beneath it the more basic unindividualized transcendental ego. /18/ The concept of the life-world is especially important for phenomenological literary criticism, for it suggests the possibility of discovering or recovering the authentic personality of a character in fiction or of the author implied in the fiction which cannot be encountered historically or psychologically.

The essences are the "objective sides of experience" and are exposed, in Husserl's system, through the eidetic reduction. /19/ They can be defined most easily by contrast to the empirical-logical understanding of essence. For Husserl, the phenomenological essence is precisely what remains present to consciousness after everything that contributes to the *empirical* constitution of an essence is excluded: factual data such as measurement, temporal-spatial description, and causal relationships. An essence need not have a correlative in the bracketed world of fact, and should not be thought of as a particular, as a Kantian thing-in-itself, or as an absolute. It is the *eidos* not of idealism (not an idea as mental construct) but of the eidetic reduction. As such, it is not a building block in an inductive construction but a momentary particle in a shifting field of consciousness.

Essence is virtually the same as *noema,* and in the description of *noesis* and *noema* (Husserl's terms from the Greek) the concept of the object within the embrace of universal subjectivity becomes clearer. All acts of consciousness are performed by a person, and in that sense they are subjective —of the subject. But the acts are also objective in that they, and not facts or real objects, constitute the substance of consciousness and hence of meaning. This essence of the acted act of consciousness is the *noema* (that which is perceived), while the acting act of consciousness in the *noesis* (the act of perceiving). Alfred Schütz identifies *noesis* and *noema* with *cogitare* and *cogitatum* respectively and says that the noetic refers to that which originates in the mind's activities, while the noematic refers to that which originates in the intentional object. /20/ What happens in the noetic act is closer to the object of study of conventional psychology (although not the same), whereas what happens in the noematic act belongs purely to the realm of phenomenological psychology.

The concept of the transcendental ego springs from a major change in Husserl's thought. In his earlier view consciousness is constituted entirely by intentional acts, and there is no need or place for the ego—a view that Sartre elaborated and defended later against Husserl's shift of position, arguing that the ego is not in consciousness but in the world. But in his *Ideen* Husserl argued that through the transcendental (the second) reduction, in which the eidetic residuum is bracketed, one encounters not a personal or individual ego but the ultimate structure of consciousness, the pure flow of consciousness, the transcendental ego which makes possible the individual ego and its universe. /21/ One sees immediately the great germinal power of this concept that could inspire Heidegger's substitution of *Dasein* for consciousness, or Tillich's "ground of being," or even Jaspers' "borderline situations." For Husserl this transcendental ego is apodictic and hence the source of meaning and value, because it knows itself as the final knowable. One senses also how Husserl could accept this bedrock of consciousness as the foundation for practicing phenomenology as an exact science, indeed as the foundation that the empirical sciences need but have not struck.

This last paragraph leads us out of what is properly merely phenomenological psychology and into areas of phenomenological philosophy, the discipline that treats not only the transcendental ego but also intersubjectivity, time and space, death, etc., and this is as far as we can go and need go to provide a background for phenomenological literary criticism and comparison with structuralism. But before turning to structuralism I wish to provide a more direct transition from this complicated cluster of concepts to my later treatment of phenomenological literary criticism through five interpretive remarks. First, in dealing with phenomenology in connection with literary criticism or any other discipline, one must always seek to keep in mind the effort to reunite subject and object, reflected best perhaps in the tension between Husserl's all-embracing subjectivity (which encompasses all objectness because consciousness constitutes the meaning of the world) and Merleau-Ponty's stubborn insistence on the primary thereness of the world (without which consciousness would have no locus or context for meaning).

Second, and particularly in dealing with the reductions, one should recall that the subject-object reunification functions in another fashion, in the relationship between imagination and reason. In his discussion of the eidetic reduction, Kockelmans says that one must employ "acts of phantasy." /22/ I would say that the genius of reductive thinking is *disciplined* fantasy, exercises of the imagination balanced by systematic attention paid to the imagination's play while it occurs. /23/

Third, to comprehend phenomenology one should practice it. As Merleau-Ponty says, "Phenomenology is accessible only through a phenomenological method." /24/ It resists critical analysis from the outside but opens up to an empathetic "thinking-along." Whoever is not willing to take that step will find it difficult to experience the power and value of the method. Whoever does try to understand from the inside discovers that the objects of consciousness give themselves to one in a peculiar way. Because consciousness intends its world that is already there, waiting to be realized, the act of recognition is a two-way affair, a convergence, a mutual yielding up of self and world. Not only does phenomenology seek to unite subject and object; every successful phenomenological act is precisely this fusion of subject and object.

Fourth, although the previous paragraph may seem to carry mystical overtones, phenomenology is not a kind of mysticism — nor is it yet, in spite of Husserl's description of it as radical empiricism, founded on a single-minded dedication to reason. Speaking to both of these, Merleau-Ponty remarks that

"Rationality is not a *problem*. There is behind it no unknown quantity which has to be determined by deduction, or, beginning with it, demonstrated inductively. We witness every minute the miracle of related experiences, and yet nobody knows better than we do how this miracle is worked, for we are ourselves this network of relationships. The world and reason are not problematical. We may say, if we wish, that they are mysterious, but their mystery defines them. . . . True philosophy consists in re-learning to look at the world." /25/

Fifth, that last sentence reminds us of what Eugen Fink has stated so faithfully: phenomenology wishes to instill, or reinstill, in us the sense of wonder. /26/ Phenomenology does not wish to control the world; it is not a philosophical imperialism. Rather, it wishes to reveal the richness, variety, promise, and infinite potential of the experience of existence. Life is above all awesome, and phenomenology desires not to domesticate that awesomeness but to make it constantly present to us.

B. Structuralism

Although it may seem inappropriate at first, a reminder of phenomenology's sense of wonder is a good place to begin a discussion of structuralism. The structuralist attitude may appear predominantly detached, aloof, and bloodless, the result of an obsession with system, yet as Susan Sontag pointed out over a decade ago, Claude Lévi-Strauss, a founder of structuralism, has exhibited much passion along with his precision in his anthropological research. /27/ In any case, the exotic dimensions of structuralism along with its mathematical complexity have inspired awe as well as confusion among those who meet it initially, and I should like to show both its rationale and its humane and luminous depth.

One cannot refer as confidently to a group of "original" structuralists as we did in introducing phenomenology, for even more divergence exists within structuralism than within phenomenology. But it is customary and essentially correct to mention the linguist Ferdinand de Saussure, the Bourbaki group of mathematicians, and the Russian formalists as the immediate forerunners of contemporary structuralism, and then to identify the linguist Roman Jakobson, the literary critic Roland Barthes, the psychoanalyst Jacques Lacan, and above all the anthropologist Claude Lévi-Strauss as the founding fathers of the movement. /28/ One way of starting to create coherence out of the many directions represented here is to accept Michael Lane's description of structuralism as "a method whose primary intention is to permit the investigation to go beyond a pure description of what he perceives or experiences *(le vécu)*, in the direction of the quality of rationality which underlies the social phenomena in which he is concerned." /29/ Key concepts of the structuralist search for "the quality of rationality," which I will treat individually, are those of system, the signified-signifier-sign relationship, binary opposition, laws of transformation, deep structure and surface structure, synchrony and diachrony, and metaphor and metonymy.

Lane's definition implies a basic difference between structuralism and phenomenology. At the risk of some misunderstanding, we might continue that contrast by stating that the effort of structuralism, unlike phenomenology, is not to discover how consciousness forms a system of being and meaning, but how system forms the being and meaning of consciousness. This statement sounds as though it has more affinities to Merleau-Ponty than to Husserl, and indeed, Merleau-Ponty has exerted a strong influence on the structuralists through his emphasis on the givenness of the world. Structuralists, unlike all phenomenologists, however, would not say that consciousness, or being, or the world intend their objects but rather that system or structure is "intentional." Consciousness moves to the periphery in structuralist thought and exists only as a phenomenon among others that can be configured and transformed. One system, the system of language, underlies all others for most structuralists, so that the linguistic model provides the basis for structural analysis in many disciplines.

Specifically, the structural linguistics that offered a new theory of signs and was introduced in the early 1900s at the University of Geneva by Saussure became the foundation of the structuralist undertaking. According to Saussure in his *Course in General Linguistics*, a linguistic sign consists of two components, a signified *(signifié, significatum)* and a signifier *(signifiant, significans)*. /30/ The signified designates the unarticulated concept or the whole area of unexpressed cogitation, while the signifier is the "sound-image" (in Saussure's terms), the actual articulation or expression. These two together constitute the sign. Further, says Saussure, no natural relationship obtains between words and things or between the signified and signifier; the connection between them is arbitrary ("tree" stands for tree only because we have decided that it should), and hence the linguistic sign itself has no natural roots but exists as a societal creation. Out of such a network of arbitrary signs a linguistic system develops that is paradigmatic for the arbitrary formation of all human systems.

The new theory of signs was radical and comprehensive enough to serve as an inspiration for the new science of semiology, the study of signs, and directed attention primarily toward what happens in the area of the signifier. /31/ Jakobson and others showed how it was possible to reduce the sound-concept to a basic constituent unit, the phoneme, and from there systematize it through a series of increasingly complex terms: morphemes, somemes, sentemes, paragraphs, whole passages of discourse. In every instance it is the structure, the relationship among phonemes, sentemes, and other elements of discourse, and not the individual elements by themselves that produces meaning. /32/

With the arbitrary nature of the sign and of the language system established, Jakobson in linguistics and literary criticism and then Lévi-Strauss in ethnology proceeded to offer evidence that general consistencies exist within and among the signifiers, no matter what system they belong to. The reduction of images and patterns of experience to binary oppositions and the discovery of laws of transformation that explain how the patterns of experience gain coherence and depth should apply to all human systems. The term binary opposition, as Lane points out, is used in structuralism in two ways; it can refer to absolute opposites in the sense of the logician's division of "a" and "not a" or, more commonly among structuralists, it can refer to less precisely delineated oppositional pairs, such as earth-sky, male-female, and include pairs from non-Western cultures that do not even strike us as oppositions, such as head-liver or honey-ashes. /33/ Barthes has speculated that binary oppositions may be universal and physiologically or neurologically based—that human behavior and the human condition are determined by fundamental binary oppositions (although he grants that such a thesis has many opponents), and Lévi-Strauss himself complicates the simple binary oppositional pattern in writings such as "The Sex of the Heavenly Bodies." /34/ The theory of binary oppositions was already implicit in the associative aspect of Saussure's linguistics, but as Barthes says, Saussure did not seem to be aware of it. /35/

The laws of transformation are similarly derived from the observations of how one level of language components changes into another ("higher") level or how the linguistic message of the sender is decoded by the receiver, and these laws are presented as the process by which any system develops and assumes integrity. The laws of transformation take the place of laws of causality. Changes in a structural configuration occur not because of the pressures of history or the master plan of nature; we cannot claim, according to the structuralists, that changes occur "because" at all but can only say that transformations take place as part of the process of the system's self-realization. Thus Jean Piaget's "genetic epistemology," for example, illustrates ultimately in a complex fashion the grand series of transformations by which human intelligence expands from elementary awareness into mature perception and cognitive experience. /36/ Lévi-Strauss in his anthropological myth studies, Barthes in his studies of fashion and advertising (among many other subjects), Louis Althusser in his study of history, Lacan in his psychoanalysis, for example, treat their subject matter as a "metalanguage" (Barthes' term) in order to discover the rules of transformation that operate synchronically in a number of different "sets" or situations and thus suggest universality. The method is comparative (although markedly different from the normal comparatist approach, as we shall see); the goal is to find, through the language paradigm, the laws of human behavior.

Although the linguistic model is paramount, the transformational theory goes back beyond Saussure at least to Marx and Freud. Marx's laws of transformation (the transformation of slave into wage-earner, for example, or of scattered private property into capitalistically consolidated private property) certainly inform Lévi-Strauss' description of endogamic and exogamic exchange among so-called primitive tribes; and Freud's explanation of how dream experiences are translated into the language of consciousness through condensation, displacement, representation, and transference is at the core of Lacan's effort to comprehend the unconscious as a language system—to express, in effect, the grammar of the unconscious. /37/ Noam Chomsky's transformational linguistics, in markedly different ways, also aims at locating the linguistic rules in the deep structure of language and analyzing their application within the surface structure, or actual articulation, of language. /38/

Although the discovery, elaboration, and universalization of laws of transformation are said to be at the heart of structuralist activity, scholars tend to explore rather the ramifications of their individual areas of competence, an effort that is inevitable, and for the time being necessary. As Lane reports, "At the Paris colloquium on structure Lévi-Strauss took the position that the most important line of future advance, the development of laws of transformation, ultimately depended upon the ability of anthropologists to formulate their structures algebraically. But despite this intense concern with formal expression his feeling for the 'lived reality' remains pre-eminent"—and, one should add, is articulated mainly in terms of his own discipline rather than mathematically. /39/

The concepts of deep structure and surface structure are also key terms with roots in Marx and Freud. The societal division between infra-structure (economic base) and super-structure in Marx, and the psychological division between the determining unconscious and the conscious in Freud have prepared significantly for the deep structure-surface structure contrast in structuralism. Lévi-Strauss has remarked that geology was one of his "three mistresses" (along with Marxism and Freudianism), and Michel Foucault has explored thoroughly the archeology metaphor; both of these writers' orientations suggest the need for "digging" beneath the surface to unearth the hidden patterns of existence. /40/ Where does one dig? According to Saussure, one would dig through spoken discourse *(la parole)* to uncover the fundamental laws of language *(la langue),* but following Chomsky, one would plumb still deeper in hope of striking upon a linguistic structuring capacity innate in humans themselves. Lévi-Strauss would sift through the myths of various tribes to locate the strata of kinship patterns denoting basic social laws (incest taboos, dietary practices, etc.) that, in turn, may be innate. Barthes wishes to find beneath the code of items of apparel in vogue the dynamics of decision-making groups. Jacques Derrida digs beneath the ground of metaphysics to examine laws of *différance* that suggest a radically new ontology. /41/

In every case the object under scrutiny exhibits a "vocabulary," a surface *Gestalt* that covers an essential "grammar" or "syntax"—the deep structure that consists of the *unconscious* laws of transformation. This theory is not like the common theory of symbols, because for most structuralists no natural relationship exists between the elements of the surface and deep structure that would explain their conjuncture, whereas in traditional idealist terms the symbol is considered as somehow partaking of its object. Structuralism, we recall, is founded on a theory of signs, and specifically of signs as arbitrarily composed, and not on a theory of symbols, and hence the unity is sought on the level of sub-surface strata (to return to the archeology metaphor) rather than on the surface level. For example, the myths of a number of tribes may be quite discrete; only when they are analyzed on the deep structural level and transformed, usually through binary oppositions, into categories, do their common qualities appear.

One sees that the foundation of semiology, the theory of the arbitrary nature of signs, has extensive epistemological and ontological implications. The arbitrary sign, functioning on the surface level, denies the conventional belief in causality and suggests instead a discontinuous universe, whereas the patterns of the deep structure point to a unity not of naturally-related objects but a unity made possible through interchangeable (or at least transformable) components in different systems. The hope is that we can eventually express the world and find a communicative unity through our many modes of discourse just as we express language itself through the conjunction of created and discovered grammars of articulation.

Synchrony and diachrony as structuralist concepts are often misunderstood. The structuralist emphasis on synchrony does not mean that the structuralists ignore or attack the pre-eminence of history in Western culture, although one could gain that impression from a superficial knowledge of Lévi-Strauss' quarrel with Sartre on history and dialectic. /42/ As Lane remarks, structuralism is atemporal but not ahistorical, and certainly structuralists such as Sebag, Goldmann, and Althusser have worked skillfully and profitably with historical perspectives. /43/ The two terms derive their structuralist usage from Saussure's linguistics, in which he distinguishes between traits of language that are synchronically determined (static language-states) and evolutionary aspects of language that are necessarily diachronic, for example semantic changes. Barthes uses astronomy as an illustration of a mainly synchronic discipline and geology as a mainly diachronic one, whereas economics and linguistics, he says, are a balance of the two. /44/ But all systems exist through some sort of interplay between the synchronic and diachronic. The synchronic aspects of a system are characterized by the equilibriate components (i.e., components seeking balance) that interact and cause the system to function, while the diachronic aspects are marked by disequilibriate units that make the system change. A cultural system such as a closed society would seem to be largely synchronic, since it could produce little stimulus for change, while an open society would appear to be more diachronic as a result of the strong impulses toward disequilibrium and change.

The effect of this kind of thinking that organizes systems in terms of synchronic and diachronic elements is to deny the predominance of causality and to neutralize, or demythologize, the concepts of time, change, and history as active, inexorable forces. In a system sustained by the interaction of parts and altered by the introduction of new parts, cause and effect are subordinated to the laws of transformation; time is understood not as a continuum but as the condition produced by the constant of interacting units; and change is the name for the result of the transformational acts. History likewise is not a dynamic agent but rather the expression of the awareness of the configuration of cultural-social systems and the attempt to predict the future shape of systems. Or as Lane says, "History is seen as the specific mode of development of a particular system, whose present, or synchronic nature must be fully known before any account can be given of its evolution, or diachronic nature." /45/ The synchrony-diachrony dichotomy could be of great value for literary criticism, for example for describing the differences between the static systems of traditional works and the evolutionary systems of experimental works.

The extremely important distinction between metaphor and metonymy was developed by Roman Jakobson. /46/ In the formulation of the various kinds of linguistic components (phoneme, morpheme, senteme, etc.), the potential units that can fit a particular position are selected according to the principle of similarity or metaphor, while the order of the units chosen is determined by the principle of contiguity or metonymy. As Barthes recounts, a list of subsidiary terms has arisen that describes the metaphor-metonymy polarity. /47/ The metaphor pole is called, variously, the associative, substitutional, paradigmatic, systematic, correlational, oppositional, *parole*-related plane, while the metonymy pole is labelled the syntagmatic, contiguous, linear, relational, contrasting, *langue*-related plane. Jakobson also pioneered in applying the metaphor-metonymy axes to non-linguistic systems, and the dichotomy seems to hold great potential for literary criticism and other disciplines.

Jan Kott, who is not a structuralist, offers an exotic example that clarifies the two concepts and demonstrates their utility. /48/ A believer in magic who wishes to cast a spell on an enemy can, Kott says, either make an effigy of the enemy and curse or mutilate it (which would be a metaphoric act), or he can acquire an actual part of the enemy such as hair or a fingernail and work his spell on it (which would be a metonymic tactic). As an oversimplification, one could say that the terms represent the difference between poetry (metaphor) and discourse (metonymy), but the distinction is in actuality of course not that neat; all linguistic operations (and perhaps all mental activities) make use of the two axes in an intricately combined fashion. Structuralists hope that an analysis of the interaction of the two in various metalanguages will contribute significantly toward general semiological clarification.

The arbitrary nature of the sign that Saussure insisted on is at the base of some structuralists' stress on interalterity, the interaction of discrete elements whereby the system exists and performs efficiently. Just as no "natural," organic relationship exists between sign and referent, so also systems consist of unique, distinct units conjoined by position rather than by species. Each thing is itself and remains itself; it is not absorbed into a whole, does not forfeit its identity, but becomes a confederate with other units to comprise the system, the result of pragmatic rather than of familial dynamics. Through this emphasis structuralism again reveals its anti-causality; things are not explainable or related naturally but must be made to relate and to perform together, in ever-shifting patterns, in an infinite play of interconnections that can sometimes be refined into systems and sometimes represented by formulae. As Cervantes Gimeno says, "The real novelty of structuralism is that it is no longer confined to the comparison of types, but instead examines distinct wholes, paying particular attention to their differences. . . . The same procedure is followed in linguistics; the linguist orders oppositions, not similarities. Similarly, the structuralist anthropologist examines the differences between societies and tries to explain them. The anthropologist, like the psychiatrist, searches for alterity or otherness." /49/

Lacan, inspired by Freud and Lévi-Strauss, elevated the concept of the Other to one of supreme importance in order to show that the encounter with alterity, as in the meeting with the psychotic or neurotic, is not necessarily an encounter with aberration but perhaps with a different system, a different code, a different set of values which one can seek to transform into his own system or use to expand his system. /50/ Lévi-Strauss himself, in arguing that "primitive" thinking is not inferior to Western logical thought but rather a different system that should be appreciated by Westerners, supports the concept of interalterity; but the Husserl specialist Derrida above all is the philosopher who (first by way of attacking Lévi-Strauss' confusion of philosophical and anthropological "difference") founded a revolutionary philosophy on otherness or, in his own term, on *différance*.

For Derrida the recognition of the absolute dissimilarity of each moment of existence from every other means the end of Western metaphysics as it has been practiced, based as it is on the assumption of the continuity of moments, so that one must "defer" meaning (a negative revision of Heidegger's "waiting") and accept alterity until it matures sufficiently to relate authentically to itself and produce interalterity. Obviously, this startling line of argument, if taken seriously, constitutes a crisis for structuralism, for it implies at best the impossibility of comprehending the systems within which one abides (suggesting an alterity so strong that interalterity cannot occur) or at worst a despair over the alienating power of otherness that prohibits systems from forming at all. Yet structuralism, like phenomenology, thrives on the edge of chaos and seeks to renew itself from the depths of disorder. In the following chapters, and in the context of literary criticism, we will try to discern how phenomenology and structuralism have responded to (and sometimes precipitated) a chaos of the word and have sought to discipline it.

NOTES

/1/ Edmund Husserl, *Logische Untersuchungen*, Vol. 1 (1900), Vol. II (1901); 2nd rev. ed. in 3 vols. (Halle: Niemeyer, 1913); *Ideen zu einer reinen Phänomenologie und phänomenologischen Philosophie*, Vol. 1 (Halle: Niemeyer, 1913).

/2/ Introductory statements on phenomenology by first-generation phenomenologists are, for example, Husserl's article on "Phenomenology" in the *Encyclopedia Britannica* (first published there in 1929 and retained until 1956); and Maurice Merleau-Ponty, Preface to *Phenomenology of Perception,* tr. Colin Smith (London: Routledge and Kegan Paul, and New York: The Humanities Press, 1962), vii-xxi.

Among the many introductions to phenomenology are the following that I have found helpful:

James M. Edie, Introduction to Pierre Thévenaz, *What is Phenomenology?*, ed. and tr. James M. Edie, with Charles Courtney and Paul Brockelman (Chicago: Quadrangle Books, 1962), pp. 13-36.

Vernon W. Gras, ed., Introduction to *European Literary Theory and Practice: From Existential Phenomenology to Structuralism* (New York: Dell, 1973), pp. 1-23. This is an excellent concise introduction to both methods.

Joseph J. Kockelmans, ed., *Phenomenology: The Philosophy of Edmund Husserl and Its Interpretation* (Garden City: Doubleday, 1967).

Quentin Lauer, *Phenomenology: Its Genesis and Prospect* (New York and Evanston: Harper and Row, 1965).

Robert Magliola, "The Phenomenological Approach to Literature: Its Theory and Methodology," *Language and Style*, 2, No. 2 (Spring, 1972): 79-99.

Maurice Natanson, ed., Introduction to *Essays in Phenomenology* (The Hague: Nijhoff, 1966), pp. 1-22.

Alfred Schütz, "Some Leading Concepts of Phenomenology," in Natanson, ed., *Essays in Phenomenology*, pp. 23-39.

Herbert Spiegelberg, *The Phenomenological Movement: A Historical Introduction,* 2 vols., 2nd ed. (The Hague: Nijhoff, 1971).

David Stewart and Algis Mickunas, *Exploring Phenomenology: A Guide to the Field and its Literature* (Chicago: American Library Association, 1974).

Erwin Straus, ed., *Phenomenology: Pure and Applied* (Pittsburgh: Duquesne University Press, 1964).

Pierre Thévenaz, *What is Phenomenology?* Still the best general introduction.

/3/   Natanson, ed., *Essays in Phenomenology,* pp. 19-20.

/4/   Cf. Natanson, *Essays,* p. 5, on Brentano. Thévenaz in *What is Phenomenology?*, p. 46, says that Husserl moved from a non-psychological analysis of consciousness to an analysis of non-psychological consciousness.

/5/   Cf. Edie's Introduction to Thévenaz, *What is Phenomenology?*, p. 26.

/6/   Cf. Gras, *European Literary Theory and Practice,* p. 1.

/7/   Cf. Michael Kullman and Charles Taylor, "The Pre-Objective World," in Natanson, ed., *Essays,* p. 118.

/8/   Cf. Kockelmans, *Phenomenology,* pp. 29-30.

/9/   Magliola, "The Phenomenological Approach to Literature," pp. 90-92.

/10/   Cf. Husserl, "The Thesis of the Natural Standpoint and Its Suspension," in Kockelmans, ed., *Phenomenology,* p. 77. W. R. Boyce Gibson, who translated Husserl's *Ideen* as *Ideas: General Introduction to Phenomenology* (London: George Allen and Unwin, 1931), renders *epoché* as "abstention," but in Volume I of the German text Husserl does not translate it from the Greek at all.

/11/   Cf. James Street Fulton, "The Cartesianism of Phenomenology," in Natanson, ed., *Essays,* pp. 71-72. Unlike Descartes, Husserl never really doubts reality but merely puts it out of play.

/12/   Lauer, *Phenomenology,* pp. 51-57.

/13/   Natanson, pp. 11-13; Kockelmans, p. 30.

/14/   Magliola, "The Phenomenological Approach," p. 88.

/15/   Cf. Thévenaz, p. 55.

/16/   Quoted by John Wild in his Preface to Thévenaz, p. 7.

/17/   Merleau-Ponty, *Phenomenology of Perception,* xiii.

/18/   Kockelmans, p. 195.

/19/   Cf. Natanson, p. 15.

/20/   Schütz, "Some Leading Concepts of Phenomenology," p. 30.

/21/   Cf. Natanson, p. 18. For Husserl the term "transcendental" refers
consistently to the constituting activity of the ego. For Heidegger it refers to being as
the absolute foundation to be disclosed to consciousness, and for Merleau-Ponty it
refers to the world itself experienced phenomenologically.

/22/   Kockelmans, p. 31.

/23/   Ray L. Hart's *Unfinished Man and the Imagination* (New York: Herder,
1968) is an outstanding example of a text that both examines and uses such "disciplined
fantasy" from a theological perspective.

/24/   Merleau-Ponty, *Phenomenology of Perception,* viii.

/25/   *Ibid.,* xx.

/26/   Cf., for example, Eugen Fink, *Das Spiel als Weltsymbol* (Stuttgart:
Kohlhammer, 1960).

/27/   Susan Sontag, "The Anthropologist as Hero," in her *Against
Interpretation* (New York: Dell, 1969), pp. 77-89.

/28/   Roland Barthes is a first generation structuralist who has written an
introduction to the method: "The Structuralist Activity," tr. Richard Howard,
Partisan Review, 34 (1967): 82-88. Other introductions that I have found helpful are:
Jean-Marie Auzias, *Clefs pour le structuralisme* (Paris: Éditions Seghers, 1971).
Peter Caws, "What Is Structuralism?" *Partisan Review,* 35 (1968): 75-91.
Richard and Fernande De George, eds., Introduction to *The Structuralists from Marx
        to Lévi-Strauss* (Garden City: Doubleday, 1972), xi-xxix.
Jacques Ehrmann, ed., *Structuralism* (Garden City: Doubleday, 1970).
Helga Gallas, ed., *Strukturalismus als interpretatives Verfahren* (Darmstadt und
        Neuwied: Luchterhand, 1972).
Howard Gardner, *The Quest for Mind* (New York: Knopf, 1973).
Michael Lane, ed., Introduction to *Introduction to Structuralism* (New York: Basic
        Books, 1970), pp. 11-39. I consider this the best general introduction.
Henri Lefebvre, *L'Idéologie structuraliste* (Paris: Éditions Anthropos, 1971).
Daniel Patte, *What is Structural Exegesis?* (Philadelphia: Fortress Press, 1976). Patte's
        book is indispensable for biblical exegetes who wish to learn structural exegesis.
David Robey, ed., *Structuralism: An Introduction* (Oxford: Clarendon, 1973).
Günther Schiwy, ed., *Der französische Strukturalismus* (Reinbek bei Hamburg:
        Rowohlt, 1969).
Robert Scholes, *Structuralism in Literature: An Introduction* (New Haven: Yale
        University Press, 1974).
François Wahl, ed., *Qu'est- e que le structuralisme?* (Paris: Seuil, 1968).

/29/   Lane, p. 31.

/30/   Saussure's *Course in General Linguistics* (New York: McGraw-Hill, 1966) was first published on the basis of his students' notes in 1916.

/31/   Cf. Roland Barthes, *Elements of Semiology*, tr. Annette Lavers and Colin Smith (Boston: Beacon Press, 1970) for a concentrated discussion of semiological terminology and method.

/32/   This paragraph and the preceding one present an extremely simplified version of the linguistic model adapted by Lévi-Strauss for anthropology, by Barthes for literary criticism, by Lacan for psychoanalysis, etc. For an authoritative discussion of the development of structural linguistics from Saussure to Chomsky, cf. Giulio C. Lepschy, *A Survey of Structural Linguistics* (London: Faber and Faber, 1970).

/33/   Lane, p. 34.

/34/   Barthes makes this speculation in *Elements of Semiology*, p. 82; Lévi-Strauss' "The Sex of the Heavenly Bodies" is published in Lane, pp. 330-39.

/35/   Barthes, *Elements*, p. 81.

/36/   Jean Piaget, *Genetic Epistemology*, tr. Eleanor Duckworth (New York: Columbia University Press, 1970).

/37/   Cf. De George, *The Structuralists from Marx to Lévi-Strauss*, pp. 20-23, regarding Lévi-Strauss on exchange, and xvi-xvii regarding Freud on dreams.

/38/   Cf. Noam Chomsky, *Language and Mind*, Enlarged Edition (New York: Harcourt Brace Jovanovich, 1972).

/39/   Lane, p. 34.

/40/   Cf. Michel Foucault, *The Order of Things*, tr. A. M. Sheridan-Smith (New York: Pantheon, 1970); and *The Archaeology of Knowledge*, tr. A. M. Sheridan-Smith (London: Tavistock, 1972).

/41/   Jacques Derrida, *L'Écriture et la différence* (Paris: Seuil, 1967). Derrida sometimes spells *différence* as *différance*, a punning tactic to suggest both "to differ" and "to defer."

/42/   Lévi-Strauss' attack on Sartre appears in "History and Dialectic," the final chapter of *The Savage Mind* (Chicago: The University of Chicago Press, 1966), pp. 245-69. A response from Sartre appears in *L'Arc*, No. 30 (1966): 87-96.

/43/   Lane, p. 16.

/44/   Barthes, *Elements*, pp. 54-55.

/45/   Lane, p. 17.

/46/   Cf. Roman Jakobson and Morris Halle, *Fundamentals of Language* (The Hague: Mouton, 1956). The distinction was already present, however, in Saussure's *Course in General Linguistics.*

/47/   Barthes, *Elements,* p. 59.

/48/   Jan Kott, "The Icon and the Absurd," in *The Discontinuous Universe,* ed. Sallie Sears and Georgiana W. Lord (New York: Basic Books, 1972), p. 31.

/49/   F. Cervantes Gimeno, "The Structuralist Approach in Psychiatry," *The Human Context,* 5, No. 1 (Spring, 1973): 121.

/50/   Cf. Jacques Lacan, *The Language of the Self: The Function of Language in Psychoanalysis,* ed. and tr. Anthony Wilden (Baltimore: The Johns Hopkins Press, 1968).

Chapter II

Phenomenological Literary Criticism

A. THEORY

The obvious next step, following the definition of phenomenological and structuralist terminology, is to place that
terminology in its literary critical framework. I will begin by
sketching the positions of representative phenomenological
theorists and then offer brief critical summaries of
phenomenologically-oriented analyses of religious and secular
material that illustrate various ways of doing such analysis.
Although in the preceding section I stressed Husserl's vocabulary
as the originating language of phenomenology, Husserl himself
was not a literary critic, and hence I have turned first to Roman
Ingarden as the philosopher who adapted Husserl's thought to
literary theory. I have selected Merleau-Ponty as the thinker who
formed the bridge between essentialist and existential phenomenology, and Heidegger, of course, as the founder of existential
phenomenology itself. Sartre will represent the existentialist
criticism that he developed and that has flourished popularly as
distinct from Heidegger's version, while Georges Poulet will
exemplify the criticism of consciousness. Hans-Georg Gadamer
will be our hermeneutical critic, and Paul Ricoeur will serve as the
critic who combines an essentialist and hermeneutical approach.

Ingarden, Merleau-Ponty, and Poulet have practiced and
influenced mainly the criticism of secular texts, whereas the others
have been instrumental in determining the evolution of phenomenologically-based analyses of both secular and religious texts. In
spite of the fact that both kinds of texts have been addressed by
phenomenologists for nearly a half-century, very few
comprehensive surveys of these efforts exist; the best of these few
for the analysis of secular texts is Zoran Konstantinović's *Phänomenologie und Literaturwissenschaft,* while John

31

Macquarrie's *Twentieth Century Religious Thought* provides a concise and good overview of the phenomenological criticism of religious texts. /1/

Roman Ingarden

The Polish philosopher Roman Ingarden was one of the first, in the 1930s, to attempt an application of Husserlian phenomenology to literary criticism. His work, in fact, constitutes the most careful and thorough transposition of essentialist phenomenology into literary critical terms that has yet appeared. It is perhaps because Ingarden remained so faithful to Husserl's thought that his theory has not, ironically, come to represent the major direction that phenomenological literary criticism has taken. As Magliola points out, critics of the "Geneva School" (Richard, Poulet, Starobinski, Miller) and others influenced more by Heidegger than by Husserl constitute the dominant group of phenomenological literary critics, while Ingarden and Mikel Dufrenne have remained in the background, in good part because they reject, in the spirit of Husserl, the psychologistic tendencies of the search for the author's consciousness hidden in the experiential patterns of his works. /2/

Evidence that Ingarden's criticism has had little impact on American criticism until recently can be seen in the fact that his 1931 book *Das literarische Kunstwerk,* still a major text of literary theory, was not translated into English (as *The Literary Work of Art*) until 1973. /3/ This text is forthrightly committed to the Husserlian project and asks the question, *"What are the essential properties, the invariant logical conditions, of that mode of being which the literary work of art uniquely possesses?"* /4/ Ingarden in this book states that the literary work is the product of the artist's life-world and can be comprehended as a "fictive universe" (a position with which the dominant group would agree) but goes on to pay more attention to the phenomenological structure of the text itself than to the relationship of text and author. After eliminating the elements that do not belong to the structure of the work (the author, psychological states of the reader, questions of value, etc.), Ingarden examines the basic structure of the work and describes it as a "stratified formation" consisting of four levels or strata contained in language and coexisting in polyphonic harmony. The first level is that of linguistic sound formations, consisting of words and word sounds, sentences, and sentence rhythms. The second level, which grows out of the first, is that of meaning units constituted by intentional or fictive objects that emerge through the various sentence functions and sentence complexes. The third level, called the stratum of represented objects, organizes the fictive objects of the second level into the unity of characters and events that characterize a particular literary work and give it its individuality. The fourth level, that of schematized aspects, is the perspective through which this particular fictive world is recognized and described, and here, of course, the modes of temporality and spatiality are among the most important for establishing perspectives.

Because the elements of the fictive universe are not grounded in the real world, the author's selection of perspectives through which to present the elements appears as the centrally creative act and as that which comprises his style. Yet in his presentation of the fictive world the author cannot construct a fully dimensional world but only fragments thereof, created through perspectives, so that the artist's intentionality in choosing the vantage points must be met by the reader's intentionality in reading depth and dimensionality into those fragments.

For Ingarden, then, the author's and reader's intentionality, the life-world of the text, and the reductive strategy through which one discovers the four strata that comprise the structure of the text are the major phenomenological concepts to be applied to literary criticism according to *The Literary Work of Art*. /5/ In his next major text, *The Cognition of the Literary Work of Art,* Ingarden addresses himself to a second question from the phenomenologist's standpoint: "What process or processes lead to the cognition of the literary work of art, what are the possible ways of cognizing it, and what results can we expect of this cognition?" /6/ In the introduction he identifies three cognitive attitudes, the aesthetic, pre-aesthetic, and the reflective cognition of the aesthetic, as a way of projecting his concerns in this book, then in the first chapter reviews the four strata described in his earlier work and emphasizes the necessary synthesizing effort of the reader in actualizing the literary work of art. /7/ In the second chapter he introduces the concept of the active memory, which is the capacity to relate the present moment of cognition to others in the continuum of experience, and also utilizes this typology of memory to speak of temporality in the literary art work.

In chapter three Ingarden differentiates between the scientific work and the literary art work, arguing that the scientific work provides knowledge separate from the work itself, whereas the literary art work provides a basis for aesthetic experience. In chapter four he distinguishes various kinds of cognition of the literary art work and shows that the attitude of the scholar reading for research purposes is unlike that of the reader seeking his own aesthetic realization of the text. He makes a further important distinction here between the work's artistic worth and the aesthetic object—which takes shape as the reader's concretization out of the literary art work. In the final chapter he stresses two problems: first, how to know if the reader's concretization of the literary art work is an authentic rendering of it, whereby he describes some of the possible kinds of falsifications and reiterates that they can be avoided by paying careful attention to the reconstruction of the first and second strata. The second problem is how the aesthetic experience proceeding from the reader's crystallization of the aesthetic object generates ultimate values.

Although Ingarden's phenomenological literary criticism has not been the dominant kind, it has in the past few years helped to provoke new research by European critics such as Wolfgang Iser and Hans Robert Jauss on the reader's participation in the interpretive process that has found resonance among American scholars as well. /8/ Further, his approach to the problem of literary evaluation has influenced especially Continental criticism; his position here is that the aesthetic qualities a literary art work displays can never be translated into independently valid judgments because they do not represent the total significance of the work. /9/

Maurice Merleau-Ponty

Merleau-Ponty's phenomenology is in one sense more faithful to Husserl's than is that of Heidegger and Sartre, yet in certain deceptive ways he turns Husserl's essentialist thought inside out. For example, he accepts Husserl's concept of intentionality but denies that intentionality is always conscious and self-sufficient. It is, he says, at its most fundamental level pre-conscious and interactive with one's body, world, and peculiar situation. Likewise, he refers to Husserl's eidetic reduction but argues that rather than using it to uncover an essential core—a primary aim for Husserl, we recall—one should recognize this maneuver as made necessary by the ambiguous quality of language and thus as a stage to be worked through on the way toward a more vital existential relationship with the world. The goal of the reduction for Merleau-Ponty is not, in other words, Husserl's goal of pure consciousness but a richer, more intense involvement with the world; what remains after exercising the reduction (one can never finish it) is not the discovery of a human essence but the body-subject interpenetrating the world more completely.

Like Heidegger, Merleau-Ponty focuses his literary criticism on language and the special nature of the poet, but since he recasts some of Heidegger's presuppositions, the literary critical results are also different. As Thévenaz points out, whereas for Heidegger the transcendental is being, for Merleau-Ponty it is man's phenomenological experience of the world. /10/ Thus (to restate my description in the preceding paragraph), in practicing the reduction, Merleau-Ponty brackets the world in order to disclose our original pre-conscious perception of it and present thereby this resultant life-world as the true transcendental.

The act of perception is central for Merleau-Ponty. Through one's body the perceptual relationship with the world takes place, so that the body becomes consciousness incarnate through which being shows itself indirectly; in the act of perceiving the world, the body undergoes a pre-reflective experience that reveals the action of being and that one strives to realize in thought. As Gras explains it, "Meaning, thus, becomes a dialectical movement of bringing to explicit foreground what is only potentially and latently present to the tacit incarnated cogito"—a process that sounds much like Michael Polanyi's epistemology as well. /11/ Hence cogitation is a symbolic act, for it attempts to represent a deeper original experience in the language of consciousness. This language is neither arbitrary in its choice of referents nor a mere signalling mechanism to express mental formulations but is rather creative; it participates in the expression of being and is intentional. As such, according to Merleau-Ponty, language is "gestural." The term suggests how language shares the bodily perception of the world, how language is an act, and how it points to meaning instead of just reflecting it. Merleau-Ponty shows, in fact, how meaning is expressed through the various forms of language: it inhabits first gestures or signs, then conceptual terms, then the speaking word, and finally the spoken word.

Literary language is particularly rich because it displays the emotional as well as the conceptual dimension of experience and hence creates and conveys more of one's total life-world. Literary criticism for Merleau-Ponty means examining the literary artist's *parole* (his personal language style, composed of emotional and conceptual aspects) to elicit its meaning not as an end in itself but as an example of the phenomenology of perception. Or, since literary expression is a kind of excess, an addition to what has already been expressed discursively, the critic concentrates on the author's style as the locus of what constitutes his excess, what shapes his *projet* or the total integration of levels of meaning that make up his life-world. As Gras points out, this attempt to share the author's life-world through his style is like the critics-of-consciousness orientation; I would add that it is also similar to Derrida's emphasis on *différance*. /12/ Another way of applying Merleau-Ponty's criticism would be to carry through its Heideggerian elements: to discuss literary examples of inauthentic modes of existence, specifically activism (an exaggeration of body-orientation) and fascination (an exaggeration of world-orientation) as failures of expression. /13/

Martin Heidegger

The influence of Martin Heidegger on secular and theological literary criticism has been massive and profound, but it has rarely been direct. Even where it has been direct, as in the New Testament studies of Rudolf Bultmann, it has usually taken the form of the transposition of existentialist categories into the critic's own framework rather than of a rigorous phenomenological reduction. /14/ A main reason why Heidegger's influence has been oblique is that he does not offer a specific literary critical procedure for a critic to appropriate—or at least none that anyone has so far been able to distill clearly from his complicated texts. One observes rather how he strives to radicalize the language of poetry from which conventional reality is already bracketed off. Literary criticism is for him at first a part of the process of *Zurückfragen*, a relentless questioning-back toward the essence of being, an effort that he practices until he reaches the point where this interrogation itself is revealed as a part of the outmoded metaphysical tradition and superfluous. Through his increasing play with words he exercises the disciplined fantasy that Kockelmans calls for. He becomes poet and critic simultaneously; subject and object coalesce in the confrontation with being and the drawing out of being. In this effort the relationship among language, thought, and poetry is clarified further: fundamental language *(die Grundsprache, Sage)* expresses itself as event *(Ereignis)*, as *Dasein* happening, so that language shaping *Dasein* generates thought; since poetry both celebrates the experience of *Dasein* already confirmed and establishes a new *Dasein*, it articulates the *Grundsprache*—so often silent—and thus causes events to happen.

Thus for Heidegger literary criticism is a means of discovering one's relationship to language, especially to poetic language, which in turn is an avenue toward the authentic experiencing of one's role in (and as) *Dasein*. In reading literary artists (the

Dichter), who have a privileged position with words, one learns that we reside in language and that language uses us—surrounds us and works through us to confirm being. To clarify such confirmation of being, Heidegger analyzes the texts of individual poets such as Hölderlin, George, and Trakl to discover the true relationship between word and thing. The word does not reflect the thing nor does it, on the other hand, create the thing; rather, it articulates the thing, allows it to speak, to come to words. We can observe Heidegger's development from the era of *Sein und Zeit* (1927), in which the word required the nurturing of human care *(Sorge)* to protect it from the abuse of "thrown" man, to the writings of the matured philosopher such as *Unterwegs zur Sprache* (1959), in which the word has established itself and offers sanctuary to thrown man, and finally to the attitude whereby the word covers itself with silence and waits for a new revelation. /15/

Even though Heidegger does not offer a literary critical method to follow, one can apply his approach in various ways. Most obviously, one might follow Ludwig Binswanger's lead in psychotherapy and literary criticism and use Heidegger's ontological *existentialia* (the basic categories of human existing) as categories for analyzing characters, motifs, settings, actions, etc., in a text or in analyzing the artist himself. /16/ Just as obviously, one could develop Heidegger's hermeneutic of *Aufweisung, Freilegung,* and *Auslegung* into a literary critical technique; in fact, the familiar new-critical technique is a good deal like the Heideggerian hermeneutic, even to the point where the new-critical effort to display the text's meaning in the context of its artistic integrity is like Heidegger's attempt to recall "forgotten" being. /17/ Or one could imitate Heidegger's own literary critical inclination and pay attention to poetry about poetry, such as Hölderlin's verse on the nature of the poet or George's on the essence of poetic language; this is Heidegger's way of allowing language to speak itself, and it seems an appropriate tactic in our age of fiction adopting various self-conscious guises. /18/

These and other ways of appropriating Heidegger have found practitioners in the United States only recently. Stanley Romaine

Hopper has, of course, been faithfully and skillfully interpreting Heidegger for years, but his writing has been mainly that: interpretation of Heidegger rather than analysis of literary artists in a Heideggerian mode. / 19/ Joseph N. Riddel, however, in his 1974 *The Inverted Bell: Modernism and the Counterpoetics of William Carlos Williams,* has done a study that is strongly determined by the poetics of Heidegger (as well as by Derrida's thought); Paul de Man in his *Blindness and Insight* collection (1971) reveals an indebtedness to Heidegger in the various essays dealing with literary history, theory, and practice; the Winter 1976 issue of the journal *Boundary 2* is devoted to Heidegger and literary criticism; whereas in theological circles John Macquarrie in *An Existentialist Theology: A Comparison of Heidegger and Bultmann* (1955); and James M. Robinson and John B. Cobb, Jr., eds., in *The Later Heidegger and Theology* (1963) have shown the centrality of Heidegger in the modern dialogue between American and Continental (mainly Swiss and German) theologians. /20/ In my sketches, in the following section, of Heidegger's 1936 Hölderlin essay and of a 1952 New Testament essay by Bultmann I will expand on the significance of Heidegger for secular and theological literary criticism.

Jean-Paul Sartre

The existential critical vogue stimulated by Sartre in the 1940s and '50s has a much more profound foundation in Sartre's own existential phenomenology. Sartre in *Being and Nothingness* defines two levels of consciousness, a pre-reflective intending consciousness and a reflective self-consciousness that has the ego (which Sartre sees as part of the world) as its object. /21/ Pre-reflective consciousness, as pure consciousness with everything exterior to it, is necessarily consciousness of nothing, consciousness as negation, and in this void human freedom emerges as man's ability to create, from nothing, himself and his world. Yet because pre-reflective, intentional consciousness always aspires to the unattainable state of thingness, of the *en soi,* man exists ambiguously between being and nothingness. Or one could say that intentional consciousness forces existence without essence, so that man's creative effort becomes a frustrating endeavor to experience precisely what he cannot. Consciousness is therefore always project, always world-transforming engagement, because in order to realize itself, to continue to function as pure consciousness, it must forever deny an essential fulfillment. In this restless, paradox-fraught philosophy is the root of existential-critical terms such as anguish, alienation, and bad faith. /22/

Sartre's existential stance applied to aesthetics stresses the power of the imagination, which he makes practically identical with consciousness as a whole, to attempt liberation through negation. His literary critical studies such as those on Baudelaire and Genet also illustrate the various modes of negation at work, and some of his best creative pieces anticipate those modes in a clearer form than they assume in the philosophical texts. His first novel *La Nausée* (1938), for example, conveys the whole affectivity of disgust better than any of his later writing does, while the early plays *Les Mouches* (1943) and *Huis Clos* (1945) are excellent dramatic renditions of, among other things, the paradox of guilt and freedom and the inescapable objectifying gaze of other persons. /23/

Sartre's criticism also contains a strong historical emphasis: language is for communication, style serves content, the literary artist addresses a particular audience at a particular moment in time in order to change that moment, although the revolutionary aspect of an author's writing is always condemned to brief duration. In this political program of literature, described chiefly in *What is Literature?*, one sees also the paradox of freedom and nothingness at work, the doomed drive of pre-reflective consciousness to realize its fulfillment in essential form. /24/

In *The Psychology of Imagination*, particularly the final chapter on "Consciousness and Imagination," that theme is treated thoroughly. /25/ Sartre's argument there is that in order for consciousness to imagine an object it must deny the real, for if it intends the real (and thus constitutes it) it cannot imagine it. Hence the imagination is a projection of nothingness, which is really the converse of consciousness intending something. Since the imagination always negates (nihilates), and by this negation constitutes its unreal object, it is a basic element of the intending consciousness. If it were not for the negating capacity of the imagination, consciousness as intentionality would be pointless, because it would not have (nor be) the freedom to intend but could only be the act of recording the already-there. The imagination makes the intending consciousness possible and constitutes consciousness as freedom; the imagination is not a superaddition to consciousness, but *is* consciousness as intentionality. If we could not imagine, which is to say posit the unreal, we could not constitute the real and could not think.

Among the traits that distinguish Sartrean existentialism from essentialist phenomenology and that give his literary criticism its peculiar sense of risk are his denial of the reductive process and of the transcendental ego. /26/ Natanson explains it thus: according to Sartre, "Phenomenological reduction and the transcendental ego rob intentionality of its genius by relinquishing the immediate world seized through intentional consciousness. What Sartre calls the transphenomenality of being is lost in the reduction." /27/ How Sartre can ignore the formal reductive steps and write prose that maintains the originality of a perception of the immediate world is demonstrated in brilliant essays such as "Faces." /28/ Yet even in these a Husserlian epoché is employed that frees the intending consciousness for its work of negation and liberation. One has the sense that in Sartre's literary criticism as well the dialectic of negation and anticipation serves the same purpose as the transcendental ego and the reduction and indeed is not very different in function from them. Yet the existential stakes for Sartre seem to be greater because, in his system, he wagers a world view with every sentence, and one responds readily to that creative daring. /29/

Georges Poulet

The distinguished Belgian literary critic Georges Poulet is the most prominent advocate of the critical direction known variously as the "Geneva School" (because a number of its practitioners have taught at the University of Geneva), the "criticism of consciousness," the "criticism of experience," and "genetic criticism." Other critics identified with this approach are Marcel Raymond (its originator) and Albert Béguin, and the "new Geneva school" critics Jean-Pierre Richard, Jean Starobinski, and J. Hillis Miller. /30/ As the term "criticism of consciousness" suggests, the movement has roots in phenomenology and existentialism and stands in opposition at least to the extreme forms of "objective" criticism that do not acknowledge the influential presence of the author in the text and the effect of the reader upon the text's explication. Thus the "consciousness" that "criticism" refers to is the interacting intentionality or life-worlds of author, characters, and reader that constitute the literary experience and even, at least in Poulet's case, literary history.

Poulet, in fact, combines a genetic approach with a unique kind of literary history. According to Sarah Lawall, Poulet's criticism is characterized by an interest in "the pre-verbal substructures of literature," an Arthur Lovejoy-style stress on "shifting patterns of perception throughout generations of literary history," the theory that a text's "structure is keyed to a central core or *foyer* that generates each work's interlocking themes and governs its spiritual identity," and a "refusal to submerge himself in purely intellectual, purely 'classical' formulations." /31/ In his monumental *Studies in Human Time,* viewing literature as the "history of human consciousness," he tries to discover through a close reading of the text the experiential patterns of the author's life-world detected therein (the process that Roman Ingarden condemns as psychologistic) to empathize with the author's creative impulse and thus to locate the originating moment in the work's evolution. /32/

This effort Poulet undertakes mainly in terms of time and space as essentialist modes of consciousness or as Heideggerian *existentialia.* He broadens this discovered moment of genesis into epochs of literary history and establishes literature as the expression of consciousness intending self and world through the works of various writers (Racine, Goethe, Balzac, James, etc.) in particular time spans. For example, an intensification of self-consciousness in the Renaissance brought on by Descartes produced a shift in European literature that gradually led away from a sense of time initiated and sustained by divinity and resulted in the modern author's felt need to create his own durable moment.

J. Hillis Miller says that most of Poulet's work can be grasped as an effort to describe the attempts of major authors since the Renaissance "to escape from the fluidity and instability of everyday time. . . by one form or another of spatialization." /33/ Underlying such criticism is the premise of the inception of the creative act in a foundational self-consciousness of the artist that is met and fulfilled by the critic in his own sympathetic response. Pervading all authentic literary experience is the quality of presence—presence of the mind to itself, of the author's mind to the mind of the critic, of the past to the new, etc.—a concept that betrays Poulet's dependence on the spatial grasp of time characteristic of the Western philosophical heritage. This uncritical use of the Western philosophical tradition is matched by Poulet's relatively uncritical attitude toward his authors' language. /34/ His concern is for their imagery, for the construction of typologies that will reveal the experiential patterns; he does not distrust the language that produces the imagery: if consciousness is fundamental, then the artistic language it generates can also be taken as basic. The criticism of consciousness is thus really a criticism *by* consciousness of consciousness at work as it originates itself and its universe through fiction—an undertaking at once more naive and more ambitious than that of most other phenomenologically-oriented directions. /35/

Hans-Georg Gadamer

Hermeneutical criticism has probably been mainly identified in the modern American mind with biblical scholarship, for it was the "new hermeneutical" dialogue among Continental and

American theologians in the 1950s and '60s that brought the approach to the attention of Americans. /36/ Since then the publication of two texts in the United States has done much to increase the awareness of the potential of secular hermeneutical criticism: Richard E. Palmer's *Hermeneutics* (1969) and Gadamer's *Wahrheit und Methode* (1960) in English as *Truth and Method* in 1975. /37/ Yet biblical and secular hermeneutics have been, in their development, intertwined. Erich Dinkler remarks that the first impulses toward biblical hermeneutics appear in the New Testament itself in allegorical and typological interpretations of Old Testament scripture, and goes on to describe how Schleiermacher during the height of Romanticism and working in both a theological and philosophical framework sought to apply an expanded Aristotelian theory of hermeneutics to biblical analysis. /38/ Schleiermacher maintained that the hermeneut must undertake a formal study of the style and structure of the text, a philological analysis of the foreign languages on which the text is based, must achieve a historical comprehension of the text's framework and a psychological appreciation of the author's situation.

The philosopher Dilthey, then, in the nineteenth century, starting from the achievement of Schleiermacher, sought to turn hermeneutics into a method specifically suitable to the interpretive efforts of the humanities as distinct from the methods of the natural sciences and emphasized the need to consider personal experience and expression as part of the process of interpretation. For Dilthey hermeneutics came to mean, beyond the method of textual interpretation, the study of how understanding occurs at all, and at this point the hermeneutical approach assumes a strong phenomenological thrust, since it comes to include a phenomenology of understanding, both in the essentialist sense (what are the intentional characteristics of understanding?) and existential mode (how does one's being-in-the-world affect understanding?). /39/

Gadamer, as a pupil of Heidegger and Bultmann (both of whom have contributed importantly to the evolution of hermeneutics) and as an astute Husserl scholar, has gained recognition largely through his *magnum opus, Truth and Method,* as the major authority on hermeneutics for secular and biblical, essentialist and existentialist proponents of the hermeneutical approach. Like Dilthey, Gadamer is motivated by the desire to separate the languages of the humanities from those of the sciences, to explore the relation of feeling and intuition to intellect and analysis, to examine the context and history of a text in terms of its possibilities for modern interpretation. He is always concerned with the problem of *how* the experience of the text is transmitted to the reader, which means that questions of method or of the text's nature are subordinated to the question of transmission and reception.

Gadamer emphasizes that the hermeneutical act is a total experience rather than just intellectual analysis, that it is a historically significant event rather than an isolated study, that it is a linguistic encounter transcending conventional linguistic categories. To call it a total experience means that one allows oneself to be grasped by the text, to open one's life to it and to the possibility of change through it, rather than trying to bring the text under the control of one's already crystallized system. At the same time, one must bring prior experience to the text and have it interact with the text's self-understanding to produce something (and someone—the reader) new: this is the historical aspect of the hermeneutical act (and Gadamer criticizes Dilthey for not stressing this historical dimension enough) and the aspect that shows the dialectical nature of history. The act occurs through language in the Heideggerian sense that not the form of articulation is of primary importance but rather what the text says, a position that can be understood only if one abandons the subject-object dichotomy and sees the text as part of the language that surrounds one, that provides the expression of our *Dasein* and that we must listen to rather than dominate. Hence also the aesthetic experience of literary interpretation is always absorbed into the ontological experience: the text tells us, along with other expressions of language, who we are at this particular historical moment.

Gadamer, like other hermeneutical critics, is inevitably much concerned with the notorious hermeneutical circle: what one sees in the text is already implicit in one's pre-understanding. Yet he argues that the hermeneutical act grasped as encounter and event means an invasion of new experience that indeed releases one from solipsism. /40/

Konstantinović's summarizing statement on Gadamer is worth quoting. He says that in *Truth and Method* "Aesthetic understanding becomes almost a paradigm of historical-humanistic knowledge. Gadamer places the mode of being of the aesthetic object at the center of his research and reaches the conclusion that it is impossible to isolate a pure aesthetic substance from all that is non-aesthetic. The work of art is not an autonomous poetic pseudoworld ontologically distinct from prosaic reality but is closely related to reality, and its meaning is identical to the structure of the meaning of practical existence." /41/

Paul Ricoeur

Whereas the impact of most of the other phenomenologically-oriented critics (Heidegger, Merleau-Ponty, Sartre, Poulet) I am treating in this section has been felt in the United States over the past two to three decades, Ricouer's influence has emerged strongly just in the past ten years, and one has the sense that it has not yet reached its height. Indeed, my own study stands more under the influence of Ricoeur than of any other single critic. Since I will discuss his career-long phenomenological projects in the context of sketching his *The Symbolism of Evil* in the next section and then will come back to him again in a final discussion of ways of reconciling phenomenology and structuralism, I will content myself here with a brief synopsis of a 1974 essay called "Metaphor and the Main Problem of Hermeneutics." /42/ This essay shows how Ricoeur, like many other phenomenological and structural critics, moves from a discussion of ordinary language to poetry and how his long-advertised "poetics of the will" may eventually take shape.

Employing his usual dialectical method, Ricoeur in this essay opposes explanation and interpretation, work and word, sense and reference, whole text and individual metaphor to emerge with a revival of an Aristotelian conception of metaphor that is also, of course, a phenomenological-hermeneutical conception. He wishes to demonstrate that the explication of metaphor, rightly undertaken, can serve as a model for the explication of a whole text, and that conversely the interpretation of the text gives us clues as to the nature of metaphor. He sees this also as an opportunity to resolve misconceptions concerning the hermeneutic circle. Ricoeur separates explanation from interpretation according to the by now familiar critical tenet that explanation treats the clarification of the text's information whereas interpretation refers to the critic's involvement in a response to the text. Similarly, sense has to do with the text's "objective" qualities, while reference includes the critic's perspective and prior knowledge—his intentionality—that determines his response. Metaphor, then, does not consist merely of a "sense" operation whereby the juxtaposition, the new contextual situation of words provides new material for explanation; it does not merely increase the polysemic possibilities of a word. Rather, a novel metaphor (one that has not already been absorbed into the polysemic lexicon) is a "semantic event" that has no linguistic status but is the author's construction of a "network of interaction, which makes of this context an actual and unique context," a "point of intersection between several semantic lines" where "all the words taken together make sense." /43/ This explication of metaphor is the model for the explication of the text because it shows how the construction of both is a guess based on clues within them and how the construction involves the selection of one probability over another.

Text interpretation, in turn, illuminates metaphor interpretation because it reveals the problematic significance of the relationship between reference and self-reference that arises only when the discourse becomes a work, "a closed chain of meaning." /44/ Ricoeur offers a mode of interpretation in which, unlike the

Romantic effort to match the spirit of the author, one opens oneself up to the existential possibilities suggested by the text. This shift also suggests a shift in the comprehension of the hermeneutic circle. Ricoeur wishes to correct the concept of the hermeneutic circle as a "circle between two subjectivities" of author and reader and "as the projection of the subjectivity of the author in the reading itself" in order to view it as the circle between one's mode of being and the mode of self-disclosure "by the text as the work's world;" it is a "dialectic between disclosing a world and understanding one's self in front of this world." /45/

This concept of text interpretation acts as a model for metaphor interpretation through a reconsideration of Aristotle's view of metaphor. According to the *Poetics,* in Ricoeur's interpretation, diction (and metaphor as an element of diction) makes *sense* only in relation to the plot or "mythos" of tragedy (which is the paradigmatic literary genre) and establishes *reference* through *mimesis;* Ricoeur considers *mimesis* as equivalent to the modern phenomenological "world disclosure." Hence, inspired by Aristotle, Ricoeur declares that the originary function of metaphor (for him its prime function) "is related to the function of poetry as a creative imitation of reality." /46/ Metaphor works to transform ordinary language into the revelation of new landscapes of the imagination. Ricoeur means to treat imagination as an element of language, and it begins to become clear that through the language of imagination he will create his poetics of the will. /47/

Other phenomenologically-oriented critics deserving attention are, from the secular side, for example, the Husserlian Mikel Dufrenne, Wolfgang Kayser, Emil Staiger, Gaston Bachelard, Jean-Pierre Richard, Gabriel Marcel, Maurice Natanson, and J. Hillis Miller, and from the religious side Paul Tillich, Fritz Buri, Heinrich Ott, Gerhard Ebeling, and Ernst Fuchs. I have not referred to prominent phenomenologists of religion such as Max Scheler and Gerhardus van der Leeuw because their work has not focused primarily on specific texts—and in a wide-ranging study such as mine I have had to limit myself to critics who are, at least in some important aspect of their critical endeavor, text-oriented.

B. Application

The discussion of phenomenological and phenomenologically-derived literary theory must be reinforced by illustrations of applied criticism, for such illustrations, better than anything else, show one the possibilities for adapting the various approaches to one's own interpretative methods and purposes. In this section I will briefly summarize five examples of phenomenological analysis of religious texts and five of secular texts. The studies that I have chosen range through the history of phenomenology and over the variety of its literary critical approaches. Thus I have included an important Heidegger essay from 1936 as well as a Poe study by David Halliburton from 1973. I have not discovered any good examples of a thorough-going essentialist analysis that might be sketched here, although a number of the writers I have selected do use aspects of the Husserlian method, but I have been able to incorporate specimens of all other prominent phenomenological approaches: Heideggerian, Sartrean, criticism of consciousness, hermeneutics, and combinations of them, all as they are applied to religious and secular texts.

Unlike the situation that obtains, as we shall see, in structuralist literary criticism, little difference can be marked between the phenomenological critics of secular and religious works. Both are relatively uncritical and unself-conscious regarding their methodology and apply it as an interpretive instrument without attempting to defend it as an ideology or a dimension of an ontology.

Mircea Eliade, "Mysteries and Spiritual Regeneration"

One of the world's foremost scholars of the history of religions, Eliade appropriates phenomenology in a more Husserlian than

Heideggerian sense by bracketing the questions of the "truth" of archaic or contemporary "primitive" religious forms and seeking instead to describe how the myths and rituals that constitute these religions are experienced from the standpoint of the participants in them. Since "Myths reveal the structure of reality, and the multiple modalities of being in the world" and are thus "exemplary models for human behavior," a study of the myths (and of the rituals accompanying or preceding them) illuminates the ontology apprehended by the believer and practitioner. /48/ Such study also involves a hermeneutical effort, for Eliade compares the "primitive" uses of myth with the uses of myth in the modern world and takes the former to demonstrate both the continuity with the latter and (particularly in the case of Christianity) the differences between the two.

Although Eliade's approach is decidedly unlike Bultmann's, Eliade too, finally, emphasizes a peculiar Christian understanding of history in relation to myth and the need for existential behavior as a way of transcending the sway of mythological thinking. According to Eliade, the Hebrew religion and then Christianity escaped the cyclical context of other religions marked by the endless repetition of archetypes—the prototypal deeds of gods and men that humans are obliged to duplicate in order to keep the world intact and secure. By substituting historical revelation for cyclical repetition, Judaism and Christianity introduced the need for a faith unconfirmed by ritual re-enactment and support of myth, and placed man in a situation of utter dependency on the God who acts in history toward a linear future and asks that humans do the same. Modern Western believers must, in fact, guard against lapsing into the old archetypal patterns that shelter them from the "terror of history" and must constantly meet the challenge of history. /49/

The chapter "Mysteries and Spiritual Regeneration" from Eliade's *Myths, Dreams, and Mysteries* can legitimately be included as an example of a phenomenological study of sacred texts because, although no biblical exegesis is undertaken here, the focus is centrally on non-Christian myths and rituals—sacred

stories and acts that incorporate religious perspectives susceptible
to interpretation both in terms of their self-understanding and of
modern man's comparative treatment of them. /50/

Eliade begins the chapter with a summary of the cosmogonic
myths of the Australian Karadjeri and of their initiation rite. The
myths center on the two brothers named Bagadjimbiri who name
the plants and animals, create a tribal structure, fashion genital
organs for humans, teach hunting, originate rituals, etc. The
initiation rite itself, undergone by boys beginning at age twelve
and continuing for several years, involves anointing with blood,
symbolic death, a ritual journey, circumcision, subcision, and
various other ceremonies. Eliade emphasizes that the rite,
intended as a repetition of the rites instituted by the two brothers,
introduces the boy to the terrors of the supernatural, causes him to
"die" to childhood, and makes him confront the adult world
imbued with the holy, with death, and with sexuality. These
constitute the mysteries of existence, and as the tribe introduces
the initiate to them through repetition of the old rituals, in his
"death" and new mode of being a new cosmogony takes place.

Not only among the Karadjeri but among other tribes similar
initiatory mysteries are cultivated. Five common to most tribes
are the novice's departure from his family and isolated sojourn in
the forest (actions with symbolic overtones of death), the use of
isolated huts or cabins for the novice (signalling a return to the
womb or to loneliness and darkness preceding a new beginning),
outright initiatory death symbolism (partial burial, ghost-like
behavior, torture and mutilation), the symbolism of mystical
regeneration (new names, treating the neophyte like an infant,
etc.), and the practice of killing and sometimes eating another
human. Through all of these the neophyte is instructed, through
rituals affecting his total being, that emergence into adulthood
means an encounter with the sacred that demands his acceptance
of adult responsibility; above all, this initiation into a new life is
conveyed by the powerful symbolism of death.

In the next section of the chapter Eliade treats another kind of
initiation ceremony, that of men's societies and male secret

societies. He argues that their origin is not an attempt to challenge the female supremacy of matriarchal cultures, as scholars of the historical-cultural school surmise, but in the same need to participate in the mysteries of death and rebirth rituals evidenced in the puberty ceremonies. In fact, the adult societies are characterized by an intensification of the elements of the initiation rites, with the difference that secrecy is more important in the rituals of the secret societies, obviously, than in those of the initiation rites. Although relatively little is known of the secret rites themselves, enough has been learned to enable one to comprehend their symbolism. Symbolic burials, swallowing by monsters, imbibing of "drinks of death," etc., and rebirths from all of these constitute initiation into the secret societies, but what the societies themselves consist of is largely unknown.

In a brief next section Eliade explores the meaning of the tortures that comprise part of many secret society rituals. Since they are believed to be perpetrated by divinities, they are thought to transform the individuals who endure them. As such, in combination with other rituals symbolizing death and rebirth that are employed in other ritual situations (puberty rites, shaman initiation) they reveal that "the mystery of spiritual regeneration consists of an archetypal process . . . effected whenever the need is to surpass one mode of being and to enter upon another, higher mode." /51/ In the section on women's rituals, in spite of the dearth of information, Eliade finds that both the puberty rites and the female secret society rituals are remarkably similar to their male counterparts and that they, like the male counterparts, are grounded on "a profound religious experience" and seek to provide "access to the sacred." /52/ Childbirth especially, however, since it discloses to women their creative force, forms the substance of a religious mystery that has no equivalent in masculine experience. But in the myths and rituals of the women's societies and secret groups, giving birth does not of itself comprise the mystery; rather, the mystery resides in the recognition of the mystic oneness between the female, the natural, and the divine. On the whole, among women as among men, the "scenario" of torture and symbolic death and rebirth at various stage of maturation appears whenever spiritual regeneration takes place.

In the section on swallowing by monsters, then, Eliade pursues this single archetypal theme in order to demonstrate how it pervades the different ritual structures and gives them meaning. In the Maori myth of Maui, for example, that hero comes home after a life of adventure and enters the gigantic body of his sleeping grandmother. Although he forbids the watching birds to laugh when they see him emerge, they do so nevertheless when he is but part-way out of her mouth, so that she bites him in half and kills him. This is why all men must die; if Maui had emerged whole, humans would be immortal. As this and other myths suggest, to be swallowed by a monster is to descend into hell, and thus one recognizes the familiar death symbolism again. But Eliade believes that this devouring also indicates a return to the womb and hence to a primal state. Being swallowed by a monster denotes simultaneously death and birth, an end and a primal beginning.

Eliade begins the final section on the symbolism of initiatory death with the observation that death as presented in such myths and rituals means not an ultimate end but rather the first step toward a new beginning. All such symbolic journeys into death are also attempts to gain wisdom, for those who have been initiated into death plumb the most mysterious knowledge of all. The knowledge that one gains is that beyond profane existence, traversed through death, is a rebirth into a superior mode of life. The mystery is present even in Christianity, where symbolic death also precedes spiritual regeneration. Speaking existentially, Eliade says that if man is involved in such experiences of death while living, he is already entering immortality, and that if this is so, then he should not think of immortality "as a survival *post mortem,* but rather as a situation one is constantly creating for oneself, for which one is preparing, in which one is even participating *from now onward* and from this present world."

/53/ From this last quotation it becomes clear how Eliade can move smoothly from a phenomenology of archaic sacred texts and rituals, distilling their essential traits and meanings, to an application to the lives of modern Western man.

John Vernon, "The Garden and the Map"

Vernon has composed this essay as the introductory chapter to *The Garden and the Map: Schizophrenia in Twentieth-Century Literature and Culture.* /54/ The first section of this chapter on the Genesis Garden of Eden myth uses the phenomenology of Merleau-Ponty and Eliade in inventive and instructive ways to initiate the enterprise of the whole book, which is, as the subtitle indicates, a study of how modern literature and culture reveal and express a pervasive and often unhealthy split between fantasy and reality. Vernon wishes to show, somewhat like Roland Barthes in *S/Z,* that what we have come to call "reality" is only one kind of structure whereby we experience the world and not the only kind, for fantasy as another such structure that we have suppressed is now insisting on taking its place as a culturally acceptable experiential mode. Because Western culture has rigorously divorced reality and fantasy, sane and insane, and forced these modes to exist in mutually exclusive fashion, human being-in-the-world has been distorted, and schizophrenia as a dominant form of illness has emerged to disclose a fundamentally mad dimension to our dividing of the world of experience.

Vernon begins the chapter by defining God as "the first schizophrenic," for the very creation of a world by divinity means a "fall" from wholeness into a division that also characterizes humans; Western man in particular has grounded his thought in structures of separation and needlessly and harmfully partitions his life into areas that do not interrelate. /55/ The Genesis myth of the Fall is the most forceful representation of this decline from wholeness to fragmentation in Western culture, and the images of the garden and the map project best the contrasting Oriental (dynamic) and Western (static) ways of accommodating this process. Since Vernon states that his approach is neither historical-critical nor biblical-exegetic but rather "structural analysis," it will afford an example of how a phenomenologist comprehends such analysis and applies it to a text that we shall encounter later from the structuralist perspective as it is more commonly understood, namely after the fashion of Lévi-Strauss.

Adam and Eve before the Fall inhabit the Garden of Eden, Vernon says, in a naive condition of synthetic wholeness. "Synthetic" in this context means not the reunification of things previously separated but, in the sense of Durkheim, Cassirer, Eliade, etc., refers to an original sense of unification in consciousness that precedes organized knowledge.

The Garden is filled with objects that are sacred because they embody what they express, because the mark of divinity and humanity is a literal part of them—an insight that Vernon derives from Merleau-Ponty. Things proliferate into individual forms inside the Garden, but because all is alive with the undiffused holy, the proliferation does not mean fragmentation. Vernon accepts Eliade's claim that plants especially image such dispersion and identifies the Tree of Life as the most fitting symbol, for it acts as model for the vital life patterns of the whole universe. Before the Fall, the relationship of parts as symbolized by the Tree is perfectly integrative, whereas after the Fall, outside the Garden, that relationship is disintegrative or segregative. The body itself, as Merleau-Ponty has described it, conveys this primal dynamic unity symbolized by the Tree of Life; the synthetic functioning of the body's parts is an excellent instance of the pre-reflective experience of integration. That bodily unity, in fact, is expressed even more radically by the story of Adam's androgyny from apocryphal and rabbinical writing. The very creation of Eve from Adam and then the postlapsarian acts of eating and sexual intercourse produce a twoness and an objectification of the body and the other that destroy wholeness.

In the view of the mystic Jakob Boehme, eating the fruit of the Tree of Knowledge of Good and Evil represents a yielding to desire, a twofold desire consisting of acquisition and consumption. Outside the Garden, then, these aspects of desire become objectifying needs that control man and alienate him from himself and his world. Both the sacred objects and sacred spaces of Eden are profaned and transformed into things and places useful for sheer survival and hence no longer valuable in themselves—no longer gratuitous and hence holy. Beyond Eden, the map rather than the garden becomes the representative image, standing for systematically and economically organized space into which the body is fitted instead of the body and space being coextensive.

Both the map and the labyrinth function as modern symbols of separation, confinement, and containment, for unlike the ubiquitous center characteristic of sacred space in the Garden, the spaces of the map or labyrinth do not interpenetrate or overlap; they exist in radical discreteness and thus, in this objectified and controllable form, can be exploited. The world of the map is the arena of having in contrast to the world of being inside the Garden. The map represents property and owning, while the Garden represents total sharing.

The map, finally, is grounded on the principle of contradiction, the division between being and non-being. Because contradiction underlies formal logic which in turn underlies knowledge, one can say that the fall from wholeness in the Garden is connected to the advent of knowledge. The other tree in the Garden, the Tree of the Knowledge of Good and Evil from which Eve and Adam eat the forbidden fruit, represents the duality and even the polarity of this knowledge. That Adam and Eve are thrust out of the Garden after eating the fruit shows that the knowledge they derive is not merely of good and evil but above all of the gulf between good and evil; although Vernon does not say so at this point, he might have added that the freedom created in this first act of disobedience is also the fundamental loss of wholeness, the separation from God that dictates all other separations and thus precipitates the schizophrenic experience.

This is, then, a "structural" analysis in the sense that the elements of the Genesis myth are made to illuminate the shape of the modern Western epistemological and existential crises. The components of the story of the Fall are demythologized into the language of consciousness. In the succeeding chapters of the book Vernon goes on to specify how the configuration of reality in the writing of authors such as Sartre, Robbe-Grillet, and William Burroughs is stretched to its extreme and turns into fantasy because Western reality at heart is schizophrenic and expresses itself in fantastic hallucinatory form. This is the static, fragmented world of the map, where all things are eternally separate from each other and where objects can point to a meaning but can never coincide with it. But schizophrenia, as R. D. Laing has argued, can also have a healing dimension, and Vernon uses the case of the poet Theodore Roethke to illustrate how his vision "of a totally unrepressed world in which all things open upon each other and exist in a kind of intimate erotic community" is a return to the mythical garden. /56/ This is the kind of madness that is the sanest reaction to the fragmented universe and that may at least suggest how the debilitating split between being and non-being may be approached and perhaps overcome. Vernon's literary-critical and cultural-critical use of phenomenology is not systematic, obviously, and one would have difficulty in taking it as a model. Yet it is an informed and worth-while appropriation. Particularly the success of the application of Merleau-Ponty's body-world categories to literary texts and authors encourages one to attempt such analyses of other artists.

Paul Ricoeur, The Symbolism of Evil

The Symbolism of Evil is Ricoeur's third book in a multi-volumed and still incomplete phenomenological study of the will. /57/ In the first of these, *Freedom and Nature: The Voluntary and the Involuntary,* Ricoeur presents an "eidetics" of the will, a bracketing of the symbolic, empirical, and poetic elements of the will in order to discover and describe its basic possibilities. /58/ In the second, *Fallible Man,* he removes the brackets, introduces an "empirics" of the will, and traces the passage from innocence to guilt via a concrete mythics to depict a phenomenology of fallibility. /59/ In *The Symbolism of Evil* he turns to a hermeneutics of the will as a third "reading" and as a way of further examining the relationship of self, other, and will. This strategy involves the study of a different kind of material, the adoption of a new attitude, and a focus on another dimension of existence. The different material is the archaic symbol and its narrative extension in myth. The new attitude is the as-if stance (somewhat like Coleridge's suspension of disbelief) assumed by the symbol analyst that permits him to comprehend the believer's state of mind without actually assuming his conviction. The new dimension now the object of focus is language itself, the field of expression that hermeneutics is equipped to treat.

Now, instead of attempting to study the structure of the will eidetically (by reducing it phenomenologically to its essences), and instead of studying it existentially, in the context of actual human thrownness in the world, Ricoeur wishes to explore how the condition and action of the will have been experienced and expressed in the context of the encounter with evil in the history of cultures. The pathos of misery that led to the discussion of finite and infinite dimensions of the will in relation to evil in *Fallible Man* here becomes the confession of acquaintance with evil that leads to the hermeneutical interpretation of such confession and hence to a recognition of how this confession confirms and clarifies the first and second readings in the two earlier books. To put it another way: since fault, the reality of evil in man (the actualization of the possibility of evil called fallibility), cannot be treated philosophically (because it is a personal experience), it must be approached through the confession, and the confession must be studied in terms of its symbolic-mythic properties, for apart from linguistic indirection, there is no way of scrutinizing the experience of evil. That is to say, the primary language of fault is the language of symbols, the myths of fault that are the narrative extensions of the symbols are already also interpretations of the symbols, and the "gnostic" speculation on the myths and symbols (which Ricoeur does not indulge in here but projects for the still unwritten volume) is a secondary interpretation. These three—symbol, myth, speculation—comprise a totality of interpretation of the experience of fault that rests on the premise that the symbol is the fundamental mediator between pre-linguistic and linguistic experience. Hence to study the symbolism of evil through confessions of fault is to study basic epistemology and ontology that will illuminate the nature and interaction of self, will, and other.

Ricoeur further defines symbols in terms of their double intentionality: they first show forth spontaneous and obvious denotative meaning, but they then also call forth references to the hidden, the other, and the connotative, and in this second intentionality the archaic symbol reveals a cosmological, oneiric (psychic), and poetic dimension. The cosmological is the objective projection of the symbol onto the world, the oneiric is the "subjective" reaction of the symbol within the self, and the poetic is the joining of the previous two in the image that permits the symbol's communicative expression.

Ricoeur identifies the primary symbols of defilement, sin, and guilt as the three expressing the confession of evil in Western culture and proceeds to describe their dimensions. The cosmological dimension of defilement is represented by infection, its oneiric aspect by a sense of dread, and its poetic moment by words and rituals of purification. Sin symbolism shows a movement from the primitive stage of defilement to an ethical context. The cosmological moment of sin is the broken contract with God, the psychic dimension is the fear of divine anger, and the poetic the call to repentence. The symbol system of guilt exhibits a total subjectification of the sin symbolism. Here the cosmological dimension is internalized into a feeling of the weight of guilt upon one's awareness, the psychic aspect is the experience either of forgiveness or despair and estrangement, and the poetic dimension is the imagery of the tribunal (a sophisticated, self-conscious examination of one's guilt) and of a scrupulous conscience.

As Don Ihde skillfully summarizes Ricoeur at this point, in this reinterpretation of the defilement and sin symbols through the subjectivizing symbol of guilt, a reduction of sorts takes place and the symbol produces thought: the subjectivization of the symbols makes them accessible, indirectly, for philosophical reflection. /60/ When, for example, the symbol of defilement no longer participates in the primary image of stain but is "purified" to the point of representing the servile will, then it suggests the *concept* of servile will (which for Ricoeur is the will enslaved by the passions). This is, in fact, the concept that the series and subjectivizing trend of primary symbols seek to articulate. Yet paradoxically, because the concept of the servile will can be considered only indirectly, being closed to philosophical reflection, Ricoeur approaches it in a more germane manner—through an analysis of myths involving evil.

Although myths also do not yield to the systematic analysis of philosophy, they are themselves a spontaneous interpretation of the archaic symbols, and in treating them, Ricoeur sees himself dealing in an ontological exploration through which one can discover man's condition. The narrative structure of myth (which distinguishes it from symbol) describes primordial man in a universal fantasy-history traversing concrete space toward the illumination of his existential situation. Through a combination of mythic stories, Ricoeur delimits again, hermeneutically, his understanding of fault: the characters of the myths, gods and men, move from a primal time and place where evil has originated toward an endpoint in fantasy-history where evil has been destroyed or at least tamed. Ricoeur sees Western myths as reducible to four types: cosmogonies and theogonies, tragic myths, anthropological myths, and myths of the exiled soul. In examining first the cosmogonies and theogonies, he treats the Babylonian Gilgamesh epic, the Hebrew Genesis myth, and the Greek Titan theme. In the Babylonian epic, chaos is the primordial state, and the principle of evil is present in and with chaos and enters the world with the creation of the gods. In the Genesis myth of the Hebrews, the world created by Yahweh is good, and evil arises through an act of the human will, although the presence of the serpent suggests a residual sense of primordial evil already there before man's volitional generation of it. In the Titan stories, the origin of evil is located in a vague region between the human and the divine, which placement Ricoeur interprets as a tentative attempt to approximate the Hebrew view of evil originating in an act of will but nonetheless already present in the world.

In the second kind of myth, the stories of Greek tragedy treating the evil gods and blind fate, Ricoeur sees no distinction drawn between the divine and the demonic. Man, like Prometheus both guilty and innocent, is transformed through courageous suffering yet without averting his inevitable doom. In the Adamic (or anthropological) myths, evil begins in ancestral man, who is not a superhuman figure—unlike Prometheus; evil here is a deviation from man's essential humanity. Moreover, this evil originates in man who himself has been created in a context of primordial goodness. Yet the other characters in the Adamic drama (Eve, the snake) hint at a connection of this myth to others in which evil arises as part of cosmic creation from chaos and show that even in the Adamic myth the origin of evil is not totally in and through deviant man. Adamic man, however, unlike Promethean man, is not doomed by blind fate and wicked gods but has the chance for justification and acquittal through an interceding god at an eschatological judgment. In the myth of the exiled soul (or the Orphic or Gnostic myth), a dualism of body and soul is conceived and the origin of evil is assigned to the creation of the physical. Man strives to escape his doom through transcending his body and finding salvation in knowledge.

Ricoeur takes the Adamic myth as the pivotal one (since it is a "self-reflective" myth) and uses it to reinterpret the other three (which he calls "speculative," since they are directed toward the natural world instead of toward consciousness). He wishes to contrast the Adamic, reflective myth with the three speculative myths in order to present dialectically what Ihde calls the reciprocity of evil as act and state—a reciprocity that is parallel to that of voluntary and involuntary in *Freedom and Nature* and to that of infinitude and finitude in *Fallible Man.* /61/ More specifically, Ricoeur tries to explain, through a dynamic re-reading of the myths, how fault (man's involvement in evil) is not merely in the structure of the will (condition) but also in the will's self-seduction (act). Essentially, Ricoeur has the three other myths act as qualifiers to the predominant Adamic myth—the one he "believes in"—to show that the evil in and initiated by man is also already there in an *other* against which man fights, and invades one's selfhood through the body-soul dualism. The mythic narratives thus read together show how man experiences what he expresses in his archaic symbols: he generates (the act, the voluntary) the evil that he discovers to be already there (the condition, the involuntary).

This insight is a way of giving specific content to the general phenomenological insistence that one apprehends (intends) a life-world already given—which is to say that the intending consciousness intends an evil that is in both the structure of consciousness and of the world. But Ricoeur, in his famous final chapter ("The Symbol Gives Rise to Thought"), says that the phenomenologist cannot get a distance on this situation but can analyze it only within the reduction. To escape the hermeneutic circle (which maintains that one must believe in order to understand and understand in order to believe), Ricoeur proposes, paradoxically, an enlargement of it: one must make a commitment, take a stand, and attempt not a presuppositionless philosophy but one starting from the point of faith, which in this text arrived for Ricoeur when he accepted the predominance of the Adamic myth for the interpretation of all his Western myths of evil. In basic methodological terms, this means accepting the predominance of the symbol as that from which one begins thought and interpretation, not that which one allegorizes to expose a deeper, hidden truth beneath it. One accepts the symbol to interpret and transcend it, in the faith that it will lead forward—not back—to thought and truth, just as one accepts the symbolism of evil to transcend it, in the faith that through experiencing and expressing evil in the paradox of the servile will one can make and find not primordial goodness but a goodness of the "second naivete"—that one experiences by fashioning this goodness out of will and thought: one *chooses* to believe that goodness exists, and in that choice is the liberation of the will and the beginning demise of evil's power. In literary terms, one could say that the individual imagines the existence of goodness and then sets about creating the conditions whereby he can experience it wholly.

Rudolf Bultmann, "Man between the Times according to the New Testament"

Rudolf Bultmann, one of the most influential and controversial figures in twentieth-century theology, begins this essay (originally published in German in 1952) with an explanation of its theme: he wishes to explore the attitude of the primitive Christian community as it experienced the delay of the eagerly awaited parousia of Christ—an experience conveyed in terms of mythological eschatology (Jesus coming again from Heaven to render judgment and to initiate the new era)—and to compare it with the attitude of modern Christians who have lost the sense of living in an interim. /62/ Many of the early congregations, as we know from the New Testament literature and the Apocrypha, expressed impatience and disappointment when it became apparent that the event of Christ's return was taking longer than expected, yet this was not the only reaction; in Colossians, Ephesians, and Hebrews, for example, one finds no indication of an expected imminent parousia nor of frustration that it has not occurred. The anticipation of the immediate event fades, yet the belief in an ultimate cataclysmic end of the world marked by Christ's return remains; in our day, however, the awareness of living in an interim time, the time between the first and second comings of Christ, is gone.

Because, with the loss of this interim awareness we have also forgotten the possibility of the new era of the Spirit, we are alienated from the church of the New Testament. In seeking to discover why eschatology did not vanish altogether in the New Testament era, and particularly why it could survive in a way that stressed a continuity with pre-Christian Hebrew prophecy, Bultmann suggests that in the concept of the interim, which itself is located within mythological eschatology, is a view of paradoxical human existence characterized by Jesus' manifestation as its most crucial moment. From many synoptic references we know that Jesus believed himself to be living between two epochs (Matthew 12:28, Mark 8:38) and that he likewise saw all persons contemporary with him as inhabiting an interim. The fact that his message calls for a total, unconditional conversion and at the same time offers complete forgiveness reflects his awareness of the two aeons that he bridges and preaches in mythological form as the end of one cosmic era and the beginning of another, as the eras of God the Judge and God the Father. Paul above all sees Jesus as the one whose entry into the world signals the new era that occurs not as a cataclysm but as a historical event. "One can say that mythology . . . begins to be historicized." /63/ Paul also, and John as well, respond to the question of how man's interim existence is to be understood by showing that the age before Christ is the age of sin that is overcome through the Christ event, so that the passing of this era can also be grasped existentially—in a way that demythologizes the mythological language—as a passing of one's individual sinful life. Both writers recognize sin as the human desire to live self-sufficiently rather than from God's power, and both present God's grace as a gift that liberates man from sin thus understood and delivers him from his past, but because grace is a gift it must always be accepted anew. One renews that acceptance by acts of discipleship and by the repeated acknowledgement that one nonetheless always stands in need of forgiveness. If one does not recognize the intensity and power of sin, in fact, one cannot appreciate the totality of freedom from sin through God's grace.

Especially the presence of the Spirit signifies the complex nature of existence between the times, for the experience of the Spirit confirms that the new aeon is dawning, yet the fact that the Spirit is necessary at all reminds one that the old era persists and that men are still imprisoned in mundane conditions. Although Paul does not deny the spectacular, myth-oriented evidence of the Spirit's power—the miracles performed in its name—he tends to stress instead the importance of the Spirit for enabling one to live a daily life in a holy fashion, to live eschatologically. But the post-Pauline writings lose this perspective and emphasize instead the special and unique gifts of the Spirit, to the point that soon (as revealed, for instance, in Ephesians and Hermas) the Spirit is viewed as mediated mainly through the ecclesial offices and the sacraments rather than as directly effective in individuals. Hence the precarious paradoxical sense of the interim is displaced, for now the church as an institutionalization of the new era takes its place in the world. The interim is absorbed by the church rather than preserved by it.

How to behave in one's daily activities during the interim is problematical for the early Christian, but the tenor of Paul's instruction (I Corinthians 7, for example) is to continue in a wonted relationship with worldly matters while maintaining an attitude of "as though not"—an awareness that one actually belongs to a new, liberating era. Similarly, although the Christian is now totally free and guided by the motivation of love, he may well decide not to exercise that freedom, out of consideration for others who are weaker and do not understand the nature of a freedom determined by love. After Paul, however, this recognition of the paradoxical nature of freedom is blurred, and freedom from the world is presented as Gnostic libertinism or asceticism or as a release from evil behavior. Ancient Catholicism, projecting a double standard that dictated a strict ascetic code mainly for those in religious orders, caused the church rather than the individual, in this distorted fashion, to incorporate an interim morality.

Finally, the New Testament Christians look for the second coming as the time when death will at last be overcome, although they confess, in the interim, that new life through Christ's resurrection is theirs now, that they now experience a simultaneous having and not-having. Paul employs the Gnostic myth of lineage to clarify this faith: mankind inherited death through Adam but now inherits life through the new lineage of Christ. Because the actuality of this life over death cannot be tested in the interim, it can be made viable only through hope, a hope that by enduring and suffering becomes aware of its *existentiell* possibilities—that is to say, a hope that realizes the concrete potential of its individual being-there. This hope tends to be an anticipation that one's present suffering will be recompensed by a beatific afterlife, but Paul apprehends hope in a more vigorous and affirmative way. Through the metaphor of dying and rising with Christ Paul grasps how a radical surrender of the self in the present produces a hope that liberates him from a fear of death and allows the power of the new aeon to be immediately effective through him. The Gospel of John and Letter to Diognetus also convey this paradox of life in death, but for the most part the Pauline dialectical expression disappears and is replaced by the interpretations of baptism as the sacrament that insures immortality or by the view that living a righteous life is evidence of Christ's vital presence.

Bultmann wishes, of course, to emphasize the need to revive Paul's comprehension of the paradoxical relationship of death and life in Christ: "It seems to have been forgotten that it is precisely in suffering and dying that the life of Jesus is revealed and the power of God made perfect. When suffering and death are nothing more than an affliction that will one day be followed by a time of happiness, then the 'interim' in which man now stands in the present has been deprived of its *existentiell* meaning." /64/ New Testament anthropology is dialectical and teaches that man is defined historically, and our interpretation must reflect this self-understanding.

Since it may not be easily apparent why and how Bultmann's essay is a phenomenological analysis, I will describe briefly its phenomenological features. /65/ Bultmann's writing is in key ways a transposition of Heidegger's existential analytic into theological terms, so that one must turn to Heidegger in order to follow Bultmann's use of phenomenology. Heidegger preferred to call himself an ontologist rather than an existentialist, and his prime interest was indeed in being *(Sein)* rather than in human existence, yet man as the place where being is disclosed is nonetheless important to him, for the *Dasein* (being-there, man as ontological being) that characterizes man is much more revelatory of being than the mere *Vorhandenheit* (present-to-hand) of inanimate things or dumb creatures. Therefore by studying the understanding of being by man as being-there, one may be able to uncover some of the nature of being itself. This project undertaken in *Being and Time* consists of examining the *existentialia* or fundamental structures of human existing *(Existenz)*, a phenomenological inquiry addressed to *Existenz* that reveals the centrality of the concept of care *(Sorge)*. This concept combines three other primary structures: possibility, facticity, and fallenness. For Heidegger, *Dasein's* incompleteness or man always being ahead of himself and showing potential is expressed as possibility, while the limitation of this potential by man's thrownness into the world where he must willy-nilly function is called facticity. Fallenness, then, is the term for a feeling of at-home-ness in the world and man's flight from anxiety and responsibility.

Heidegger carries through a similar analysis of the concept of death to show how it is, first, the ultimate possibility of *Dasein* but, second, also constitutive of man's thrownness, for being is always being that anticipates certain death. Death is related, third, to fallenness in that man flees from the thought of death, driven by anxiety, and thus forfeits authentic existence.

We would have to develop a similar analysis of concepts such as body and history even to begin to do Heidegger's phenomenology of *Dasein* justice, but the preceding comments will suffice to show how Bultmann borrows from him in his New Testament theology. John Macquarrie remarks that Bultmann sees his theology as a phenomenology of faith, for his effort is to describe the content of faith and render it conscious to the believer. /66/ His grand project of demythologizing the New Testament, for example, is at heart a way of bracketing the superfluous material in order to reach the kerygma that is the essence of the content of faith.

In "Man between the Times" the direct influence of Heidegger is easy to detect. For example, the discovery of the Christian's tendency in the interim to abandon the tension of his paradoxical existence between two aeons is a theological version of Heidegger's existential analytic that traces the decline of care in *Dasein* from possibility to facticity to fallenness. The examination of interim man as described in the New Testament, in fact, gives special tangibility to Heidegger's analytic. What Heidegger characterizes, for instance, as a double fallenness into the world and into collectivism can be viewed more clearly through Bultmann's interpretation as the interim sojourner's propensity toward transforming the elements of his paradoxical life—the presence of the Spirit, one's daily behavior, the hope of immortality—into non-dialectical modes that represent either an adjustment to "facticity" (i.e., the double morality of ancient Catholicism) or a yielding to institutionalizing (Heidegger's collectivism), as in the absorption of the new aeon by the church or the mystery of life in death formalized in the sacrament of baptism. In like fashion, an investigation of how Bultmann uses Heidegger's being-in-the-world to inspire his interpretation of body in the New Testament (based on the contrast of *soma* and *sarx)* would illuminate much of Bultmann's controversial commentary on the meaning of Christ's resurrection. Similarly, a sketch of Bultmann's adaptation of Heideggerian historicity (involving, for example, the difference between *historisch* and *geschichtlich* or the renewable possibilities of authentic existence) would serve to elucidate the all-important relationship of mythological expression to existential attitude that Bultmann wishes to emphasize as the way of learning to live in genuine faith. /67/

Above all, the stance of the paradoxical risk of faith that Bultmann insists must be maintained by the Christian between the times is the same as Heidegger's challenge to live authentically, through constant choices toward meaning, in the confrontation with the nothingness of death. One learns through the combination of Heidegger and Bultmann that all men exist always between the times and that human freedom achieved through Christ is the paradigm for *Dasein* seeking openness toward being-itself.

Robert W. Funk, "Word and Word in I Corinthians 2:6-16"

Funk's essay is the final chapter of his 1966 *Language, Hermeneutic, and Word of God.* /68/ The book is strongly influenced by Bultmann and Heidegger but goes beyond them in its attention paid to the "new hermeneutic," the increasing awareness in theology since the Second World War that language, rather than functioning merely as an instrument of communicating, is a crucial part of the interpretative act itself. In a way both remarkably similar to linguistically-based structuralism yet radically different from it, the new hermeneutic posits "that language itself says what is invisibly taking place in the life of a culture." /69/ Even more than that, for the new hermeneut language itself is said to speak, and "The subject matter of which language speaks is primarily being." /70/ The overtones of Heidegger are distinct here: man is the locus of language speaking, and therefore the theologian must attend to the language of faith disclosing itself in man. Ernst Fuchs, a prominent German proponent of the new hermeneutic, argues that language like faith is a gift rather than a tool at one's disposal and that faith is dependent on God's *word.* For Fuchs, therefore, "the historicness of existence" is "the linguisticality of existence." /71/

Gadamer especially, in his investigations of how understanding is possible and indeed occurs, is the scholar who reveals most readily the relationship of hermeneutics to phenomenology. He wishes to describe the conditions under which interpretation takes place as a way of recognizing "what is," and in the process declares that hermeneutics is primarily a matter of translation—a new actualization of the text in every new interpretative effort—and of seeking agreement with another on the content of the text rather than grasping the view of the text that another holds. Gadamer also claims that what emerges in the interpretation of a text, biblical or otherwise, is not the author's self-understanding but a revitalization of the subject matter. Thus, rather than projecting Bultmann's dialectic between mythological language and existential awareness, Gadamer stresses the interplay of language and subject matter. /72/

Funk's essay is composed against this background of the new hermeneutical dialogue among contemporary theologians. His exegesis of Paul's First Letter to the Corinthians 2:6-16, which consists of Paul's defense of his preaching "the word of the cross" against the Gnostic-oriented Corinthian schismatics, uses the interpretations of Bultmann and Ulrich Wilckens as a foil for his own combination of linguistic analysis, close reading, and the new hermeneutical concern for permitting the text to speak itself. /73/ His argument consists of the following main points: 1) Paul presents a kerygmatic word of the cross that is intended to conteract the emphasis on "sophia," wisdom interpreted by the schismatics as secret knowledge possessed only by initiates. Although he wishes to resolve the strife, based on sophia versus the word of the cross, among the members of the church at Corinth, he is even more concerned to speak to the theological issue itself in the sense of determining how God comes to word. 2) The fact that Paul uses typical Gnostic terminology and syntax does not mean that he was seduced by the Gnostic view in spite of himself but rather that he employed the language of Gnosticism against the schismatics in order to destroy their argument and direct them toward the kerygmatic truth. 3) Paul understands language not as mere words, not only as tools for communication, or in this instance to convey a mystery to the initiates, but as an event, as a process in which people participate and by which their lives are transformed. 4) One must discover the intentionality of the text in order to arrive at a full and balanced understanding, an endeavor that means neither too limited a reading of the text itself nor too broad an inclusion of the context.

Regarding the basic conflict between sophia and the word of the cross, Funk shows that Paul is not trying to persuade the schismatics to accept his christology but rather to recognize the crucified Christ as the foundation of faith. This is necessary because the Corinthians have become infected by Gnosticism to the extent that they view sophia as divine wisdom accessible to them and through which they can attain redemption—a redemption, moreover, that bypasses the need to practice a this-worldly eschatological faith.

Paul sets out to accomplish his task by using the language of Gnosticism against itself. Funk disagrees with the contention of Bultmann and Wilckens that in the midst of his argument Paul himself succumbs to the Gnostic heresy and is drawn into a strategic acceptance of the Gnostic redeemer myth in order to contrast it to the crucified Christ. Rather, as Funk carefully and skillfully demonstrates, the only word *(logos)* with power is not the word of wisdom but the word of the cross, precisely the word that appears weak and foolish to the "sophist," the one who deems himself wise. The only effective sophia is the sophia belonging to God, and the only way of sharing this sophia is through acknowledging the crucified Christ. Wilckens and Bultmann think that Paul has simply offered a Christian version of Gnostic sophia here, but Funk argues, by viewing the whole passage in context, that for Paul the helplessness and absurdity of the word of the cross, through which God's sophia is made available, is not illusory but substantial: "To the Gnostic the foolishness and weakness of the Redeemer must be ephemeral; to Paul they are the substance of his redemptive work. Gnostic wisdom delivers man from the world; the sophia that comports with the word of the cross leaves man, as it were, at the mercy of the world. For Gnosticism hiddenness is transhistorical; for the Christian it is nothing if not historical." /74/ Thus Paul finally shatters the Gnostic position. By connecting sophia with the crucified Christ, by identifying the Gnostic Lord of Glory with the humiliated Christ he robs Gnosticism of its arrogance and grandeur and forces the schismatics to listen to his kerygma of the cross.

In presenting this proclamation of the cross after dissolving the word of sophistic wisdom, Paul expands the meaning of language in the modern hermeneutical sense. He wants the Corinthians to respond to the preaching of Christ crucified with an existential decision, and he wants them to reach a common confessional agreement as a Christian community—both actions which grasp language as event and render it as event instead of taking it as a solely mental construct. Because language is event, further, Paul attends it and brings it to speech before the congregation. It comes alive in his preaching and attains a power in the midst of the listening congregation (he projects an imminent visit to them) that the ungrounded mythological images of Gnosticism cannot share. The intentionality of this text that Funk underscores, therefore, is to transcend itself as words, to provoke interaction among speaker, subject matter, and hearer, and to evoke response. For the modern interpreter, this means pushing the text to the limit of its "linguistic horizons," which is to say comprehending what it wished to say, as far as possible, in its original context and also transferring that intention to one's present situation. Thus Paul's intention is to let "Jesus come to speech." /75/

Transferring the event to the modern situation means regaining clarity about the hermeneutical situation itself. Funk frequently addresses implicitly the questions of contemporary hermeneutics. For example, his stress on Paul's desire, in the context of discussing language as event, to see the divisive Corinthians achieve a common confessional understanding is reminiscent of Gadamer's insistence that hermeneutics consists in large part of seeking agreement with another on the basis of the text. Similarly, Funk's tracing of the way the Pauline word is absorbed into its utterance is like Gadamer's assertion that in genuine hermeneutical understanding language disappears into its subject matter. Or yet again, Paul's attempt to enter into the language world that his auditors inhabit in order to subvert it toward his evangelistic-corrective ends is a dramatic version of what every hermeneutical project entails: a personal and historical involvement with language and others in order to achieve the growing self-and-communal understanding that meaning, in one important sense, consists of.

Martin Heidegger, "Hölderlin and the Essence of Poetry"

This short, difficult essay was first published as "Hölderlin und das Wesen der Dichtung" in 1936 and thus represents the period in which Heidegger had already moved beyond a Husserlian essentialist phenomenology to found existential phenomenology. /76/ Although critics like Magliola claim that "Heidegger's own literary criticism (on Hölderlin, Rilke, and others) belongs to his post-phenomenological period," Zoran Konstantinović argues in a more convincing fashion that Heidegger's influence on literary criticism can be traced primarily to *Being and Time*, published in German in 1927. /77/ Thus even though *Being and Time* consists of a fundamental revision of Husserl's thought, it is still sufficiently marked by his vocabulary and spirit to permit one to call it phenomenological. Konstantinović shows the close relationship clearly: "If Husserl's transcendental reduction led to pure consciousness, whose essence is the constitutive act, or intentionality, then in Heidegger intentionality becomes transcendent and surpasses all experience; it is pure consciousness, existential primal consciousness." /78/ I believe, therefore, that one can look upon the Hölderlin essay as one that incorporates both the older essentialist influence and the emerging existentialist "poetry as primary word" direction.

Heidegger begins the essay by justifying the choice of Hölderlin as the poet to reveal the essence of poetry; the reason is not that Hölderlin's verse incorporates the essence of poetry better than many others but that he himself as poet writes about that essence. Heidegger then turns to five "pointers" from Hölderlin that help us to recognize "the essential essence of poetry." /79/ This last sentence should alert one that Heidegger is attempting here a brief phenomenology of poetry, for to look seriously for the essence of poetry means a willingness to submit to the spell of poetry, and thus again Hölderlin, who writes about this power of poetry, is the ideal choice for the subject of the study.

The first pointer is a quotation from Hölderlin referring to the writing of poetry as "that most innocent of all occupations." /80/ Heidegger uses this phrase to declare that writing poetry first, as a playful preoccupation with words, "is harmless and ineffectual," yet this insight, of course, does not yet penetrate to the essence. /81/ The second pointer is a Hölderlin citation that reads, "Therefore has language, most dangerous of possessions, been given to man. . .so that. . .he may affirm what he is." /82/ This affirmation means a human confession of belonging to the earth and at the same time accepting the responsibility for one's worldly existence, a decision that is actualized as history and for which articulation language is offered to man as one of his possessions. Language is not only the "most dangerous of possessions" but the prime danger of all because it is what first shows man the potential for non-existence, yet language also carries in itself the additional danger of presenting a confusion between genuine and ·inauthentic utterance, because the essential can show itself only as the ordinary and the redundant. Language is, finally, in this ultra-dangerous form, actually a human possession in that it assures man that he can exist as a historical being. It is not therefore a possession as a mere communicative instrument but as an event there for man to share in to confirm the reality of his existing in the world.

The third pointer consists of a quotation from an unfinished Hölderlin poem:

> Much has man learnt.
> Many of the heavenly ones has he named,
> Since we have been a conversation
> And have been able to hear from one another. /83/

The fact that human *being* is constituted in language is realized only in conversation, which is both dialogue and encounter. We not only *hold* but also *are* conversation, which means that we are part of a universal dialogue that always focuses on the essential word. Yet Hölderlin says that *we have been* a conversation, suggesting a historicity to this universal focus on the essential word: we have been part of a single conversation since the human awareness of time, for this awareness is the unity that makes us one in conversation. Further, man has named the gods and thus rendered them present (just as he has caused the world to appear) through language; but naming the gods means that they have addressed and claimed man, and through this divine linguistic creation of human existence man is asked to decide if he will accept or reject the gods. Thus through conversation with the gods the idea of language as the highest occasion of existence assumes significance and receives grounding.

The question of who effects the naming of the gods and the essence of things is answered by the fourth pointer from Hölderlin: "But that which remains, is established by the poets." /84/ Thus, "the poet names the gods and names all things in that which they are"; this is not a simple labeling but an act whereby

what is named also acquires an identity as existence. /85/ "Poetry is the establishing of being by means of the word," but because being can never be an existent, human existence itself is given a foundation when the gods and essence of things are named. /86/
The last pointer from Hölderlin reads

> Full of merit, and yet poetically, dwells
> Man on this earth. /87/

Even though man constructs his worldly home through words, his foundation is not labor but poetry, which is to say, his existence is given as a gift. But if human existence is at its base poetic and poetry is not decoration but the very grounding of existence in history, how can Hölderlin refer to poetry, as in the first pointer, as "that most innocent of all occupations?" One must recall that because poetry names the gods (being) and the essence of things, it does not emerge from ordinary language but rather the essence of language emerges from poetry. Poetry is also "the most dangerous of possessions," as is evident in Hölderlin's descent into madness, yet Hölderlin on the verge of madness could call poetry innocent because he saw that a necessary innocence attaches to its essence, so that the poet can carry out his task protected by this patina of harmlessness. Although poetry looks like an innocent game it is not, for while a game joins men in self-forgetfulness, poetry brings them to the foundation of their existence.

Poetry grounds being through intercepting signs from the gods and passing them on in human form. Yet because the poet is also the voice of the people he mediates between gods and men, and in standing between them he is an outcast. Thus the man who dwells poetically in the world is at once alienated from it. Hölderlin saw himself as an inhabitant of this Between realm, but the Between for him was also temporal, with the No-more on the one hand and the Not-yet on the other. The Between therefore is the Nothing that the poet inhabits, a lonely post from which he mediates the historical essence of which poetry consists.

To sketch Heidegger thus is self-defeating, since one cannot hope to catch the multiplication of nuances on which his style and philosophy build—unless one recognizes in the process that one's interpretation of the essay (as is the case with all of Heidegger's writing) forces or seduces one into practicing his kind of epoché. Heidegger makes an existential phenomenologist of Hölderlin, of course, and demands such a phenomenological reading of his reading of Hölderlin if one is to grasp his (Heidegger's) sense. In other words, in order to understand Heidegger one must ponder each phrase first according to his reduction—already a radical remove from conventional argument—and then undertake one's own bracketing of Heidegger's reading in order to arrive at one's own existential analysis. This ultra-close reading (assuredly a different sort than what Barthes, for example, exercises in *S/Z*), then, both explains Heidegger's literary criticism and involves one directly in it.

Georges Poulet, "Balzac"

Poulet's book *The Interior Distance* (original French version 1952), of which the Balzac essay comprises the fifth chapter, is the second in the series of his multi-volumed project *Studies in Human Time.* /88/ In the first volume, published in 1949, Poulet was concerned to show, through an empathetic reading that attempted to identify with the *cogito* of representative authors such as Montaigne, Baudelaire, Flaubert, and Proust, how the artists of succeeding eras experience and express their identities temporally; or in more formal phenomenological terms, he employed time as a mode of consciousness to disclose how authors of various epochs define themselves and their art through temporality perceived as both an element of one's subjectivity and of the object world that one must apprehend. In *The Interior Distance* (which contains essays on figures such as Marivaux, Hugo, and Mallarmé) Poulet expands his effort to include space as a mode of consciousness that interacts with time, but it is a space that is seldom objectively considered. Rather, as *la distance intérieure,* it refers both to "my thought" as "a space in which my thoughts take place" and to the space "which separates me from, or draws me closer to, that which I am able to think." /89/

It is obvious from these quoted definitions that Poulet is interested less in exploring space (and time) as a realm in which literature exists and more in describing a creative consciousness in which a literature is born that shapes its own space and time as a reflection of the objective space and time that can never be known in themselves. Or one might suggest that Poulet's method here is a phenomenology of artistic self-consciousness, an internal description of how a writer experiences the reception and absorption of images, largely through the categories of space and time, that are transformed into his text. The point of this complicated exercise is "to bring to light that interior vacancy in which the world is redisposed," in other words to illuminate the operation of the mind that reconstitutes for itself a world through words, the components of which it assimilates in fragmented and inchoate form. /90/ In Husserl's terms, Poulet examines the process of consciousness intending its literary world through the interplay—the arena of the "interior vacancy"—between *noesis* and *noema*. Poulet's method is, in fact, as Magliola points out, a literary critical version of Husserl's own. Magliola sees Poulet as establishing essential typologies in his writing, which task consists of the description of "the major features of an author's collective work in terms of systemic experiential patterns" which parallel "the procedures of Husserlian eidetic typology." /91/

Poulet's prose is self-referential and difficult to follow, although elegantly inventive and even lyrical. The first of the eight sections that comprise the Balzac chapter offers the typical Poulet strategy: by studying Balzac's *personae* and trying to identify common characteristics of their projecting and experiencing consciousnesses, by citing and commenting on passages that convey such traits, Poulet hopes to construct an inside view of Balzac's own passion-ridden consciousness as one example (among nine in the whole book) of how an artist's creative self is formed and communicated by his comprehension and utilization of space and time. Thus "the Balzacian being" experiences himself first in negative terms as desire and void existing in vacuity and wishing to be surrounded by substantiality. He is moved by primitive will and the need to expand that will into the world and the future. The whole of *The Human Comedy* (Balzac's many volumes of interrelated fiction), in fact, is an expression of the simultaneous pure impulse and fulfillment of the will. Through the twin forces of concentration and projection the thought of Balzac's characters both asserts and enlarges its hold on the world. Here one already sees, at the beginning of the essay, Poulet's emphasis on spatiality, his depictions of the mind filling its own latitude or travelling beyond itself, as a way of imaging the motions of the self defining itself.

The second section deals with the Balzacian being discerning space only to forget it immediately. Through memory and anticipation Balzac's characters range freely through past and future, without a sense of trespassing, nostaligia, or anxiety, and this uninhibited wandering permits a grand multiplicity of experiences to fill the interior distance and obliterate space-time; in the creative moment, then, this "prodigious density" explodes again into the world in the plenitude of fictive images. /92/

The third section reveals the next step: the surfeit of imaginative energy that generates the explosion of images on the world causes the mind to overextend itself, so that it finds itself again empty and faced with the void. Suddenly all it can imagine is a hellish darkness. "Mind, conqueror of space, is reconquered by space. Thought, left to itself . . . traverses everything, and finally loses itself in an imageless night." /93/ The will or desire that shaped a world turns destructive and not only annihilates the world but threatens also to dissolve the self. And even though the characters avoid this self-destruction, they sink into an apathy caused by an awareness of how great the distance is that again separates them from the objects of their desire. Left solely with their desire, they feel impotent and caught up in an inevitable temporal drift toward aging and death.

The way out of this enervation, one learns in Poulet's fourth section, is to abandon the purely mental landscape and venture physically into the external world. The character who embarks on this "adventure" learns that his total desire can fix on individual objects. This passion, that discovers the *other,* redirects the character's energies and reshapes his whole perspective. Now the object of desire is literally there, a real gap exists that must be bridged, and the will exerts itself in an immense effort to invade the space of the other by an intensification of the sensory faculties—as, for example, the young sculptor Sarrasine (Poulet mistakenly calls him a painter) attempts in the Balzac short story when he is infatuated by the prima donna La Zambinella. But the influence is also reciprocal; the other, the object of passion also manages to traverse the space dividing it from the desirous subject, and in this "mystery of Balzacian intersubjectivity" (as expressed, for instance, in the scene describing the violently passionate exchange of glances between Rodolphe and Francesca in *Albert Savarus*) one finds the proper setting for a similar transformation of time. /94/

Poulet treats that metamorphosis in the fifth section. The character passionately involved with the other experiences time as his fortune surging toward him to engulf him in a climactic and self-annihilating union. This anticipation that marks Balzac's fiction Poulet describes as a "magic moment," some of which are infused with joy and others with foreboding. /95/ The characters (usually women) who express these premonitions rife with passion or death transcend the divisions of past, present, and future, for in encountering such moments they sense time as a part of the fulfillment of their imminent destiny. This kind of existence constitutes a two-fold kind of duration, one (which the reader observes) an actual becoming of what the character is already determined to become and the other (which the character undergoes) a confused sense of re-experiencing a future already anticipated in the past. Yet eventually the passionate engagement with the real world, no matter what the quality of its duration, degenerates, like the isolated passion within the mind, into a monomania, and the character is again left with a realization of the void.

In the sixth section Poulet argues that Balzac's own consciousness, as revealed for example in personal letters, was racked by this fear of life's combustible tendencies and the growing awareness of diminishment, both of which forces he tried to counter with a drive for longevity. His inverted strategy is to lapse into inertia, to achieve constant duration by giving up passionate activity in favor of an automatism, but he cannot really stand to endure in such minimal fashion, of course. Thus he is faced with the central dilemma: "a life without duration or a duration without life." /96/ Since life, however, necessarily decides for the former, his problem becomes how both to survive and to live intensely.

Therefore, in the seventh section Poulet explains how Balzac and his protagonists strive to detach themselves from the world in order to possess it. Having foundered in his attempts to control the imagination's inner world of ideas and the external world of events inhabited by passion, Balzac turns to a realm of thought, the realm of abstraction, in which neither desire nor passion can reach him. He seeks to understand and participate in the world that anticipates both the motions of the will—of desire exerting itself—and of passion—of desire pursuing its objects in the world; this is the world of causes rather than of effects. This penultimate step brings him, as artist, into the circumference (the space) of God the creator.

This shared space is the subject of the final section. Balzac intends his fiction to function as a dynamic of cause rather than a depiction of effect, and this absorption with the divine and paternal dimension of being causes him to maintain a sympathetic involvement with his characters. As *The Human Comedy* grows to its hundred-plus components, Balzac becomes more and more preoccupied with his creator powers, and his formation of his fictive world replaces his concern with the merely mental or physical world. The sheer voluminosity of Balzac's production mirrors both the occupation of the inner distance and of duration, yet Balzac as god of his universe even attains to a kind of transcendence: because he *intervenes* in his characters' fortunes, he is like a divine power interposing his will from afar, and this action at least seems to affirm Balzac's belief in the force of transcendence. In the end, however, Balzac the creator slips once more into despair, not because of impotence but precisely because he has poured himself into his world and is empty again. This kenosis, after Balzac's life-long effort has filled all space and duration, brings about a nothingness that opens up to ultimate space and time, so that the Balzacian being is left in a posture of separation and waiting.

Such a sketch cannot convey the combined pellucidity and opacity of Poulet's prose that is communicated even in the English translation. Like Heidegger, although less resolutely so, Poulet presses his reader to slow down and struggle to penetrate the poetic complexity of his style in order to grasp the import of his criticism, which is to say that Poulet's style itself effects an initial phenomenological reduction that the reader must recast in terms of his own life-world. One must read Poulet on his own terms, but even after that one is left with the responsibility of translating his vision into one's own; otherwise the criticism of consciousness assumes a false objectivity that defeats its unique purpose.

Jean-Paul Sartre, Saint-Genet, Actor and Martyr

Sartre's Genet study was composed at a time (1952) when Sartre no longer promulgated a Heideggerian-based philsophy of existential essences that can be discovered in the vacuum of the epoché. /97/ He does, however, proceed in a phenomenological manner already established in his Baudelaire book of 1947, whereby he juxtaposes the *en soi, pour soi,* and *pour autrui* of Genet with the world of his imagination as it merges with the artistic consciousness. But in the Genet study (Genet being who and what he is) Sartre stresses the social-historical context more than in his previous writing. The existential-phenomenological biography takes form according to the stages of Genet's life and the mythic roles that he assumed (at least in artistic retrospect) at every stage.

Sartre's method becomes immediately clear in the first section on Genet's childhood. First he describes Genet at age seven from the *en soi* perspective—from the vantage point of being-in-itself, as an existing object—as an illegitimate child already out of place among foster parents in the farmers' village, among those whose *being* and *having* are connected to the land and to the lawful acquisition of goods. But when he views Genet from the *pour soi* viewpoint—the perspective of man's conscious free choice—he detects in the small boy already the exhilaration of the one who purposefully aligns himself to saintliness and, paradoxically, also to thievery as ways of denying the kind of being and having represented by his surroundings. Then, from the perspective of the *pour autrui,* being from the standpoint of others, Sartre sees the child Genet viewed suspiciously by the peasants and discovered in thievery. From this point on the *pour soi* and *pour autrui* interact: because Genet is labelled as a thief he now consciously accepts himself as such; society's "gaze" has transformed him into its object.

The next section takes Genet through his career as thief from adolescence to young adulthood. From the *en soi* position Sartre shows how Genet decides formally to be a thief because others have changed him into one; from the *pour soi* position he reveals how this decision affects Genet's consciousness and leads to contradiction: because he accepts what others have made of him, his being wicked is innocent, but because he does evil, which involves acting on free choice, he is guilty. From this contradiction Genet evolves a two-fold position: if evil is predetermined, he is a martyr and saint (with feminine connotations), but if he takes it freely upon himself, he is the prince of crime. Thus the dialectic of being and doing resolves itself into the two corresponding roles of saint and criminal; in terms of the *pour soi* and *pour autrui* relationship, then, as a teenager Genet attempts to perfect this dual role especially, as Sartre stresses it, through sexuality. Particularly through pederasty Genet confirms the paralyzing power of the gaze of others; he becomes the submissive partner, the martyr or "female" saint who suffers the satisfaction of the lust of the others but still reaffirms his identity through a conscious choice of an involvement in a criminal sexuality.

Describing Genet from the ages of eighteen to twenty in terms of a dialectic of being, Sartre treats Genet's awareness of his being as revealed by others in his accompanying inability to grasp himself as other, illustrative of the universal attempt of consciousness to locate being through others and the inevitable discovery that consciousness, always ahead of itself, can define itself only as the freedom of nothingness. In terms of a dialectic of doing, in this same stage of growing up, Genet's childhood decision to do evil is an admission of the power of goodness, for only the non-reflective creature can act evilly without acknowledging the good; thus one cannot do absolute evil.

In the "Caîn" chapter Sartre undertakes a recapitulating analysis of Genet at age eighteen from many angles: Genet in relation to world, language, affectivity, history, and reason. In the passage on language, for example, Sartre translates the already established insights into Genet's consciousness into Genet's linguistic practice to disclose how his criminal behavior is connected to a perverse language usage: how he employs language to hide rather than communicate meaning. Or again, Sartre looks at Genet in relation to history to point out that because of his acquiescence in his objectification through the gaze of others he is ahistorical.

The third section concerns Genet in a period of aesthetic absorption from the ages of twenty to twenty-six and speaks to the three concepts of image, gesture, and word. Because Genet viewed *en soi* desires evil he shifts acts to images in order to project antagonism into them. His solitary imagination working in such a transformational fashion turns above all to the fantasies of sexuality and particularly to masturbation. But seen *pour soi,* Genet through fantasy and dreams changes acts into gestures, yet even in this context Genet, in his dedication to the realization of evil, appropriates his aesthetic freedom of choice and employs beauty to invalidate the gesture. Seen again *en soi,* Genet reconciles image and gesture through words—which, as we have already observed, both disguise and disclose his intention.

The fourth section at last treats Genet as author at age thirty. His evolution into a writer is comprised, of course, of the same contradictory elements that characterized the earlier stages of his life, but now the passive (female saintly, martyr) side becomes more assertive and the defiant criminal side, without in the least retracting its perverse rejection of goodness, finds a way of communicating itself to others that transcends the paralyzing power of the gaze of others. At last he can grasp his objectification by others and in objectifying it through his writing can come to terms with it. This last then leaves Sartre free, in the final chapter, to describe the effects of Genet's writing on the reader. The analysis uses Genet's efforts at self-liberation as an illustration of Sartre's general understanding of consciousness: because Genet through his literary work has managed to find himself *pour soi* as the thief, he is freed of the *en soi* objectification of himself as thief, but this means that his consciousness is now void and empty and functions solely as consciousness to create. He has emptied himself into his art and finds now only pure negativity remaining—a situation that Sartre sees as inescapable for everyone who realizes and accepts responsibility for his condition. One might say that just as Melville's Ishmael, according to Paul Brodtkorb's analysis, is left at the end only with his artistic vision and his story to tell, so also Genet is left with bare words—or as he puts it, "My victory is verbal." /98/ Yet unlike Ishmael, Genet, whose life has been aligned to betrayal as the worst kind of evil, commits an ultimate betrayal of and through his art, for he does not permit his art to accomplish anything other than his own liberation toward nothingness. Thus even though he has "won," in forcing recognition of himself from others through his art, it is an empty victory, for he is recognized and accepted in spite of his perversity and crimes. "His is the horrible and grating misfortune of the damned. Thus, he has the bitter experience of never being taken *for what he is*." /99/

As Otto Hahn says, "Sartre's technique then is a phenomenological and differential analysis, followed by a spiraling totalization which constantly passes back through the same points, and each progression leads to totalization on a higher level. . . .By reproducing the totality in the process of its objectification, one restores life to the author's aggressivity, his frustrations, his struggle, the meaning he attributed to language, and thus one discovers the significance of the work." /100/ One might add that this significance at last is always transformed into a new project of consciousness that seeks futilely but meaningfully to transcend nothingness—futile because the consciousness that seeks transcendence is itself negation, and meaningful because this is all there is to do.

Paul Brodtkorb, Jr., Ishmael's White World

For close to a decade following its 1965 publication, Brodtkorb's Melville study held a lonely position in American letters as virtually the only book-length attempt to use a phenomenological approach to a work of fiction. /101/ The study is not based on a broad background in phenomenology; in fact, as the author readily admits in a note to his introduction, his categories are derived largely from a single text, J. H. Van den Berg's *The Phenomenological Approach to Psychiatry,* and indeed, the direct influence of Husserl, Heidegger, or Merleau-Ponty is nowhere to be found in the study, although strong hints of Sartre are present. /102/ Nevertheless, Brodtkorb does have a solid grasp of elementary phenomenology, and the study is a tight, skillful, imaginative demonstration of how the method can be applied to a literary text—a major text, moreover, that has undergone much previous analysis.

Brodtkorb begins by projecting his study as an examination of Ishmael's consciousness, which is, after all, all we know about him and the world of *Moby Dick* that he creates and inhabits. Brodtkorb quotes Hillis Miller's statement that literature is a form of consciousness and that the critic's duty is to acquaint himself with the subjectivity indwelling the words of the text, in order to re-experience that subjectivity from the inside, as much as possible, and then re-create it in his criticism. This is possible with *Moby Dick* (as with any other text) because Ishmael's re-creation of *his* world and self in the story is expressed in his narrator's strategy, and because a discovery of such a unity of subjectivity in the text is in good part the result of the reader's attitude that he brings to the text.

Following these structuring comments, Brodtkorb treats mood in the first chapter (as what seems to be for him a mode of consciousness), defining it as that which inhabits situations, which determines the situation, and accounts for differing perceptions of similar experiences by a single consciousness. Mood, in other words, is the *Gestalt* of emotions whereby we initially experience our world, and this is especially important for *Moby Dick,* which begins with an emphasis on mood and relies heavily on it throughout.

In chapter two Brodtkorb undertakes a phenomenology of the physical elements—earth, water, air, and fire—as the components of world that he treats as one of the contents of consciousness. Earth conveys familiarity, stability, predictability, confinement, while water signifies strangeness, emptiness, formlessness, and motion; air and fire (which seem much less important for Brodtkorb's purposes) express formlessness and motion, and spirit and light respectively. This description of world becomes significant when related specifically to Ishmael's being-in-the-world. For him, for example, such being is like living in an inn; his sojourns are temporary, and he is always in motion, just as nature is in process, for this motion distinguishes the living from the dead. The world's roundness determines its motion; its circularity underscores the futility of his incessant travelling, yet the calm vortex he intuits at the center of the world remains unknown; although it suggests a spiral and hence a verticality that hints at an escape from his horizontal round-the-world movement, it is not really an option for him; for humans can escape the futility of circular motion only through madness or death.

In chapter three Brodtkorb turns to body, another content of consciousness. Ishmael seems to view the soul "as a kind of ghost animating the body," and thus Brodtkorb equates soul and self, using "self" here as spontaneous consciousness or pure pre-reflective ego. /103/ For Ishmael body and self are very closely related but still not the same. Body generally reflects self, but close scrutiny is necessary to learn what is reflected, and the results are often ambiguous. Ahab, for example, feels estranged from his body, and his body reflects that internal schizophrenia, a division of the self, yet his body also helps to cause his alienation of self from body. Ishmael himself suffers from the paradox of the simultaneous identity and separation of body and self and the recognition that no escape from this condition is possible.

Chapter four focuses on others as a content of consciousness and shows first that just as the self never reveals itself totally through body, so also the selves of others remain partially hidden. In fact, as *Moby Dick* reveals so eloquently, men are fundamentally isolatoes who try to interact through social roles, so that humanity and brotherhood mitigate against the natural isolation of persons. Brodtkorb finds four clear patterns of self-other relationships in *Moby Dick*. One is the assumption that the self of the other can explain itself to one—as it turns out, a false belief. A second is the acceptance of love as the way of temporarily bridging the self-other difference. A third is a comic, wry acceptance of the otherness of the other, and a fourth is the attempt to become the other through fictional projection; one imagines the self of the other. A primary reason why Ishmael will not judge Ahab at the end of the novel is that he can understand Ahab's difference, the otherness of his self, only partially.

In chapter five Brodtkorb takes up time as a mode of consciousness and discusses it in terms of causality, eternity, and death. When Ishmael ponders time he generally thinks of fate, yet fate for him is not the gods but his own character. However, since he does not understand the origin of fate in character, he is no closer to a solution to the problem of fate. He is willing to let the idea of fatality as a universal stand valid for Ahab and his view of the world but for himself he remains uncertain. Likewise he is fascinated by the possibility of eternity but will not commit himself to it, just as he is much concerned with death but will not take a stand on its nature and substance. What he can do, and does, is to describe what it is like to live in time, how he wishes to escape its endless circularity into eternity but cannot. Unlike Ahab, who has cast his lot with eternity, Ishmael is a time-bound man who must make his temporality—his present—meaningful.

In chapter six, the central chapter of the book, Brodtkorb shows how these phenomenological descriptions join in the totality of Ishmael's self, how his character and history are consistent with his moods—that comprise his world of time, space, body, and others—and how this world is coherent. Thus one recalls that Ishmael's boredom originally led him to sea, a boredom that consists of a sense of the emptiness of self and world and that began in experiences of rejection in Ishmael's childhood. The conscious encounter with boredom turns to dread, and the realization that this boredom and dread have no end leads to despair. Ishmael seeks the exotic to escape boredom, dread, and despair, and for awhile at sea, in the plentitude of new experience, overcomes them, but the cycle always begins anew. Ishmael's discourse on whiteness gives tangible expression to the sense of boredom, dread, and despair that afflicts him and to the ineffability of the universe that permits no explanation for this condition.

Ishmael is fundamentally a storyteller, but as the narrator of this story he is unreliable—a failing that points to the irony of his refusal or inability to take a position on things. The irony is that he will not or cannot take a position on things because his profound sense of despair makes such choices meaningless. Brodtkorb at this point rehearses some of the theological criticism on *Moby Dick* and declares that Ishmael's despair is more than theological; it is attached to the deepening realization, with every failed attempt, of the impossibility of ever attaining a true and unequivocal self. The self that emerges is thus the self of the artist, the one who gives provisional meaning to despair by shaping a something from nothing, by at least dramatizing his spiritual universe in story and thereby providing something substantial for his self. This is, however, a reading of *Moby Dick* that is perhaps uniquely accessible to the phenomenological critic, for one can gain this vision of Ishmael's self, of his struggle with boredom, dread, and despair only by sympathetically experiencing Ishmael's moods oneself. Only in this way can one comprehend the unity of Ishmael's consciousness and the peculiar unity of the novel and relate it to the construction of one's own meaningful life-world.

David Halliburton, "The Fall of the House of Usher"

Halliburton advertises his 1973 book, *Edgar Allan Poe: A Phenomenological View,* as "the first general interpretation of an American author from a phenomenological point of view," and his claim is correct (Brodtkorb's Melville study is restricted to a single text, while Hillis Miller's analyses of Wallace Stevens and W. C. Williams are not exhaustive treatments of those poets). /104/ Unlike Brodtkorb, who derives his phenomenological categories from a single source, Halliburton displays a sophisticated knowledge of the Continental phenomenological tradition, ranging from Heidegger and Sartre to Bachelard, Poulet, and Ricoeur, yet he also draws on the venerable philological tradition represented by Leo Spitzer and Erich Auerbach and orients himself to the native American scholarship of C. S. Peirce and Kenneth Burke as well. His study is comprehensive: after a short description of methodology he treats, one way or another, Poe's entire creative literary corpus, proceeding chronologically within the genres of poem, tale, and dialogue. His stance as a phenomenological critic, along with adhering to a rigorous close reading of individual texts throughout, is not to impose his subjectivity upon the texts but "to reach the subjectivity of the character in the work. To render the situation of another is to stand outside of myself, and to draw the subjectivity of the other toward a kind of objectivity." /105/

Because Halliburton's strategy of close reading results in a plenitude of information that makes coherent summary almost impossible, I will sketch only one of his analyses, a twenty-page passage on "The Fall of the House of Usher"—to my mind also one of the best interpretations in the book. Halliburton begins his "Usher" essay with a lengthy explication of the story's opening sentence to forecast the interdependence of elements that characterizes the whole tale and to describe the sentence as "the process by which the narrator *comes to consciousness.*" /106/ The interdependence reveals itself first in a twoness, a parallelism of elements that determines not only the narrative structure but the ontological structure of the story as well. All important events and components in the story have their analogies, a situation that, in turn, creates a network of interrelationships the realization of which effects the narrator's development of consciousness. More than that, the narrator is intensely *self*-conscious, which means that he is constantly checking his own responses to the fantastic events in the mansion and skeptical of the reality of those events. When, at the end, those events turn out to be indeed reality rather than illusion, the impact upon the reader is that much greater, for one has expected the self-conscious narrator to be able to distinguish illusion from reality.

The house itself contributes to the false sense of unreality in the tale, for it seems to stand precariously yet does not collapse (until the end), and even the syntax used to describe this paradox embodies the contradictory relationship between appearance and reality. Yet Usher himself, rather than the house or the narrator, is the focus of the tale, and the narrator's duty is to inhabit the mansion with Usher—the edifice that Usher cannot leave because his destiny is to live out his family line there. His hyper-sensitivity is also connected to his involvement with the house. This sensitivity is an intensification of the ability to experience material sensation rather than a sensibility, which is a way of relating in a balanced fashion to the world and which in Usher has deteriorated, so that he cannot live adventurously without threatening his sense of self. Usher's attachment to the house and to his sister Madeline is thus a means of protecting himself by narrowing the perimeters of his experience; through a concentration on these he can ignore everything else—although, as a result, his consciousness is strongly marked by the sense of diffused separation that pervades the house. The house, moreover, represents the establishment of a sacred space according to the dynamics such as Eliade and others describe, a private and impregnable world, yet it is also a demonic space and as such contains the impulse toward destruction. More than that, the house represents Poe's view of the universe as a tension between powers of attraction and repulsion, with Usher himself standing for the stage in which the forces of attraction are gradually overcoming resistance and are about to bring everything back to a primal unity. This means also that the physical will disappear into the spiritual, a process that Usher exemplifies as well, as his adversion toward participating in normal sensory experience suggests.

In this return to primal spiritual unity Usher and his sister act as the primal couple, a relationship that the narrator can observe from a remove, even though his is the transmitting consciousness of the dynastic dissolution. In fact, the three characters—brother, sister, and narrator—are never together as a threesome. If Usher and Madeline are together the narrator is displaced, and if Usher and the narrator are together, the sister is absent—another example of the disjunctive twoness of the tale striving toward resolution. Such twoness also characterizes the narrative tactic. At first one absorbs the vital information, as it occurs, through the narrator, but later one learns the critical facts through Usher only after they have happened. Thus Usher has probably known all along that they have buried Madeline alive, but refuses to rescue her, whereas the narrator discovers only through Usher's confession that the sister has been placed comatose in the tomb, and this confession is a convergence of two narrative perspectives, once more a unification of dividing duality. When Madeline breaks out of the sepulcher and rejoins her brother in death, the tendency of Poe's universe is imaged in the action; the sister's desperate feat is a victory both of the will and the body: she overcomes the forced separation from her brother—the twoness again—and achieves the final primal unity that is their destiny and into which, in Poe's view, the universe must contract. Attraction defeats repulsion.

The external natural forces that inform the mood and setting of the story at the start exert their importance at this climactic moment through the storm close to the end. A kind of transference occurs, as nature, represented by the storm, grows in power while Usher subsides into enervation and helplessness. Usher sitting in his rocking chair facing the door, rocking expectantly, is already seized by a force beyond his control and waiting for his destiny to be consummated. The almost human quality of the storm prefigures the sister's return from the tomb and the fatal reunion with her brother. Even this action extends into a double event—a double fall—that reinforces the twoness of the tale resolving itself into a unity that conveys a world disappearing into itself. The first phase is the fall—itself a double fall—of Usher and Madeline together, meeting their deaths in intimate physical proximity. This is also the point at which the narrator must leave, a retreat that does not constitute escape but one that is ontologically necessary, for the unifying force that draws brother and sister together in death does not tolerate any longer a complicating third entity. The second phase is the collapse of the mansion, which falls in on itself just as the Ushers die in mutual descent and as Poe's universe contracts upon itself. The sense of both disillusion and completion is very strong in this final dramatic occurrence.

The narrator is related to, but not involved in, this climactic unification through dissolution. He is on the outside, as he was at the start, an observer from the normal world where attraction and repulsion are still maintained in balance. Because he cannot grasp the symbolic importance of the fall of the Ushers and their house—although he has been forced at least to accept the reality of their world—he can, at the end, only name, and thus the last words are the recapitulating words, *"the House of Usher."* This naming, says Halliburton, is "a parodic Word within the Word, a presence of the absolute turned inward on itself, a force transforming its presence into its own absence." /107/

This last comment suggests an interpretative process that moves beyond the usual boundaries of phenomenology and toward a thinking like Jacques Derrida's, although Halliburton never mentions Derrida in his study. In any case, Halliburton's combination of close reading in the new-critical tradition, the phenomenological examination of consciousness, and an expert knowledge of Poe's own exotic philosophy results in a remarkably rich, enlivening, and instructive book that not only advances Poe's scholarship but adds importantly to the brief American enterprise of phenomenologically-oriented literary criticism. In charting Poe's drive toward unity (Halliburton notes in his conclusion that Poe, like Balzac, sought to construct a system) Halliburton has contributed a key chapter in the study of the broader process of consciousness seeking unity with itself through the narrative work of art.

NOTES

/1/   Zoran Konstantinović, *Phänomenologie und Literaturwissenschaft* (Munich: List, 1973); John Macquarrie, *Twentieth-Century Religious Thought* (New York and Evanston: Harper and Row, 1963). Robert Magliola's "The Phenomenological Approach to Literature" is the best *short* introduction to the varieties of phenomenological approaches to secular texts, while Vernon Ruland's *Horizons of Criticism: An Assessment of Religious-Literary Options* (Chicago: American Library Association, 1975) contains a useful survey of phenomenological approaches to both religious and secular texts. Ruland's brief treatment of structuralism, however, is confused and unreliable. Two other sound short studies of literary phenomenology are Zoran Konstantinović, "Über Ingarden hinaus . . . Forschungsgeschichtliche Hinweise zur Entwicklung des phänomenologischen Ansatzes in der Literaturwissenschaft," and Bernhard F. Scholz, "Literatur als Bewusstseinsphänomen: zum Ansatzpunkt phänomenologischer Literaturwissenschaft," both in Helmut Kreuzer, ed., *Phänomenologie und Hermeneutik* (Göttingen: Vandenhoeck & Ruprecht, 1975), pp. 25-34 and 35-53. This text is No. 17 of the *Zeitschrift für Literaturwissenschaft und Linguistik*, 5 (1975).

/2/   Magliola, "The Phenomenological Approach," 85. Manon Maren-Grisebach in her *Methoden der Literaturwissenschaft* (Munich: Francke, 1970) has a good chapter on phenomenological literary criticism that relies heavily on Ingarden's kind of analysis and provides a helpful contrast to Magliola, who largely ignores Ingarden.

/3/   Roman Ingarden, *The Literary Work of Art: An Investigation on the Borderlines of Ontology, Logic, and Theory of Literature,* tr. George G. Grabowicz (Evanston: Northwestern University Press, 1973).

/4/   David Michael Levin, Foreword, *The Literary Work of Art*, xvi.

/5/   Konstantinović's "Ingardens Stratifikationstheorie," in *Phänomenologie und Literaturwissenschaft*, is a sound, informative chapter on *The Literary Work of Art*.

/6/   Roman Ingarden, *The Cognition of the Literary Work of Art*, tr. Ruth Ann Crowley and Kenneth R. Olsen (Evanston: Northwestern University Press, 1973). Originally published as *O poznawaniu dziela literackiego* (Lvov: Ossolineum, 1937). The English translation, however, is based on the German translation *Vom Erkennen des literarischen Kunstwerks* (Tübingen: Niemeyer, 1968). The quotation is from the Translators' Introduction, xv.

/7/   The translators offer a summary of the whole book in their Translators' Introduction, xvii-xxx, that I have used.

/8/   Wolfgang Iser, *The Implied Reader: Patterns of Communication in Prose Fiction from Bunyan to Beckett* (Baltimore: The Johns Hopkins University Press, 1974); Hans Robert Jauss, *Literaturgeschichte als Provokation* (Frankfurt am Main: Suhrkamp, 1970). Another representative, more recent essay by Jauss is his "Goethes und Valérys *Faust:* Zur Hermeneutik von Frage und Antwort," *Comparative Literature*, 28, No. 3 (Summer, 1976): 201-32.

/9/   Cf. Ingarden's discussion of literary evaluation in works such as *Erlebnis, Kunstwerk und Wert: Vorträge zur Aesthetik* (Tübingen: Niemeyer, 1969). Such essays as those collected in that volume have influenced, for example, Manon Maren-Grisebach's *Theorie und Praxis literarischer Wertung* (Munich: Francke, 1974); and Horst S. Daemmrich's *Literaturkritik in Theorie und Praxis* (Munich: Francke, 1974).

/10/   Thévenaz, *What is Phenomenology?*, p. 6.

/11/   Gras, *European Literary Theory*, p. 6. Cf. Michael Polanyi, *The Tacit Dimension* (Garden City: Doubleday, 1966). A study needs to be done on the value of Polanyi's thought for reconciling phenomenology and structuralism.

/12/   Gras, p. 7.

/13/   Cf. *ibid*. The aspects of Merleau-Ponty's approach that I have summarized are mainly from his *Phenomenology of Perception; Sense and Non-Sense*, tr. Hubert L. and Patricia Allen Dreyfus (Evanston: Northwestern University Press, 1964); and *Signs*, tr. Richard L. McCleary (Evanston: Northwestern University Press, 1964). Remy C. Kwant's *The Phenomenological Philosophy of Merleau-Ponty* (Pittsburgh: Duquesne University Press, 1963) is a valuable aid for understanding Merleau-Ponty; Eugene F. Kaelin's *An Existentialist Aesthetic: The Theories of Sartre and Merleau-Ponty* (Madison: The University of Wisconsin Press, 1966) is also worthwhile, although it excludes, curiously, a discussion of literature as part of the aesthetic dimension.

/14/   In Europe the work of prominent literary critics such as Emil Staiger, Maurice Blanchot, and Beda Allemann has been strongly influenced by Heidegger. Cf., for example, Emil Staiger, *Die Kunst der Interpretation* (Zurich: Atlantis, 1955); Maurice Blanchot, *L'Espace litteraire* (Paris: Gallimard, 1955); Beda Allemann, *Hölderlin und Heidegger* (Zurich: Atlantis, 1954). None of these critics, however, is a mediator of Heidegger's approach, but all, rather, use some aspect of his thought in combination with or contrast to their own as methods of reinforcing them.

/15/   Martin Heidegger, *Sein und Zeit* (Halle: Niemeyer, 1927); English translation: *Being and Time,* tr. John Macquarrie and Edward Robinson (New York: Harper and Row, 1962). *Unterwegs zur Sprache* (Pfullingen: Neske, 1960); English translation: *On the Way to Language,* tr. Peter D. Hertz (New York: Harper and Row, 1971). Walter Biemel's *Martin Heidegger* (Reinbek bei Hamburg: Rowohlt, 1973) has been very helpful for this discussion, especially the chapter on "Dichten—Denken—Sprache," pp. 125-41.

/16/   Cf. Ludwig Binswanger, *Being-in-the World,* tr. Jacob Needleman (New York: Basic Books, 1963).

/17/   Cf. Thévenaz, p. 55.

/18/   Cf. Biemel, p. 130; and Gras, p. 5.

/19/   A representative essay by Hopper is his Introduction to *Interpretation: The Poetry of Meaning,* ed. Stanley Romaine Hopper and David L. Miller (New York: Harcourt, Brace and World, 1967), ix-xxii.

/20/   Joseph N. Riddel, *The Inverted Bell: Modernism and the Counterpoetics of William Carlos Williams* (Baton Rouge: Louisiana State University Press, 1974). Paul de Man, *Blindness and Insight: Essays in the Rhetoric of Contemporary Criticism* (New York: Oxford University Press, 1971). Representative essays from *Boundary 2,* 6, No. 2 (Winter, 1976), are Stanley Corngold, "*Sein und Zeit*: Implications for Poetics," 439-53; and William V. Spanos, "Heidegger, Kierkegaard, and the Hermeneutic Circle: Towards a Postmodern Theory of Interpretation as Dis-closure," 455-92. John Macquarrie, *An Existentialist Theology: A Comparison of Heidegger and Bultmann* (London: S. C. M. Press, 1955). James M. Robinson and John B. Cobb, Jr., eds., *The Later Heidegger and Theology* (New York: Harper and Row, 1963). Macquarrie's *Twentieth-Century Religious Thought,* especially Chapter XIII on "Existentialism and Ontology," is very helpful in describing the influence of Heidegger and other phenomenologists on modern theologians, while Ruland in *Horizons of Criticism* has a brief but valuable section, pp. 172-75, on Heidegger in relation to theology and literary criticism.

/21/   Jean-Paul Sartre, *L'Être et le néant: Essai d'ontologie phénoménologique* (Paris: Gallimard, 1943), translated as *Being and Nothingness* by Hazel Barnes (New York: Philosophical Library, 1956).

/22/   Cf. Gras, pp. 8-10.

/23/   Jean-Paul Sartre, *La Nausée* (Paris: Gallimard, 1938), translated as *Nausea* by Lloyd Alexander (New York: New Directions, 1949); *Les Mouches* (Paris: Gallimard, 1943), translated as *The Flies* by Stuart Gilbert (New York: Knopf, 1948); *Huis Clos* (Paris: Gallimard, 1947), translated as *No Exit* by Stuart Gilbert (New York: Knopf, 1948).

/24/   Jean-Paul Sartre, *What Is Literature?*, tr. Bernard Frechtman (New York: Philosophical Library, 1949), is a translation of part of Volume II of *Situations* (Paris: Gallimard, 1947).

/25/   Jean-Paul Sartre, *L'Imaginaire: Psychologie phénoménologique de l'imagination* (Paris: Gallimard, 1940), translated as *The Psychology of Imagination* by Bernard Frechtman (New York: Philosophical Library, 1948). Cf. especially the conclusion, "Consciousness and Imagination," pp. 233-46.

/26/   According to Thévenaz, p. 69, Sartre practices a radical reduction whereby the ego itself is purged from consciousness and placed outside in the world.

/27/   Natanson, "Phenomenology and Existentialism: Husserl and Sartre on Intentionality," in Kockelmans, ed., *Phenomenology*, p. 343.

/28/   Jean-Paul Sartre, "Faces, Preceded by Official Portraits," in Natanson, ed., *Essays in Phenomenology*, pp. 157-63.

/29/   Among the many works on Sartre, those that I have found most useful are Robert Denoon Cumming, ed., *The Philosophy of Jean-Paul Sartre* (New York: Random House, 1965), especially Cumming's own introduction; Walter Biemel, *Sartre* (Reinbek bei Hamburg: Rowohlt, 1964); and R.D. Laing and D. G. Cooper, *Reason and Violence: A Decade of Sartre's Philosophy, 1950-1960* (London: Tavistock, 1964).

/30/   Sarah Lawall's *Critics of Consciousness: The Existentialist Structures of Literature* (Cambridge: Harvard University Press, 1968), which I have relied on here, has a good introduction on the whole "Geneva School" and chapters on individual critics of that school, including one on Poulet. Other valuable essays on Poulet are J. Hillis Miller, "Geneva or Paris? The Recent Work of Georges Poulet," *University of Toronto Quarterly*, 39, No. 3 (April, 1970): 212-28; Paul de Man, "The Literary Self as Origin: The Work of Georges Poulet," in de Man, *Blindness and Insight*, pp. 79-101; and Richard Macksey, "The Consciousness of the Critic: Georges Poulet and the Reader's Share," in Macksey, ed., *Velocities of Change* (Baltimore: The Johns Hopkins University Press, 1971), pp. 304-40.

/31/   Lawall, pp. 75-76.

/32/   The five volumes of *Studies in Human Time* are *Etudes sur le temps humain* (Paris: Plon, 1950), translated as *Studies in Human Time* (Baltimore: The

Johns Hopkins University Press, 1956); *La Distance intérieure* (Paris: Plon, 1952), translated as *The Interior Distance* (Baltimore: The Johns Hopkins University Press, 1959); *Les Metamorphoses du cercle* (Paris: Plon, 1961), translated as *The Metamorphosis of the Circle* (Baltimore: The Johns Hopkins University Press, 1967); *Le Point de départ* (Paris: Plon, 1964); and *Mesure de l'instant* (Paris: Plon, 1968).

/33/   Miller, "Geneva or Paris?", 215-16.

/34/   *Ibid.*, 217ff. In·this connection de Man ("The Literary Self as Origin," p. 100) remarks that "Language clearly matters to him only when it gives access to a deeper subjectivity. . . . A conception of literature as a language of authenticity, similar to what is found, for example, in some of Heidegger's texts after *Sein und Zeit* is not Poulet's."

/35/   Cf. Georges Poulet, "The Self and the Other in Criticial Consciousness," *Diacritics*, 2, No. 1 (Spring, 1972): 46-50, for a concise statement on how his critical position has evolved throughout his career.

/36/   Cf. James M. Robinson and John B. Cobb, Jr., eds., *The New Hermeneutic* (New York: Harper and Row, 1964), for representative essays on this dialogue. Robinson's introductory essay, "Hermeneutic Since Barth," pp. 1-77, is an important summary of the modern history of hermeneutics.

/37/   Richard E. Palmer, *Hermeneutics: Interpretive Theory in Schleiermacher, Dilthey, Heidegger, and Gadamer* (Evanston: Northwestern University Press, 1969). Part I is an excellent summary of modern hermeneutics. Hans-Georg Gadamer, *Wahrheit und Methode: Grundzüge zu einer philosophischen Hermeneutik* (Tübingen: Mohr, 1960), translated (no translator listed) as *Truth and Method* (New York: Seabury Press, 1975).

/38/   Erich Dinkler, "Hermeneutics," in Marvin Halverson and Arthur A. Cohen, eds., *A Handbook of Christian Theology* (Cleveland and New York: World, 1958), pp. 160-62.

/39/   Kurt Müller-Vollmer, in his *Towards a Phenomenological Theory of Literature: A Study of Wilhelm Dilthey's Poetik* (The Hague: Mouton, 1963), gives four pages to the relationship among Dilthey, Husserl, and Heidegger, but his study of Dilthey is not phenomenological. Müller-Vollmer pays no attention to Gadamer nor to the modern biblical hermeneuts in his book. He has, however, written a fine overview of phenomenological criticism in America in his "Rezeption und Neuansatz. Phänomenologische Literaturwissenschaft in den Vereinigten Staaten," Kreuzer, ed., *Phänomenologie und Hermeneutik*, pp. 10-24.

/40/   Cf. Wallace Martin, "The Hermeneutical Circle and the Art of Interpretation," *Comparative Literature*, 24, No. 2 (Spring, 1972): 97-117, for a good study of recent criticism of the hermeneutical circle that shows sound acquaintance with phenomenology and structuralism.

/41/   "Das ästhetische Verständnis wird dort fast zum Paradigma der histor-
ischgeisteswissenschaftlichen Erkenntnis überhaupt. Gadamer stellt die Seinsweise des
ästhetischen Objekts in den Mittelpunkt seiner Untersuchungen und gelangt zur
Schlussfolgerung, dass es dabei nicht möglich ist, eine rein ästhetische Substanz von
allem Nicht-ästhetischen zu isolieren. Das Kunstwerk stellt keine autonome poetische
Scheinwelt dar, die sich ontologisch von der prosaischen Wirklichkeit unterscheidet,
sondern ist eng mit der Wirklichkeit verbunden, und sein Sinn ist der Sinnesstruktur
des praktischen Lebens homogen" (Konstantinović, pp. 145-46, my translation).
While Konstantinović endorses Gadamer's work, E. D. Hirsch in Appendix II of his
influential *Validity in Interpretation* (New Haven: Yale University Press, 1967)
launches a vigorous attack on *Truth and Method,* arguing mainly that Gadamer is
unsuccessful in his attempt to reconcile past and present through his concepts of
tradition, quasi-repetition, and horizon-fusion. Gadamer, he says, ignores the
important difference between the unchanging meaning of a text and the changing
meaning of a text for the present-day reader. Cf. *Validity,* pp. 254-55. Another largely
negative critique of Gadamer's work is Heinz Schlaffer's "Die Entstehung des
hermeneutischen Bewusstseins. Eine historische Kritik von Gadamers *Wahrheit und
Methode,*" Kreuzer, ed., *Phänomenologie und Hermeneutik,* pp. 62-73.

/42/   Paul Ricoeur, "Metaphor and the Main Problem of Hermeneutics," *New
Literary History,* 6, No. 1 (Autumn, 1974): 95-110.

/43/   *Ibid.,* 103.

/44/   *Ibid.,* 104.

/45/   *Ibid.,* 107-108.

/46/   *Ibid.,* 109.

/47/   The most comprehensive and representative example of Ricoeur's work
available in English in his *The Conflict of Interpretations: Essays in Hermeneutics,* ed.
Don Ihde (Evanston: Northwestern University Press, 1974). Ihde's *Hermeneutic
Phenomenology: The Philosophy of Paul Ricoeur* (Evanston: Northwestern
University Press, 1971) is an excellent critical summary of Ricoeur's work up to *The
Conflict of Interpretations.*

/48/   Mircea Eliade, *Myths, Dreams, and Mysteries: The Encounter between
Contemporary Faiths and Archaic Realities,* tr. Philip Mairet (New York and
Evanston: Harper and Row, 1967); French original: *Mythes, Rêves et Mystères* (Paris:
Gallimard, 1957).

/49/   Cf. Macquarrie, *Twentieth-Century Religious Thought,* pp. 222-23, for a
concise description of Eliade as a phenomenologist who contrasts archetypes with
historical acts.

/50/   The chapter appears on pp. 190-228 of *Myths, Dreams, and Mysteries.*

/51/   Eliade, *Myths,* pp. 208-09.

/52/   *Ibid.,* p. 209.

/53/   *Ibid.,* p. 228.

/54/   John Vernon, *The Garden and the Map: Schizophrenia in Twentieth-Century Literature and Culture* (Urbana: University of Illinois Press, 1973). The section of the first chapter, "The Garden and the Map," that I am summarizing is on pp. 3-12.

/55/   *Ibid.,* p. 3.

/56/   *Ibid.,* p. 191.

/57/   Paul Ricoeur, *The Symbolism of Evil,* tr. Emerson Buchanan (Boston: Beacon Press, 1967).

/58/   Paul Ricoeur, *Freedom and Nature: The Voluntary and the Involuntary,* tr. Erazim V. Kohák (Evanston: Northwestern University Press, 1966).

/59/   Paul Ricoeur, *Fallible Man,* tr. Charles Kelbley (Chicago: Regnery, 1967).

/60/   Ihde, *Hermeneutic Phenomenology,* pp. 113-14. I have depended considerably on Ihde's summary of *The Symbolism of Evil* for my own sketch here.

/61/   *Ibid.,* pp. 121-22.

/62/   Rudolf Bultmann, "Man Between the Times According to the New Testament," tr. Schubert M. Ogden, in Rudolf Bultmann, *Existence and Faith* (New York: Meridian, 1960), pp. 248-66. The title of the German original is "Der Mensch zwischen den Zeiten nach dem Neuen Testament."

/63/   *Ibid.,* p. 254.

/64/   *Ibid.,* p. 266.

/65/   John Macquarrie's *An Existentialist Theology* has been very helpful to me for this summary.

/66/   *Ibid.,* pp. 6 and 35.

/67/   As Macquarrie (*ibid.,* p. 161) explains, *historisch* in German is used by the theologians to refer to the scientific study of history whereas *geschichtlich* is used to refer to historical reality.

/68/   Robert W. Funk, *Language, Hermeneutic, and Word of God* (New York: Harper and Row, 1966). "Word and Word in I Corinthians 2:6-16" is on pp. 275-305. Funk, like many contemporary theologians, prefers the singular "hermeneutic" over "hermeneutics." Cf. the Editors' Preface to Robinson and Cobb, eds., *The New Hermeneutic,* ix-x, for the argument defending the use of the singular.

/69/   James M. Robinson, "Hermeneutic Since Barth," in Robinson and Cobb, eds., *The New Hermeneutic,* p. 39.

/70/   *Ibid.,* p. 47.

/71/   Ernst Fuchs, "Zur Frage nach dem historischen Jesus," *Gesammelte Aufsätze II,* p. 429. Quoted by Robinson, *ibid.,* p. 55.

/72/   Cf. Robinson, *ibid.,* p. 77.

/73/   Funk, "Word and Word," p. 277.

/74/   *Ibid.,* p. 295.

/75/   *Ibid.,* p. 302.

/76/   Martin Heidegger, "Hölderlin und das Wesen der Dichtung," *Das Innere Reich,* 3 (1936), 1065-78; translated by D. Scott as "Hölderlin and the Essence of Poetry," in Martin Heidegger, *Existence and Being* (Chicago: Regnery, 1949). I have used the text as reprinted in Gras, *European Literary Theory,* pp. 27-41.

/77/   Magliola, "The Phenomenological Approach," 97, n. 7; Konstantinović, *Phänomenologie,* p. 141.

/78/   Konstantinović, *Phänomenologie,* p. 141: "Wenn die transzendentale Reduktion Husserls zum reinen Bewusstsein geführt hat, dessen Wesen der konstitutive Akt ist, die Intentionalität, so wird nun bei Heidegger die Intentionalität transzendent und überschreitet jede Erfahrung, sie ist das reine Bewusstsein, das existentielle Urbewusstsein" (my translation). Cf. also Joseph N. Riddel, "From Heidegger to Derrida to Chance: Doubling and (Poetic) Language," *Boundary 2,* 4, No. 2 (Winter, 1976), 571-92, for a good discussion of the roots of Heidegger's literary criticism as phenomenological criticism in *Being and Time.*

/79/   Heidegger, "Hölderlin," p. 28.

/80/   *Ibid.*

/81/   *Ibid.,* p. 29.

/82/   *Ibid.*

/83/   *Ibid.*, p. 32.

/84/   *Ibid.*, p. 34

/85/   *Ibid.*

/86/   *Ibid.*

/87/   *Ibid.*, p. 35.

/88/   Georges Poulet, *The Interior Distance,* tr. Elliott Coleman (Baltimore: The Johns Hopkins University Press, 1959). I have used the edition published by the University of Michigan Press, Ann Arbor, 1964. The "Balzac" essay appears on pp. 97-152.

/89/   *Ibid.*, vii.

/90/   *Ibid.*, viii.

/91/   Magliola, "The Phenomenological Approach," 92.

/92/   Poulet, "Balzac," p. 108.

/93/   *Ibid.*, p. 111.

/94/   *Ibid.*, p. 121.

/95/   *Ibid.*, p. 123.

/96/   *Ibid.*, p. 134.

/97/   Jean-Paul Sartre, *Saint Genet, Actor and Martyr,* tr. Bernard Frechtman (New York: Braziller, 1963). I am greatly indebted to the essay by Otto Hahn, "Sartre's Criticism," in Macksey, ed., *Velocities of Change,* pp. 260-76, for guiding me through my summary.

/98/   Sartre, *Saint Genet,* p. 567.

/99/   *Ibid.*

/100/   Hahn, "Sartre's Criticism," p. 275.

/101/   Paul Brodtkorb, Jr., *Ishmael's White World: A Phenomenological Reading of Moby Dick* (New Haven: Yale University Press, 1965).

/102/   *Ibid.*, p. 152, n. 4.

/103/   *Ibid.*, p. 42.

/104/   David Halliburton, *Edgar Allen Poe: A Phenomenological View* (Princeton: Princeton University Press, 1973), p. 21. Cf. J. Hillis Miller's analyses of Stevens and Williams in *Poets of Reality* (New York: Atheneum, 1969).

/105/   *Ibid.*, p. 28.

/106/   *Ibid.*, p. 279.

/107/   *Ibid.*, p. 299.

Chapter III

Structuralist Literary Criticism

A. Theory

Since structuralism is a younger critical method than phenomenology, it has not had the opportunity to evolve clearly recognizable—and recognized—variations of approach, yet some tentative ones have emerged with sufficient clarity to be identified. These are linguistically-oriented structuralism, based on the theory of Saussure, the work of the Prague Circle, and to a degree on that of American structural linguists and on the theories of subsequent scholars; the genetic structuralism of Lucien Goldmann that owes a good deal to linguistic structuralism but just as much to Georg Lukács, Marx, and Freud; and Jean Piaget's structuralism as an interdisciplinary method of the social and natural sciences that he has employed mainly in his research in genetic epistemology. Piaget's method has evolved apart from linguistic structuralism and has had almost no impact at all on literary criticism, and hence I will pay no further attention to it in this chapter. /1/ Since Goldmann's structuralism has had a somewhat greater influence, I have included a summary of one of his own literary sociological essays as an example of his method.

This leaves linguistically-based structuralism for us to categorize and examine. Within this direction one can differentiate among folklore-and-myth-oriented structuralism (Propp as precursor, Lévi-Strauss, Barthes), linguistic structuralism *per se* (Jakobson), semiology (Barthes, Kristeva), the structural study of narrative elements, or what one might call structuralist poetics (Barthes, Greimas, Todorov), structuralist textual commentary (Barthes and many others), and structuralist literary psychology (Lacan). The most popular of these among the secular literary critics have been the folklore-and-myth-oriented type, structuralist poetics, and structuralist textual commentary, and the biblical structuralists have also limited themselves largely to these three. My brief introduction to prominent structuralists in the following pages and my summaries of representative structuralist essays will further illustrate the various types and their combinations. /2/

I have had to make some strategic choices in my discussion of how leading structuralists adapt the structuralist vocabulary to literary critical ends. For instance, I have paid very little attention to Lévi-Strauss' "The Structural Study of Myth" and none at all to Propp's *Morphology of the Folktale*. Although both of these are seminal texts for structuralist literary critics, they have been summarized exhaustively elsewhere, are readily available in English, and sufficiently illustrated in examples of practical criticism that I shall present. I have, on the other hand, introduced other prominent literary critical texts by Jakobson, Lévi-Strauss, Barthes, Greimas, Todorov, and Genette that need to be rehearsed as an entry into the methodologies of the various examples of applied analysis that I shall turn to following the discussion of literary theory. Readers who wish to deepen such theoretical acquaintance should turn to Scholes' *Structuralism in Literature,* Jameson's *The Prison-House of Language,* and above all Culler's *Structuralist Poetics.* /3/ As is obvious by these initial remarks, no structuralist literary critics have yet emerged who have attempted a thoroughgoing treatment of structuralist theory in terms of its theological implications, although Dan O. Via, Jr., John Dominic Crossan, Daniel Patte, Matthieu Casalis, and François Bovon have all ventured modest statements on the theological import of structuralism in connection with actual biblical exegesis. /4/

Roman Jakobson

Roman Jakobson's criticism contains elements of his background in Russian formalism that found fulfillment in his greatly influential structural linguistics and poetics. Along with other members of the Prague Linguistic Circle such as Mukařovský, Trubetzkoj, Wellek, and Havránek, Jakobson was in good part responsible for the shift in Central European criticism from formalism to structuralism: from the concentration on the phonetic and poetic possibilities of words and word combinations to the focus on broader structures or systems within the literary works that interrelate through principles of similarity or difference (called equivalences) to form the total system that *is* the work. /5/ In his pioneering studies on the relations between linguistics and literature, Jakobson posits that poetics is "an integral part of linguistics" and that in fact "many poetic features belong . . . to the whole theory of signs, that is, to general semiotics"; that literary criticism should properly be labelled literary studies and concern itself with description rather than with normative questions; and that the synchronic dimension of poetics, like that of linguistics, must be developed through individual descriptive studies before a diachronic "historical poetics" can be built upon it. /6/

In his masterful "Linguistics and Poetics" Jakobson places the study of poetics within the framework of linguistics by describing the six factors of verbal communication

	CONTEXT	
ADDRESSER	MESSAGE	ADDRESSEE
	CONTACT	
	CODE	

with its corresponding six functions

	REFERENTIAL	
EMOTIVE	POETIC	CONATIVE
	PHATIC	
	METALINGUAL	

and pointing out that the attention to the message for its own sake is the poetic function of language, although this function should not be studied in isolation but in relation to the other aspects of language. /7/

Jakobson then proceeds to answer his central question, "what makes a verbal message a work of art?" by identifying selection, based on equivalence, and combination, based on contiguity, as "the two basic modes of arrangement used in verbal behavior"; in the poetic composition, then, the principle of equivalence is shifted from the area of metaphor (or selection) to the area of metonymy (or combination). In other words, a study of similarity and difference applied to syllabification, meter, and rhythm (Jakobson presents numerous examples) elucidates the essence and nature of poetry. /8/ Likewise, the series of semantic units in a poem produces, through equivalence counterposed to contiguity, the symbolic richness of poetry evidenced in traits such as ambiguity. Jakobson says that a similar kind of analysis should be attempted with prose fiction through an application of the metonymic principle, and that Propp and Lévi-Strauss have already provided hints on how one might proceed. If one develops another of Jakobson's propositions further—that the same metaphor and metonymy discussed in the linguistic context also correspond in good part to the Freudian concepts of condensation and displacement as categories of the unconscious—then an additional possibility for the analysis of our predominantly internalized and self-conscious prose fiction is available.

Claude Lévi-Strauss

Lévi-Strauss is not a literary critic (although he has had a tremendous impact on literary criticism) but an anthropologist who views literature as one kind of social system to be studied for the evidence it offers of the unconscious structuring patterns of a particular society and ultimately evidence of the underlying common basis of behavior that all humans share. In his essays on myth (such as "The Structural Study of Myth," and "How Myths Die") and in his *magnum opus*, the four-volume *Mythologiques*, one can trace an analytic strategy rooted in ethnological myth studies that can be applied to literary texts and indeed is done so directly in his well-known essay (written in cooperation with Jakobson) on Baudelaire's "Les Chats." /9/ The strategy involves a painstaking and complex transference of the principles of Jakobson's structural linguistics into anthropological, mythic, and (in the Baudelaire essay) literary critical terms. In the myth studies he employs the concept of binary oppositions to construct "mythemes" that are derived from sentence bundles each containing two related terms; the mythemes are arranged in "vertical" and "horizontal" patterns of similarity and contiguity (corresponding to synchronic/diachronic and metaphoric/metonymic arrangements in linguistics) to form a system that discloses the fundamental social-psychological meaning of the myth, either by studying a number of versions of the same myth or a number of different myths that are shown to have the same basic components.

In considering the relationship of myth to art, Lévi-Strauss focuses not on literature but on music. When myths die, he claims, they transfer their subject matter to the novel, where it is reworked through the free play of the narrative focus and loses the strict symmetrical form of the myth proper, but the form of the myth (which for Lévi-Strauss is more characteristic than its content) is subsumed in music; thus the novel and the musical composition become the substitutes for myth. In other words, the signified of myth becomes the property of the novelist, who gives it new definition by placing it in new arbitrary relationships through a new signifier, but the signifier of myth is taken over by the musical composer. Wagner, as one would guess, is the composer who for Lévi-Strauss illustrates best how the mythic form has been absorbed by music. /10/

In "Charles Baudelaire's 'Les Chats'" Jakobson and Lévi-Strauss apply their method to a specific text; it is a fascinating study that shows how a poem, although much more complex than a myth, can be analyzed structurally to expose the dynamics of its creation. Jakobson and Lévi-Strauss work with the text's self-contained "variants" (the equivalent of many versions of a single myth) such as its overlapping prosodic, syntactic, and phonetic levels arranged on a "vertical" (i.e., synchronic, non-linear) axis, and through the discovery of binary oppositions (masculine-feminine, lover-scholar, light-dark, animal-human, etc.) expose the sonnet as composed of systems of equivalences typical of a closed system before finally reconsidering it as an open system through the resolution, via transformation, of the implicit opposition between metaphor and metonymy. /11/ The result is a recognition of the fusion of the worlds of scholar and lover, of intellect and passion—a concrete instance of the juncture of structure and event, of the felt totality of existence. The intricate ordering process present in the composition and analysis of the poem, moreover, gives insight into the general systematizing propensity of the mind.

One could guess even from this synopsis that the Jakobson/Lévi-Strauss interpretation contains oversimplifications, and these have been challenged by some vigorous responses, the most significant early one of which was Michael Riffaterre's "Describing Poetic Structures: Two Approaches to Baudelaire's 'Les Chats.'" /12/ Riffaterre argues that not all structures in a poem are necessarily poetic structures, and hence a linguistically-based analysis may not serve to recognize the specifically poetic patterns that make a poem a poem. He accuses the two critics of turning "Les Chats" into a "superpoem" that remains an enigma because a grammatical study can produce at best and at last only a grammar of the poem. He counters the forbidding creation of a superpoem by proposing a "superreader," a tactic accomplished by transferring Jakobson's stress on the poetic "message" (one of his six poetic functions) to an emphasis on the conative or reader function. Thus, rather than studying the equivalent of mythic clusters *à la* Lévi-Strauss, Riffaterre's superreader would gather and collate the "cluster" of responses to this particular poem and from this activity derive a more proper poetically responsive interpretation.

Scholes objects that the approach of Riffaterre's superreader produces no more of a genuinely poetic analysis than Jakobson and Lévi-Strauss do and that Riffaterre's own superb interpretation of the poem (in the same essay) is not based on the superreader strategy he describes but on the excellent critical capability that he brings to the poem himself. The failure of these three critics— Jakobson, Lévi-Strauss, and Riffaterre—to shape a structuralist literary critical apparatus that will interpret a poem for one suggests to Scholes that structural analysis can help only indirectly in applied criticism, that "it can provide us with the best framework available to aid in the perception of an actual poetic text. . . .But it will not read the poem for us. That we shall always have to do for ourselves." /13/

This view seems to limit the structuralist role unnecessarily and is not quite fair to the three Baudelaire critics. Lévi-Strauss, at least, as James A. Boon reminds us, enourages a *bricolage* attitude toward poetry creation that relieves what appears to be a rigid and programmatic method applied to "Les Chats." /14/ In *The Savage Mind,* namely, Lévi-Strauss refers to the *bricoleur,* the jack of all trades of "primitive" closed societies who constructs his universe from the pre-formed materials (unlike the raw materials of the Western technologist) that surround him and whose basic uses are already determined—"like the constitutive units of myth, the possible combinations of which are restricted by the fact that they are drawn from the language where they already possess a sense which sets a limit on their freedom of manoeuvre." /15/ The implication is that the poet is a tinkerer like the "savage" *bricoleur* and that the critic can take the same approach to studying poetic composition as he can to studying dimensions of closed societies. Further, it should be recalled that Jakobson and Lévi-Strauss have stated their intention in the Baudelaire study as "an attempt to understand the *creation* of a Baudelairian sonnet" and not an examination of the poem's effect. /16/ Jakobson and Lévi-Strauss have not claimed to have invented a method that reads a literary text for one, nor has Riffaterre declared any such efficacy for his approach. What they have accomplished is the formation of new ways of comprehending the poetic process that (in the case of Jakobson's and Lévi-Strauss' innovative study, at least) has already produced further provocative interpretations through the work of other critics.

Roland Barthes

The notoriety that Roland Barthes has suffered through his

strife with Raymond Picard over Racine and the fact that he has written on popular culture subjects (James Bond, Greta Garbo, the Eiffel Tower, photography, advertising) should not obscure his remarkable accomplishments both as semiologist and wide-ranging literary critic. Susan Sontag in 1968 called him "the most consistently intelligent, important, and useful critic—stretching that term—to have emerged anywhere in the last fifteen years." /17/ He is capable of brilliant structuralist textual explication but has also repeatedly presented structuralism through the long view and the overview, relating it to the history of literature and locating literary criticism as a metalanguage within the context of semiology generally. Because he has been the most important practitioner of literary structuralism, I shall pay more attention to his theory in these pages than to the theories of other critics.

Barthes' criticism shows a concern for history (the place of literature in relation to time) that reveals his phenomenology-influenced background and that counters the charge that structuralism dismisses history. /18/ In writings such as "The Structuralist Activity," Barthes shows how a text must first be deconstructed and then reassembled in order for the critic to comprehend and appreciate the creative process and to allow him to participate in the creative act. /19/ Barthes says, in fact, that the critic is necessary to complete the literary act, that author and text without critic present an unfinished work; the critic is the entelechial agent, the one who uses language transitively to vocalize the silent or intransitive art work. In his controversial 1962 book on Racine, Barthes reveals his debt to Freud, as he analyzes the corpus of Racine's drama in terms of the primal horde model to discover the structure of dramatic action underlying the plays. /20/ Here the metalanguage of Freudian terminology is employed to erect a synchronic structure that nonetheless locates Racinian theatre historically and that shows the power of a criticism using binary oppositions to reinvigorate the language and art of an older literary epoch and make it interpret the present.

In his representative essay, "To Write: An Intransitive Verb?,"

Barthes wishes to demonstrate how language and literature are once again enjoying a reconciliation through structural analysis following the estrangement brought on by the demise of rhetoric. /21/ This reconciliation, resulting in an endeavor Barthes calls semio-criticism, contributes to the grand undertaking of "a single, unified science of culture" which is the study of culture as a general symbol system. /22/ Barthes sees his task as studying "the structure of the sentence" as a model for the structure of discourse generally (i.e., of all verbal expression) and of the human culture system, and examines three grammatical categories of equal significance for literature and linguistics: temporality, person, and the verb *to write*. /23/

Regarding temporality, he distinguishes between the time of discourse (the speaker's present enunciation) and the time of history (the aorist, or past, or preterit tense), and declares that recent creative, non-realistic literature presents nuances of temporality that undermine the old correspondence of the time of discourse with objective discourse and the time of history or narrative with subjective discourse. The indication is that some aspects of literature are developing a temporality of discourse, of the moment of enunciation, that gives literature a new actuality and "objectivity," a new determinative function like that of linguistics, in shaping and not merely reflecting the symbols of the cultural system.

Speaking of person, Barthes distinguishes between the discoursing *I* and the referent *he* or *it* as the difference between person and non-person to show that the conventional novelist "cheats" by making the subject of narration (the non-person) appear vivified through quasi-identification with the subject of discourse (the person, the *I*, the implied author), as if the *I* had to be subordinated in fiction. Some recent fiction (such as Robbe-Grillet's) shows us that the relationship among the *I* of the author, of the narrator, and of the reader is not as clear-cut as is generally assumed, and that the dissymmetry of language, the overlapping of message and code is finally appearing through the problem of person as a difficulty in literary criticism.

In discussing the verb *to write,* Barthes says that the modern tendency to understand it intransitively (to write *per se,* not to write something) suggests how the writer today uses the "middle voice" whereby he renders himself the center of *parole*—something like an application of the phenomenological notion of the artist at the service of the language which surrounds and pervades his existence. This problem of the writer's activity corresponds to the problem of the verb in linguistics: both are shifting status and seeking a new identity in the presence of discourse. Language and literature show us how reality is grasped in interrelational or intersystemic moments that can serve as cultural models.

A central essay of Barthes that has received too little attention to date is his "Introduction to the Structural Analysis of Narrative." /24/ Since there is no way of adequately summarizing this lengthy and complicated piece, my comments should be read as a guide through the essay that the interested reader should turn to himself. Barthes begins his "Introduction" by stating a generic problem: how can the many different kinds of narrative be comprehended and distinguished from each other without some model? Structuralism is involved in this problem by virtue of its effort to order the multitude of speech acts through a description of the language from which they originate. The structural analyst of narrative is in a situation akin to Saussure's in linguistics, "seeking to extract, from the apparent anarchy of messages, a classifying principle and a central vantage point for his description." /25/ One must abandon the inductive model that literary critics have adapted from the experimental sciences and proceed deductively, since the infinite number of narrative possibilities makes induction absurd. For the structuralist, the linguistic model is the obvious one, for structural linguistics has already demonstrated its ability to describe, deductively, the common properties of the world's three thousand languages.

One cannot superimpose structural linguistics upon structural narrative analysis, however, for linguistics stops necessarily with the sentence as its largest unit, whereas for narrative analysis the sentence is the smallest unit with which one can work. One must view the sentence as the basic unit in the network of the self-multiplying systems of discourse that humans create. Hence narrative language can be studied as one of the modes of discourse that is homologous with the sentence: "a narrative is a large sentence, just as any declarative sentence is, in a certain way, the outline of a little narrative." /26/

Linguistics has also supplied structural narrative analysis with the key concept of the levels of description and the resultant recognition that a hierarchy of levels exists. Just as in linguistics the description of a sentence in terms of phonemes, morphemes, words, etc. cannot be done purely distributionally (i.e., on the same level) but must be undertaken integratively (i.e., on more than one level) in order for meaning to be explained, so also in narrative analysis a theory of levels must be established. One cannot, in other words, read a story only "horizontally," to follow its linear development; one must simultaneously read "vertically," absorbing all the while the implications being revealed on a number of levels. To do so is, of course, a version of practicing diachronic, or syntagmatic, and synchronic, or paradigmatic, reading at the same time: "the meaning does not lie 'at the end' of the narrative, but straddles it." /27/ Barthes tentatively selects three levels of narrative structure for analysis, a level of functions as Propp and Bremond define the term, a level of actions as Greimas employs the term to treat characters *(actants),* and a level of narration which approximates the level of "discourse" as Todorov treats it. An examinaton of the substance of each of these levels and of how they relate, through a "progressive integration," constitutes the body of Barthes' essay.

Barthes treats the level of functions in greatest detail, beginning with a determination of the basic narrative units on the level of function. These are, he says, the distributional or functional class, consisting of elements of narrative that operate on a single level (i.e., that function metonymically and complementarily and refer to functions of actions), and the integrative or metaphoric class, made up of elements he calls indices or indicators, that convey such things as characters' personality traits and identities, atmosphere, etc., and that refer to functions of being rather than of action. Popular tales are mainly functional, while psychological narratives are mainly indicial, and in between these extremes is a great variety of what Barthes calls intermediary forms. Each of these two classes, in turn, is reducible to two sub-classes each. The distributional, functional class consists of units that Barthes names cardinal functions or nuclei, because they precipitate decisive actions, and of catalyses that fill in the space between the nuclear actions. Or as Barthes states it otherwise in a colorful way, the cardinal functions are moments of risk in the narrative, while the catalyses are "areas of security" that serve to secure contact between narrator and reader. The indicial class can be subdivided into indices proper (conveying character traits, emotions, etc.) and information fragments that merely offer data. Barthes stresses that a unit can inhere both classes at once, so that some units are mixed, and that catalyses, indices, and information fragments are developments of the nuclei—which, like the simple components of the sentence, together constitute a few finite sets from which the story proliferates.

From the functional units Barthes moves to functional syntax and states the main problem regarding it: we know that narrative structure distorts the "realistic" relationship between temporality and logic; can one discover an atemporal logic behind narrative temporality? The structural analyst seeks to comprehend temporality as part of the system of discourse rather than as an *a priori* category. Barthes reviews three attempts to describe such an atemporal logic: Bremond seeks to reveal an "energetic logic" (we might call it also an existential logic) by retracing the decisions that a character has had to make at key points of the story; Lévi-Strauss and Greimas try to locate paradigmatic oppositions in the nuclei and then superimpose them upon the syntagmatic pattern; and Todorov attempts to learn the principles that regulate the combinations, transformations, etc. that the *actants* (i.e., characters) of narrative are involved in. Barthes himself prefers a concept of sequence, "a logical string of nuclei, linked together by a solidarity relation," that is to say, joined as a series of actions that form together a self-contained totality; these sequences are always namable (Fraud, Struggle, Seduction, etc.), often by the reader through interpretative equipment he brings to the act of reading. /28/ A number of sequences join together to form a "pyramid of functions" that can be analyzed on the functional level and then opened up to the next level in the hierarchy, the level of actions. /29/ Barthes points out further that although the functional structure of narrative is fugue-like, introducing, elaborating, and dropping sequences simultaneously, sometimes sequences exist in a narrative without any connection at all on the functional level and can be grasped in their continuity only from the higher level of actions.

To this level Barthes turns next and, treating actions in Greimas' sense of *actants* or acting characters, discusses three ways of defining character that have come about from the structuralists' reluctance to deal with characters via psychological essences. For Bremond, every character "is the hero of his own sequence;" for Todorov, the basic predicates of love, communication, and assistance determine the relationships among characters through the rules of derivation and action; for Greimas, characters can be categorized in terms of three pairs of opposites (subject/object, giver/receiver, adjuvant/opposer) as they take part in the actions of communication, desire, and ordeal. /30/ The term "action" on this level, then, refers not to the acts that constitute the functional level but rather to the broader expressions of *praxis*. Barthes believes that the three articulated theories of action are generally viable but do not solve the central problem involved in the classification of characters, namely, the location and identity of the subject (the protagonist) of a narrative. The key to this problem must lie in a study of the grammatical rather than the psychological (i.e., "real") person, but since any answers must be found in relation to the third level of the narrative hierarchy, the level of narration, Barthes introduces a discussion of that level next.

Here he asks the question, who is the giver of narrative, as a way of responding on this level to the problem of the subject (the *I* and the *you*) that could not be solved on the level of action. He reviews three assumptions: one is that the narrator is the actual, real-life author and the text is thus merely the expression of his self. A second is that the narrator is an all-knowing consciousness, a "God" who both knows his characters intimately and is aloof from them. The third and most recently developed is that the narrator is the one who limits his presentation to the viewpoints of the characters. Barthes finds all of these inadequate because they perpetuate the illusion that narrator and characters are real people, whereas Barthes himself, of course, wishes to argue that they are grammatical entities. He goes on to distinguish between personal and apersonal systems of narration and shows that although the narrative mode traditionally stressed the apersonal, the personal gradually insinuated itself into the story to the extent that narratives mix the two regularly—a practice that some contemporary artists are trying to abrogate by emphasizing the formal, linguistic person; thus recent literature is often transitive rather than descriptive, wishing to verify its pure existence as speech rather than symbolizing some external reality or conveying a message. Such literature uses its referential dimension to emphasize its linguistic substance, rather than the traditional *vice versa*.

Barthes studies the self-emphasis of narrative in what he labels the narrative situation, pointing out that the writing process itself is part of the coding of narration, the role of which is not to send forth a narrative message but to call attention to the process itself. In fact, any analysis of the message belongs to the world of discourse beyond the narrative level and no longer has anything to do with structural narrative analysis. Western society, typically bourgeois and hence geared to production, is interested in ends and tries to disguise rather than accent the coding of narrative. Nevertheless, whoever makes the least gesture of response to narrative cannot help participating in the coding process that is itself before it yields to the world's interpretation.

Barthes concludes with a description of the system of narrative and, returning to the analogy of language, shows how the processes of unit-producing segmentation and unit-combining integration, producing form and meaning respectively, have their counterparts in narrative. Segmentation creates form through sign dispersion and expansion. On the linguistic level, a sign is distorted and "fractured" (dystaxy occurs) when its logical sequence or juxtaposition is interrupted by other signs, so that its signified is dispersed and taken up by other signifiers that have no meaning in themselves. A similar dispersion occurs in narrative on the functional level: units of a sequence can both constitute the totality of the sequence and be separated by other functional units, so that a broader significance occurs only through the distribution, i.e., the distortion of the units. As an example, Barthes refers to the description of two people meeting and shows how that act, coherent and whole as a "realistic" projection, is distorted by narrative depiction into smaller units that fashion their own logical time and that can be understood only by the sustained reference to the reader's "intellective memory." Thus the distortion of narrative creates suspense that is resolved by the reader's recollective effort as well as by the narrative's completion of the sequence.

Not only does sign dispersion among the functional nuclei occur but also sign expansion through the catalyses that fill the gaps between the nuclei, a possibility which shows that narrative, unlike poetry, is ultimately reducible to summary, the summary of the functional units that preserve the uniqueness of the message.

If segmentation creates form through sign dispersion and expansion, integration shapes meaning through a "vertical" or "in-depth" reading of the distorted units; the reader does not recognize a sequence because it imitates real life; rather, he puts the disparate elements of a sequence together to make them resemble real life. Narrative art does not consist of a repetition of real life but of a series of sequences that defy repetition. Literally nothing is signified in narrative except the language itself happening. If structural narrative analysis begins with the linguistic model, then also its highest point of meaning is the embodiment of the language act. In our monologues to and from each other we celebrate our participation in the language event and hence our humanity.

Although Barthes employs a number of examples from popular fiction (mainly from Ian Fleming's James Bond novel *Goldfinger*), his essay is not fundamentally an application of structuralist literary critical principles to actual texts. Rather, it is an elucidation of the principles themselves and a tentative elucidation at that, more of an attempt to identify problems of structural narrative analysis and various critics' solutions to them than an effort to present a definitive description. One could apply Barthes' categories to individual texts more or less systematically, as in fact he himself does—less systematically—in "The Struggle with the Angel: Textual Analysis of Genesis 32:23-33," but one has the sense that Barthes would not necessarily endorse such exercises. The practical application of structural analytical techniques should never be merely programmatic or derivative but should be imaginative and creative to the extent that it criticizes the techniques and alters the theories behind them. For like the metonymic and metaphoric impulses of the linguistic model that inspires it, structuralist literary criticism always seeks both a logical continuity with a critical context and, at the same time, a transcendence of it and tries to establish a productive oppositional relationship (a dialectic) between the forces of continuity and transcendence.

A main reason why structuralist critical theory has proliferated and practical application has not is that the theorizing generates codes that are never perfected, so that critical writing tends toward expression of the endless possibilities of narrative, just as narrative exhibits key traits of linguistic discourse formulating its finite sets of rules. Structuralist criticism, Barthes insists, resists efforts to use its techniques as a means of subduing a text; it wishes to open up the text to the potential of the world's discourse, so that the categorizing, paradoxically, is intended as a liberating act. In Barthes' *S/Z* we shall see that paradox in action.

A. J. Greimas

The work of Greimas is in certain key ways an extension of Jakobson's theory explained in essays such as "Linguistics and Poetics"—that the analysis of the operations whereby the elementary linguistic units produce lexical meaning can be applied to larger units of discourse, to stories and novels, to reveal the pattern of meaning inherent there also. Yet as interesting as Greimas' studies have been, they have not demonstrated the universal validity he would like to claim for them and must at this point in the history of structuralist criticism be judged as instructive failures. Much like Lévi-Strauss in his myth analysis, Greimas begins his semantic analysis in *Sémantique structurale* by positing "semes" (minimal semantic traits derived from oppositions) and then "lexemes" composed of combinations of semes; because the meaning of lexemes changes according to context, one must consider the various readings ("sememes") of a lexeme in a particular passage of discourse, derive the traits that all of the sememes have in common, and thus produce a list of variant contextual semes. /31/ The repetition of such semes in a text, recognized by the reader, produces "classemes" which provide the text with its fundamental coherence, while the repetition of classemes then leads the reader to comprehend the totality of signification or the "isotopy" of the text. The point of the whole exercise is to show how the broad range of meaning in a text can be traced to elementary linguistic maneuvers, yet as Culler says, it is an attempt that is almost doomed to fail because Greimas must be at pains to include at the basic levels all possible meanings that might be discovered at the more complex levels, a near impossibility because one must, among other things, try to allow for the idiosyncrasies of the readers. /32/ Culler suggests wisely that rather than trying to force Greimas' semantic theory to work on its own terms, one might use it where it suffices, note where it is inadequate, and fill in those gaps with methodology drawn from other critical sources. /33/

Greimas has also advanced a flawed but fascinating theory of narrational characters that, in spite of its questionable universality, has been adopted and adapted by interpreters of secular and biblical texts such as Todorov and Barthes. In his *Sémantique structurale* he borrows first the seven roles of folktale characters identified by Propp in his *Morphology of the Folktale:* the villain, the hero and false hero, the dispatcher (who sends off the hero to fulfill his task), the sought-after-person, her father, the helper, and the giver of magical aids. Although Propp did not suggest any general validity for these roles applied to other narrative forms, Greimas uses the pattern to demonstrate that a concise *actantial* model (i.e., a model based on a few consistant roles or *actants*) provides the groundwork of all semantic acts from the single sentence to the complete story. Greimas revises Propp's seven *actants* into six of his own that form a double syntactic and thematic pattern:

sender —> object —> receiver

⬆

helper —> subject<— opponent

Recast in Propp's terms, the model becomes clearer:

dispatcher —> sought-after-person —> hero

⬆

helper/giver —> hero <— villain/false hero

Culler points out troublesome problems with Greimas' model, for example, the fact that Greimas, without justification, assumes that the sender-receiver relationship is the same as that between other roles in the model; further, none of Propp's categories suggest at all the receiver role which to Greimas is central, so that Greimas must argue the uniqueness of the folktale as a type of story that has the hero fill both the subject and receiver roles. /34/ Greimas wishes to use this latter strategy to create a typology of narratives by categorizing them according to the mergings of any same two roles in a single character (thus other categories would emerge like the one in which the hero is both subject and receiver), but as Culler states, the possibililties for extending the model seem very tenuous, not least because Greimas has offered so little illustration of how to apply it. /35/

Nevertheless, Barthes in his analysis of the Old Testament "Jacob and the Angel" passage and Todorov in his treatement of *Les Liaisons dangereuses* have both applied it with some success, and Greimas continues his efforts to correct and refine it. And even if the project of discovering direct connections between linguistic and narrative analysis were ultimately to fail, Greimas' scholarship would still be worth reading for its insights into the cultural communicative process, for instance, the observation that the structure of narrative consists of a breach of contract and eventual restoration of the contract, a process reminiscent of Lévi-Strauss' discovery of the basic systems of exchange that inform and underlie human societies.

Tzvetan Todorov

The Bulgarian-born and French-educated Todorov (he studied under Barthes in Paris) develops not only Greimas' notion of narrational character but also of plot and offers a structuralist theory of reading as well. In his study of *Les Liaisons dangereuses* in *Littérature et signification* he employs the concepts of desire, communication, and participation, inspired by the relationships among characters in Greimas' *actantial* theory, and establishes rules of action that govern the behavior of the *personae*. /36/ But in his *Grammaire du Décaméron* he abandons the *actantial* model, returns to the methodology of Propp, and, beginning with the sentence as the exemplary unit, describes characters as empty subjects, as proper nouns attached to and determined by various "predicates," that is, by the cluster of actions that the reader absorbs as he follows the text. /37/

The increasing attention paid to the reader's involvement among structuralist critics results in a specific theory of reading in

Todorov's "Comment lire?" essay. /38/ Here he defines reading as a specific kind of literary activity as distinguished from projection (what is usually called extrinsic criticism), commentary (intrinsic analysis, explication), and poetics (the search for general principles in individual works). In the activity of reading one sees the text as a system and studies the structure of relationships among its components. Further, unlike interpretation, which tries to uncover hidden meanings, reading accepts and works with multiple levels of the text (cf. the influence of Todorov's mentor Barthes), and unlike description, which for Todorov means structural linguistics applied to literary texts, reading asserts a freedom from linguistic categories and a commitment to a strictly literary system that is both part of a literary tradition and transcends it. In the remainder of the essay Todorov shows how the reading process works by using the strategies of "superposition" and "figuration" to discover and examine relationships between parts of a text or between different texts. Todorov does not abandon structural linguistics, of course; he states that interpretation and description must also be undertaken, along with reading, but in his emphasis on reading and his sympathy toward formalist and generic criticism he, like Barthes, relieves structuralism of some of its first-generation attachment to the linguistic model. Indeed, he argues that even though linguistics is the basis of metalinguistic systems such as literary criticism, systems like literary criticism can extend our knowledge of linguistics and aid in forming a universal grammar. We may be reminded in the process that the language of literature is the essential form of language *per se*. One might remark, finally, that Todorov's *The Fantastic: A Structural Approach to a Literary Genre* offers a challenge to biblical scholars to adapt his immensely provocative approach to the "fantastic" literature—such as the prophetic and apocalyptic visions—of the Old Testament and the New Testament. /39/

Gérard Genette

Robert Scholes calls Genette a "low structuralist," one who, in contrast to the glamorous "high structuralists" such as Lévi-

Strauss, Barthes, and Lacan, with their sweeping claims and ingenious systems, patiently and sensibly carries on the task of careful textual analysis in dialogue with other critics. /40/ Moreover, Scholes says, since Genette is at home with English and American literary texts and critics, his writing is likely to find more long-range response in the United States than many of the more spectacular European structuralists' works. /41/ In his three volumes of *Figures,* which deal in part with Proust's *Remembrances of Things Past,* Genette reveals his overriding concern with rhetoric and the act of reading. /42/ By rhetoric he means the whole grammar of literary terminology such as metaphor, allegory, etc. (what he calls "figures") that contrary to what traditional rhetoric tried to grasp as a complicated list of rules (comparable, say, to the laws of nineteenth-century philology), functions in reality as a system of interrelationships. Genette wishes to rehabilitate rhetoric by relating it to linguistics. Like Jakobson, Genette begins with the syntagmatic and paradigmatic, the interplay between metonymy and metaphor as that which characterizes literary language and must be examined as the basic step of the critical act. Like Todorov and the later Barthes, Genette is led from an analysis of the text to the dynamics of reader involvement, but unlike Barthes (especially his *S/Z*) he does not come to emphasize the cultural codes that the text elicits but rather, more like Todorov, the reader's reception of the figures that constitute the text. Genette's description of the reading event, in fact, comes very close to a phenomenology of reading.

What Genette discovers, among other things, in his Proust interpretation are levels of fictive discourse that can be used in an approach to any literary text: the events that comprise the story *(histoire),* the actual story *(récit),* and the presentation of the story *(narration).* Of these, *récit* is central and pivotal; from it the reader recreates *histoire* and projects *narration.* Genette clarifies the interrelationships of the three levels by aligning them to three other concepts derived from the linguistic elements of verbs: tense, mood, and voice. Tense helps to explain the temporal connection between *histoire* and *récit;* mood also deals with *histoire-récit* relations but more with matters of point of view than of action.

Voice treats the relation of the narrator to *histoire* and *récit*, and also to the characters inside and the reader outside of the story. That this new way of encountering fiction has great potential can be seen, for example, in the valuable distinctions it creates between seeing and telling in a story and the ability it provides the reader to distinguish the subtleties involved in variations of seeing and telling. Particularly, then, as these textual relationships emerge as constants of human behavior and natural events, the literary text, as in Todorov's theory, illuminates the deep structure of all contexts. To oversimplify heuristically: the systems of narrative clarify other global systems.

Other structuralist theorists should be mentioned. Jan Mukařovský, Claude Bremond, Julia Kristeva, Boris Uspensky, and Northrop Frye (in another tradition) are among those who have contributed centrally to the definition and attempted solution of structuralist literary critical problems, while critics of the structuralists such as Seymour Chatman, Jonathan Culler, and Fredric Jameson have, in the process of describing and evaluating the structuralists' efforts, added important contributions of their own. But the dimensions of my own study are modest, and the introductions to the few theorists I have mentioned must suffice. The sketches of applied literary structuralism in the ensuing pages will include brief attention paid to theories of non-literary structuralists (Goldmann and Lacan) with literary ramifications and will, in any case, reinforce the theoretical discussion I have offered.

B. Application

In the course of introducing structuralist theories I have already included one textual study (Jakobson and Lévi-Strauss on Baudelaire's "Les Chats"), and I shall now turn to ten examples of applied analysis, five of them on biblical passages and five on modern secular texts. My intention has been to select studies that extend as far as possible from the earlier days of structural analysis to the present; thus the Leach essay was first published in

1962, whereas two others I have picked (by Casalis and Detweiler) are very recent. I have also chosen books and essays that represent widely varying approaches within the structuralist methodological context: two that rely heavily on Lévi-Strauss (Leach and Casalis), two by Barthes himself that illustrate different kinds of efforts by one prominent critic, and one (Goldmann) that largely forsakes the linguistic model.

It will become quickly apparent that a different strategy obtains among the critics working with biblical literature and those examining secular texts. The critics treating the Old Testament and New Testament passages are intent on adapting more-or-less developed methods to actual textual analysis and offer relatively little criticism of those methods, but the critics of secular fiction seem more interested in combining practical analysis with a refining of method. This is so even with Barthes; he is much less venturesome in his treatment of the Genesis story than in his reading of Balzac. I think that this difference is valid beyond the criticism represented by my ten selections. Structuralist biblical exegetes have wished mainly to show the utility of structuralism for providing worthy new interpretations of scripture, whereas the critics of secular literature have stressed more the dialectic between theory and application—the need to apply the theory in order to discover where and how it must be revised. /43/

Edmund Leach, "Lévi-Strauss in the Garden of Eden"

Edmund Leach the British anthropologist has taken on the role of Lévi-Strauss' somewhat quizzical but sympathetic interpreter. It is a valuable stance for this essay, for in it, without using technical structuralist terminology or committing himself to any of the structuralists' analytical directions, he situates Lévi-Strauss' myth analysis in the tradition of anthropological myth studies and then shows how a Lévi-Straussian treatment of the Genesis creation story differs from the two other prominent myth-analytical approaches. /44/

Leach first distinguishes between the symbolist and functionalist groups in anthropological myth studies. The symbolists include James Frazer, Freud, and the early Ernst Cassirer, and understand myth as a way of dealing with the great mysteries such as the origin of the world and of death, and as a way of cushioning the brutality of existence through symbolic mediations of it. The functionalists include Emile Durkheim, Malinowski, and the later Cassirer and argue against the symbolists (who deny a direct connection between myth and the social framework) that myth and society are intertwined and that myth therefore can be studied properly only in its social context. British anthropologists, Leach says, mainly accepted the functionalists' approach over the symbolists' theory and over Frazer's comparative approach as well. Lévi-Strauss, however, beginning especially with his "The Structural Study of Myth" in 1955, challenged the functionalists with a version of symbolist analysis—what he has labelled structural—that disavows the need to study myth and rite (i.e., the social component of myth) together. The method, as is well-known by now, involves the accumulation and collation of the versions of a myth, no matter what their sources or dates, in order to find a common structural pattern from which a "meaning" can be derived. The implication is that the old symbolist view of myth was correct—myths soften the impact of insoluble contradictions of the human situation, such as the fact that life also involves suffering and death, by offering mediating middle categories. The mediation is accomplished through myth clusters, rather than individual myths, that agree in certain ways but differ in others, and hence dissipate the force of the contradictory categories. For example, the Pueblo Indian myth cluster that tries to reconcile the contradiction between life and death does so in terms of the categories of farming, hunting, and war; hunting, which incorporates life-giving power as well as death to animals, is the mediating category.

Leach next treats Lévi-Strauss' analysis of the Oedipus myth that is his central example in the 1955 essay, pointing out how the Sphinx is the mediating figure between the opposition of Laios and Jocasta, Oedipus' parents, and how Oedipus' indirect destruction of the Sphinx is the mediating act that resolves the

problem of accommodating patrilineal descent (desirable) and the
necessity of being born of a woman (undesirable). In order, then,
to test Lévi-Strauss' method in the Western Christian context,
Leach applies it to the Genesis creation myth. He shows first how
symbolist, functionalist, and structuralist approaches stress
different dimensions of the narrative. For the symbolists the
Garden of Eden element is central and offers material for
projecting phallic symbolism and symbolic connections between
knowledge and death, whereas for the functionalists, the seven-
day creation narrative is more significant and projects the seven-
day week and the Israelite taboos described in Leviticus. An
analysis in Lévi-Strauss' terms, however, demonstrates the
validity of the mediating middle category theory. The first chapter
of Genesis, describing the seven days of creation, shows, for
example, how firmament mediates fresh water and salt water, and
how plants mediate land and water, but basic contradictions such
as those between life and death are not resolved. Thus Leach starts
again, this time with the Garden of Eden story in the second
chapter of Genesis, and discovers here that unitary existence (one
river, one life, one human) is restricted to Eden, while the world
beyond the Garden consists of oppositions: male-female, life-
death, good-evil, etc. Ingeniously, then, Leach draws parallels
between the Oedipus-Sphinx myth and the myth of the Fall. He
likens the serpent in the Garden to the monster of the Oedipus
tale, and finds a correspondence between the lameness of
Oedipus, the autochthonous (earth-born) hero, and that of Eve's
offspring, whose heel shall be bruised by the serpent. God's curse
upon man in this context then can refer to the opposition between
man and woman or even between father and son, for which
perhaps the circumcised child is the mediating category. Leach
sees the same oppositional pattern repeated in the Cain and Abel
story in Genesis 4: the tension between the gardener and the
herdsman leads to the death of the herdsman-brother and the
substitution of a wife for him, so that the "sterile homosexual
world," like the world of the Creation myth before sexually
bifurcated creatures are introduced and like the Garden before

Eve and the Fall, "shall become a fertile heterosexual world." /45/

Although Leach does not say so, he has also effected a compromise of sorts between the symbolist and functionalist "oppositions" of the anthropological myth analysis. The reference to the circumcision ritual, for example, neatly mediates between the phallic reading of the Eden story by the symbolists and the functionalists' insistence on a social interpretation. Further, without engaging in any sort of biblical textual criticism or theological discussion, he shows how a wholly new basis for such criticism and discussion can be laid.

Matthieu Casalis, "The Dry and the Wet: A Semiological Analysis of the Creation and Flood Myths"

Casalis undertakes, in contrast to Leach, a professional theologically-oriented structuralist study of two Genesis myths, based on Lévi-Strauss, in his 1976 *Semiotica* essay. /46/ Casalis begins with a lucid analysis of how the death of God has meant the end of hermeneutics and the beginning of the semiological age. Hermeneutics refers here to the attitude that accepted God as the Absolute Signified, whose meaning is imaged in all the signifiers in the world, signifiers which, because they refer to the same content, always reflect the same message. Because man is a privileged signifier of God as Absolute Signified, he is acknowledged as a subject, the one addressed by God, and hence is involved in the subject-object epistemology that underlies Western thought. Casalis sees the death of God as a momentous, anxiety-laden event that has, among other things, led to the disintegration of language meaning: because signs have lost their divine referent, they have become mere "semiological matter"; since they now literally refer to nothing, they open up to immanent plurisignification. Although the concept of the subject survives tenaciously in the post-death-of-God, semiological age, it must be recognized as the fiction that it is, so that signs can speak for themselves without the intervention of man as privileged signifier.

Casalis wishes his essay to serve as part of the process of

liberating the signifier and appropriates Lévi-Strauss' myth analysis in order to apply it to the Genesis Flood and Creation stories. He has chosen this material to answer the charge that Lévi-Strauss' method has been tested only on ideal contents, favorable to its successful applicaton, rather than on materials that evince a "lack" or an "excess" of meaning for Western culture. Because the biblical creation myths have helped to determine Western hermeneutics for centuries, and thus project an excess of meaning, a semiological approach to them should show the validity of Lévi-Strauss' method.

Turning to the Creation myth itself (Genesis 1) and accepting the validity of the Priestly and Yahwist traditions as defined by historical criticism, Casalis undertakes a "horizontal" (syntagmatic) and "vertical" (paradigmatic) reading, as Lévi-Strauss did in his study of the Oedipus myth, and discovers a pattern of disjunctions that expresses how the amorphous cosmos is given form through a differentiation process based mainly on the fundamental opposition of wet and dry. Moreover, the structures of the two narrative traditions mirror each other: the Priestly narrative stresses the emergence of the world through a disjunction of dry and wet, while the Yahwist story begins with the dry and tells how through the conjunction process life springs forth. The Flood story, in its two traditions, also plays disjunction and conjunction against each other; the Priestly matter conveys a conjunction of upper and lower waters (rain and springs) to get rid of the differentiation of earth/water, etc. and return the universe to chaos, while the Yahwist material takes the conjunction of earth and water to its conclusion of cataclysmic excess—the world is destroyed by water. The resultant paradigm emphasizes the need to hold both creational processes—the disjunctive dry/wet that begins with total wet and the conjunction dry plus wet, that begins with total aridity—in balance to avoid catastrophe and death.

Like Leach, Casalis argues that this kind of myth analysis supports Lévi-Strauss' claim that myths develop as mediations of logical contradictions; in the case of the Genesis material the contradiction to be overcome exists primarily between the Yahwist and Priestly versions of the Creation and Flood stories, between extreme conjunction and extreme disjunction. Comparing his analysis diagramatically to a chart from Lévi-Strauss' *The Raw and the Cooked,* Casalis illustrates how the Semitic myths of Genesis, like the Indian myths treated by Lévi-Strauss, describe the limited range, that range mediated between cosmic extremes, within which life can flourish. Further, a symmetry between the paradigms of the Indian culinary myths uncovered by Lévi-Strauss and the Semitic Creation and Flood myths indicates that both belong to a single paradigmatic set. If this is so, then one has a demonstration that Lévi-Strauss' method can be applied valuably to Western material.

One might add that Casalis is also resolute in his effort to free the signifier from the Absolute Signified, since he carries through his semiological exercise with little reference to the Old Testament creator God or to man as subject and privileged signifier. Nature and language, rather, become the central components of the study and serve as the relational entities from which the new signs are formed. One might ask whether the emergent signs are any less redundant than those produced by the hermeneutic attempt, but at least Casalis does suggest the rich complexity, almost the infinite interplay of elements that constitute the world viewed semiologically as a fiction of language rather than as an image of God.

Roland Barthes, *"The Struggle with the Angel: Textual Analysis of Genesis 32:23-33"*

Barthes explains at the start of this essay that he does not wish to demonstrate principles of structural analysis of narrative but rather intends to undertake a structural analysis *per se,* one that concentrates on the text itself, to show "which coded stages go into it." /47/ He begins with a sequential or *actionnelle* analysis and treats three sequences of the Old Testament passage on the patriarch Jacob wrestling with an angel—the crossing of the river, the struggle between Jacob and the angel, and the changes of names, all of which exhibit certain basic oppositions. /48/ Regarding the crossing of the river, first, the redundant text leaves unclear whether Jacob himself crosses the river or merely sends his household over. If he himself does not cross and wrestles the angel on the non-Canaan side, implications are present of a battle with the genie of the river and of the need for the hero to prove himself by ordeal before entering the promised land. If he does cross and fight the angel on the Canaan side, the story reveals Jacob's need to defeat the genie of the new land.

Regarding the struggle, the stylistic ambiguity creates a paradoxical structure. The vagueness of pronouns in v. 26 ("who, seeing that he could not master him, struck him in the socket of his hip . . .") leads to the situation in which the angel strikes an unfair blow that should be decisive yet which is ineffectual, for the angel must still bargain with Jacob to release him before dawn breaks: "The one who knows the secret knowledge, the special blow, is nevertheless beaten." /49/ Barthes sees this paradox as an example of the folklore of the human fighting with the divine in order to receive a special mark, a brand, and views the action as an extension of Jacob's prior strategy—using his position of weakness to extract a blessing, as indeed he did in taking away his brother Esau's birthright—and as a preview of his descendants' fortunes—the children of Israel (Jacob's new name) in their weakness conquering the land of Canaan.

Regarding the change of names, Barthes describes the emergence of a "mutation": the change of Jacob's name to Israel as a result of his demands for a blessing (the condition for the angel's release) and Jacob's request that the angel reveal *his* name (to which the angel responds indirectly by supplying the blessing but not his name) result in Jacob naming the place of struggle as Peniel—where he saw God and lived—but this "mutation of names" also signals a more pervasive change. One recognizes how in all three sequences a "crossing" occurs—of a place, of a familial rank, of a name, and—in the establishment of the taboo against eating the sciatic nerve—of a dietary practice. This multiple crossing, Barthes seems to say, is much like the way language creates new meaning by transgressing the old rules.

In the second part of the essay (actually about the last third) Barthes turns away from sequential analysis and to structural analysis *per se,* that is to say, away from a mainly textual examination and toward the *actantielle* analysis of Greimas and the functional analysis of Propp. According to the *actantielle* strategy, whereby one categorizes the characters by their functions into six classes, Jacob would be the subject, receiver, and adjuvant (the one who aids the subject), while God, in the form of the angel, is the sender and the opponent, and the transversing of a protected place is the object. In the fact of Jacob acting as his own adjuvant and of God the sender also acting as adversary, Barthes finds evidence that the story fits the form of the extortion folk narrative: God not only defends the river against the trespassing hero but also is the one who supplies the brand and the blessing when he is "defeated." In this daring narrative structure, the use of the extortion pattern, Barthes sees a parallel to the "scandal" of God's subjugation by Jacob.

According to Propp's classification of folktale structure in terms of its narrative actions (functions), the Genesis story is an excellent example of a typical folktale. Barthes describes many correspondences between Propp's thirty-one functions of the folktale and the Jacob story (the journey of the hero, the struggle of the villain and the hero, the defeat of the villain, the branding of the hero, the liquidation of a misfortune or need, etc.) to demonstrate the classic folk structure of the story. Yet finally Barthes confesses that he is not so much interested in the folklorist's model of the story that is revealed through structural analysis as he is in what he calls the "metonymic montage." The thematic components of the story are not developed, he says, but rather condensed in the unconscious fashion of metonymic thought. The richness of interpretation to be discovered, therefore, lies in the effort of such multiple readings as Barthes has attempted; these do not distill a meaning (a "signification") from the text but reinforce its original power.

Apart from the typical use of diagrams, Barthes' analysis does not readily reveal its structuralist basis, yet it is heavily dependent on structural linguistics, on Lévi-Strauss' myth analysis, and on Freud as he has been appropriated by the structuralists. The linguistic influence appears, for example, in Barthes' facile identification of narrative and linguistic sentences, resulting in a correspondence of *actantielle* analysis with the present participle of grammar and of sequential analysis with the verb; later, Barthes declares that the Jacob-angel passage "creates the precise conditions for the operation of a new *'langue'* of which the election of Israel is the 'message.' God is a *logothète:* Jacob is here a 'morpheme' of the new *langue*." /50/ More important is the largely unstated supposition that each sequence of the episode contains some kind of irritating "difference" conducive to producing new meaning, just as the differences that arise through phonemic analysis establish the bases of linguistic meaning. The influence of Lévi-Strauss is apparent in the similarities to Lévi-Strauss' analysis of the Oedipus myth; Barthes calls attention to the battle with monsters, enmity between brothers, lameness, etc., as they are treated in the Genesis story, and, like Lévi-Strauss, discovers a mythical narration of the origin of a taboo in the deep structure of the story. Finally, the debt to Freud is evident in Barthes' fascination with inversions, such as his labelling of God, who chooses Jacob over Esau, as a counterbrander; in his treatment of symbols as displacements (basic to Freud's dream analysis); and in his references to the presence of the Narcissus theme (discussed by Freud in relation to the myth of the enemy brothers) in the hostility between Jacob and Esau.

As Barthes himself warns at the start, his analysis will not be a lucid one and probably unsatisfactory to theologians, but it does serve as a rich illustration of how structural analysis can open up a text, can deconstruct it without destroying its integrity and leave it intact for the biblical exegete searching for another kind of meaning.

Jean Starobinski, "The Gerasene Demoniac: A Literary Analysis of Mark 5:1-20"

The Geneva literary critic and physician Jean Starobinski's essay on Jesus healing the Gerasene madman seems at first to employ his wonted "criticism of consciousness" approach rather than a structuralist method, for the charts, overt binary oppositions, transformations, etc. are largely missing. /51/ Yet one soon learns that he is engaged in another sort of structuralism, one that asks, for example, Barthes' kind of questions about the narrator and makes Greimas-style inquiries into the roles of the *actants* and combines these with imaginative exposition. As Sarah Lawall has suggested, Starobinski already reflected the influence of structuralism in his 1964 *L'Invention de la liberté,* especially through its addition of a sociological concern to the intrinsic analysis. /52/

Starobinski begins by explaining that he will not treat the text in a theological or historical framework but will instead proceed synchronically—paying attention to "its sequential organization" (which is not the same as Barthes' sequential or *actionnelle* analysis, as illustrated in his study of Jacob wrestling with the angel) as well as to the "quasi-simultaneity of its parts," to the text as it stands apart from redactional speculation. /53/ He turns first to the question of who is speaking through the text, discovers that the narrator is anonymous as befits a true story, and distinguishes between two levels of narration: that of the presentative mode and that of the citations from the Old Testament and from Jesus himself. The intent is to point to the centrality of Christ and to let Christ speak in the first person, so that the reader/hearer must respond with a decision to believe or disbelieve him. Addressing himself to action next, Starobinski finds that the passage is very rich in topographical information, in its attention to setting, and that this information is important for the action. That Jesus crosses the lake into foreign territory suggests metonymically his intention to universalize his saving ministry and metaphorically (through his immediate encounter in Gerasa with the madman) that he has entered a demonic region. The crossing itself assumes ontological importance: Jesus goes to the infernal graveyard site at night to rescue a man in the devil's power. Further, the double prophetic emphasis (the Old Testament passages that must be "fulfilled" and Jesus' own anticipations of what will happen) shows that all significant actions are predicted, and those events that occur without preparation can be interpreted merely symbolically (i.e., the demons entering into the swine, who fall into the lake, represent the fall of the rebellious angels into hell).

Regarding character, Starobinski observes that Jesus' relationship to the crowd, consisting of a rhythm of appearance-disappearance-reappearance, confirms the movement that he repeats for the disciples during the period of passion, death, and resurrection. Starobinski also sees a valuable opposition between singularity and multiplicity. Jesus is alone but surrounded by an increasing number of people; Jesus alone faces the demoniac who is both himself and "legion." Although Jesus speaks to the multitudes, his healing is generally performed on a single individual at a time, and in fact in this instance Jesus cures the possessed one by restoring his singularity to him. Starobinski points then to the folklore theme of cheating the devil, present here, whereby Jesus as hero fights the monster in a plural form it has assumed and liberates the victim, sending him back to his people but then accepting him, folktale style, as a follower. Psychoanalytically speaking, the "expulsive catharsis" leads to the displacement of suicidal violence: the demons flee into the swine (appropriately unclean animals) and leap into the abyss.

Starobinski concentrates next on the exorcism event itself, the pivotal action of the story. The conditions of possession and healing are oppositions that must be mediated. Possession is characterized by externality (the demoniac is outside of his community and "beside himself"—although Starobinski does not say this), alienation (he is at total odds with his fellows), and negation (all he does is meaningless action). The cured man, on the other hand, is restored to the community, reconciled to his people, and provided meaning through Jesus' person and mission. The importance of speech in the exorcism passage should not be overlooked; it is in a sense the element of mediation. Jesus is victorious through words over the demons, who have exerted control through language, and in giving the man his *own* language back to him and rendering the demons dumb by sending them into the swine, Jesus exerts his authority.

The question of *actants* causes one to inquire who has the status of Jesus' opponent. First it is the evil spirits in the madman and then the frightened Gerasenes who ask that Jesus leave their land. Jesus does in fact leave, and the resultant "residue of opposition" observed here is paradigmatic of the oppositions that lead to his death, then to later resistance to the Christian message following Christ's resurrection, and eventually to the eschatological concept of the anti-Christ.

Starobinski deals then with parabolic interpretation, referring to the parable of the sower and Jesus' ensuing words about those who cannot comprehend parables (Mark 4:1-34). He discusses the operation of crossing from one "register" of parable to another, from the literal to the didactic level, and sees in this crossing a parallel to the crossings in the exorcism story: the crossing of the lake, the crossing from possession to freedom, etc. are like the parabolic crossing from ignorance to insight. Starobinski realizes that such creative reading leads to the temptation to allegorize the whole gospel, an enticement that must be resisted in order to maintain the historicity of the narrative and to permit the theology of the parables to appear. In other words, a syntagmatic (literal) reading combined with the paradigmatic (interpretative) substitutions exposes an eschatological meaning (rather than a merely "spiritual" one) that asks for the reader's decision. The opposition of singular/plural in the exorcism story extends to the opposition of the many gospel stories and their single eschatological meaning in Christ. Further, the parable structure itself maintains the necessary opposition to Jesus discovered in the Gerasene story; those who cannot "hear" the parable (those on the outside) are the ones who continue to oppose what is for them Jesus' hermetic message.

As a physician, Starobinski is interested in the medical aspects of demon possession and treats these in the final section of his essay. Rather than projecting the presentation of possession as a contemporaneous explanation of epilepsy, schizophrenia, etc., from the "superior" position of modern scientific knowledge, we should inquire if the story might not be a way of explaining the Devil: demonic possession does not explain the abnormal behavior; the abnormal behavior "interprets" the demonic which the individual knows otherwise only theologically. "What is to be understood becomes what makes understanding possible. What is to be interpreted becomes what makes interpretation possible." /54/ This evocation of the hermeneutic circle which concludes the essay reveals at last that Starobinski, in spite of his skillful use of structuralism—although done more inspirationally than programmatically—remains mainly a phenomenologically-oriented critic; in the final sentence he refers to man as "both a speaking being and an historical being," less a structuralist perspective than one that confirms his profoundly humanistic stance. /55/

Louis Marin, Sémiotique de la Passion

Marin, a noted Pascal scholar, is also one of the most dazzling and difficult structuralist critics, one who, without a theological platform, brings a forceful and original imagination to bear on biblical texts. *Sémiotique de la Passion* (still untranslated into English) is a relatively short book (186 pages of text) divided into two main sections, the first a study of what he calls the topography of the Passion of Christ, and the second a semiotic of the traitor, both as revealed in the New Testament gospels. /56/ The section on Christ's Passion proceeds by speculating on the ontology of the proper place name. Marin's rationale for such an approach rests on the argument that the proper name exhibits a unique negative and positive trait. Negatively, it is at the limits of speech and silence in the area of *langage* (human speech), which is to say that it has a much more restricted referential capacity than other nouns, and this quality suggests the inferior dimension of *langage*. Positively, the proper name moves beyond this limit by functioning between *langue* and *parole* (i.e., between a language system and individual speech acts or, in Chomsky's terms, between competence and performance) "and in the hiatus of symbolic unfolding" by providing a more tangible orientation point by virtue of its limited referentiality. /57/ Thus the examination of place names (toponyms) in the Passion story uncovers a kind of organization that promotes the unfolding of this symbolically-charged narrative in concrete terms.

Marin is interested, along with Lévi-Strauss, one discovers, in a kind of structuralist transformation process: if, as Lévi-Strauss observes, toponyms exist at the limits of the breach dividing speech and things, how can one make a certain place name assume a new meaning without destroying its original spatial connotation—how can one describe the passage of one's "'cultural' system into another system which is in continuity with the first and also in a state of disruption?" /58/ Here one sees Lévi-Strauss' old dilemma recounted in *A World on the Wane:* how to encounter and understand the South American tribe (the Tupi) without harming their self-identity. /59/ Marin proposes a solution, for his version of the problem, that is also a general hypothesis for his study. The Passion story, he says, tries to neutralize its toponyms in a way that preserves their self-identity so that they can become "others" *(autres)* through passage into the "common" *(commun)*. The neutralizing process is a diversified one in that it can assume the form of etymological translation, of a radically new event, or of a simple excision through a common name, which substitutes for the proper name through narrative metonymy or discursive metaphor.

Having introduced this approach in the first chapter, Marin turns in chapter two to "The Locations of the Story: Death and Resurrection of the Toponyms." Since the toponyms emphasize a spatial context as the way of producing narrative meaning, Marin proposes to analyze the *trajets* (movements, journeys) of the hero in order to find the differences between them from which meaning is formed. Jesus is the hero of the gospels, obviously, so that four of his *trajets* are described, beginning with 1) Jesus' messianic entry into Jerusalem starting at the Mount of Olives, followed by 2) an episode of intermediary space leading to 3) passages in which the proper place names are effaced, and concluding with 4) the crucifixion and resurrection scenes that accompany the reappearance of the proper place name.

Comparing the versions of the first *trajet* (Jesus' triumphal entry into Jerusalem) in the four gospels, Marin finds a ternary structure in Matthew consisting of four stages of the journey (the crowd's enthusiastic worship along the way, the crowd's ready identification of Jesus upon his entry into Jerusalem as the prophet Jesus of Nazareth, the entry into the temple to expel the moneylenders, and the departure for Bethany), in contrast to a simple binary spatial structure in Mark, Luke, and John. Marin then depicts the relationships between the locations represented by the toponyms and the "actors" who appear there in terms of conjunction and disjunction. For example, in Matthew the Mount of Olives scene is characterized by conjunction between Jesus and the crowd, the temple scene by disjunction, and Jerusalem by a neutrality evidenced in the initial questioning of Jesus' identity. By charting such relationships in all four gospels Marin shows how space is shaped into meaningful locations through the encounter between Jesus, as "vector of orientation," and the other actors in the text.

Marin's discussion of the second *trajet* locates Jesus in the intermediary space between Bethany and Jerusalem and calls attention to the negative aspect of this journey caused by Jesus' cursing of the fig tree. In the remainder of this section Marin carries out an analysis similar to that of the first *trajet,* assigning values of conjunction, disjunction, etc. to the place names in these passages. In treating the third *trajet* Marin describes the gradual effacement of the toponyms in the various gospel passages through the failure of the writers to give specific names to the places of Jesus' sojourn; rather, the places are identified by the names of the actors or are translated into common nouns. In the fourth *trajet,* focusing on the resurrection and ascension, the post-resurrection apparitions of Jesus take the place of his journeys, and the proper place names—Bethany, Jerusalem, the Mount of Olives, Golgotha, etc.—are restored. Marin summarizes the chapter by recalling that at the beginning of the story the toponyms are caught up in the text of the story; they receive a "semantic charge" from the hero's displacements, joining them to the signifying systems that the text consists of, but still retain their referentiality. It becomes neessary to efface them and substitute common names for them in order to permit a narration of the story without distortion.

The remaining chapters of the first section treat "Toponymic Systems and Secondary Topics." Here Marin discusses Jesus' entrances into the town and the temple, including consideration of the New Temple, the New Jerusalem, the Last Supper; the parables found in these passages, including those of the wicked harvesters and the marriage feast; and the eschatological discourses, which include the coming of the Son of Man and eschatological parables such as those of the ten virgins and of the talents. In these chapters Marin constructs paradigms of entry and departure, return and expulsion, consummation and rejection, convergence and separation. He concludes that the ultimate effacement of the toponyms occurs in the Last Supper scenes, where Jerusalem and the temple are replaced by common nouns (Jerusalem = where Jesus is; temple = where Jesus eats), because all comes to focus on Jesus as the only proper noun, the only point where space becomes meaning; "speech in the form of the unique proper name 'Jesus' . . . becomes consumable body—that is, sacrificed thing, sacred space containing and contained in sacrifice." /60/ Thus in the end, through complicated "passages," the place names of the Passion story indeed take on new meaning without forfeiting their original connotations.

The second section, on the semiotic of the traitor, I will summarize very briefly. This section, which is only casually related to the first, centers on the role of Judas Iscariot, of course, but also deals with the satanic temptations of Jesus in the desert, and builds on the *actantial* model of Greimas and on the exchange model of Lévi-Strauss from his *Structural Anthropology*. Marin wishes to show that Judas' betrayal of Jesus is finally, in structuralist terms, a gift. The betrayal allows Jesus to join God, his signified, by means of the "exchange" that Judas' act consists of: through the betrayal Jesus as divine signifier becomes its opposite—non-divine signifier—and is empowered to rejoin the signified and become the signifier-signified, "the Son glorious in the glory of the Father." /61/

Both sections of the study, then, rely finally on a structural linguistic model, but the model itself is also enhanced by Marin's elaborate and intricate transformations. Neither the Passion story nor the transformational model can be experienced the same after Marin's treatment of them, yet what they have now become expands the horizons of both biblical exegesis and literary criticism without destroying the old contexts. One could say, borrowing an apt New Testament metaphor, that Marin has managed to pour new wine into old wineskins in a way that preserves both the flavor and the vessel.

Roland Barthes, S/Z

In *S/Z* Barthes' anti-reductionist tactic evident in his Genesis study (on Jacob and the angel) becomes central. /62/ At the end of that essay he declares that he does not wish to distill a signification from the text but rather to provoke multiple readings that will celebrate the utter plenitude of the passage and confirm its original strength. In *S/Z* he intensifies this effort, and with a vengeance. A vengeance, in fact, is subtly operative in the function of this book as yet another challenge to the French academic critics, another stage in the conflict between Barthes and the practitioners of traditional *explication* that reached the height of its furor in the dispute following Barthes' publication of *Sur Racine*. For in *S/Z* Barthes refuses to "interpret" in any conventional way at all or even in a fashion that the brief tradition of structuralist criticism (especially as practiced by Todorov and Greimas) would prepare one for. His commentary is at once strikingly illuminating and maddeningly obscure, consisting of a dazzling and complex interplay of codes that threatens to overwhelm the story it treats but at last does expose the narrative's intricate force without displacing it by another "definitive" analysis. In addition, *S/Z* is a record of the reading process itself, an activity with which the structuralists, like the phenomenologists (the critics of consciousness and the hermeneutical critics especially) and the German *Rezeptionskritiker* (Wolfgang Iser, Hans Robert Jauss) are becoming increasingly concerned.

The text that Barthes discusses is Balzac's "Sarrasine," an approximately thirty-page story within a story about a young French sculptor, Ernst-Jean Sarrasine, who in 1758 travels to Rome and there at the opera falls in love with the prima donna La Zambinella. He pursues her passionately, discovers at last that "she" is actually a castrato, in his anguish tries to kill him but is killed instead by the hired assassins of Zambinella's protector, the Cardinal Cicognara. This narrative is surrounded by a frame tale in which the narrator (the time is around 1830) takes a young lady to a Paris ball where they see a frail, ancient man catered to by members of the wealthy family giving the party. The narrator's friend, curious to know who the old man is, agrees to hear the narrator tell the story of him the next evening in exchange for an ensuing night of love. The story of the old man is, of course, the story of Zambinella, whose accumulated wealth now supports his doting relatives. Horrified by the tale, the young lady breaks her agreement to make love with the narrator.

What Barthes sees present in the Genesis passage as a "metonymic montage" he expands in *S/Z* to a network of five codes running through the 561 "lexias" (fragments) and ninety-three "digressions" into which he divides the short story. A code is what Barthes has called a metalanguage elsewhere, an efficient and concentrated vocabulary that one applies to a complicated construct to simplify and thus restate its substance. /63/ It is worth observing that Barthes' codes have the double function of a literal code. They present a helpful shorthand to the initiate but hide the significant information from those on the outside, and in this sense they enact the dual role of the New Testament parable that structuralist exegetes have stressed recently. Barthes introduces and evolves five codes in *S/Z*, under which, he says "all the textual signifiers can be grouped . . . and every lexia will fall." /64/

The five codes (a bit later he lists them as five "voices") in the order he initially names them are first the hermeneutic code, which deals with fundamental questions, enigmas, and deceptions, and with the elements of plot (including the sense of author plotting against reader) that must be solved for the reader to pursue the continuity of the story; he names this also the voice of truth, indicating that this code fixes on the veracity of what happens beyond all foreshadowings, delays, and deceits. Second, the code of semes refers to the connotations of the most elementary meaning-units, especially as they constitute characters and themes; Barthes calls this also the voice of person. Third, the symbolic code refers to theme in a broader sense—to the repetition of major units in various ways to produce a multifaceted representation. Fourth, the proairetic code is the code of actions, similar to the sequential analysis in the Genesis passage on Jacob and corresponding to the movement from the functional to the actional level in his "Introduction to the Structural Analysis of Narrative." He calls it also the voice of empirics and wishes by it to trace the syntagmatic, horizontal progression of a text. Fifth, the code of culture, or referential code, which he also names the voice of science, identifies the supra-individual voices of a society or its institutions, the general influences that speak often in clichéd form through a text.

Barthes then immediately puts these codes to work, using the hermeneutic and proairetic codes to pursue the chronological development of "Sarrasine," the connotative (semic) code to follow the creation of persons, the symbolic code to amplify broad and basic themes, and the cultural code to comment on the embodied voices of the establishment. He does not arrange these in any systematic order but rather copies shorter and longer passages of the "Sarrasine" text and then addresses them from the perspective of whatever code seems apt. Frequently he interrupts himself with "digressions" that move away from the text to face the problems of the act of reading, aspects of rhetoric and aesthetics, semiology, etc. In the treatment of the lexias and the digressions the familiar concerns of Barthes are expounded: the elusive nature of the literary subject, the fugitive and deceptive quality of language itself, the need to "explode" a text in order to experience it in its wholeness, the necessary playfulness of the critical venture and the corresponding infinite creative energy of the human imagination, the restless effort constantly to reform the world through language, the structuralist drive to replace the object with a message. Most remarkable, perhaps, is his ability to present the Balzac text through an ultra-close reading that does not draw attention away from the fiction, and simultaneously to make this commentary speak to the historical-cultural situation from a structuralist's theoretical-speculative vantage point. For example, following the discussion of Sarrasine excited in the theater by the singer La Zambinella, in the digression on "euphemism" Barthes describes a literal reading (Sarrasine enraptured by the singer and wishing to repeat the initial encounter) and a symbolic one (Sarrasine sexually aroused by the singer and turning the moment into a masturbatory recollection) to argue that the literal does not take precedence over the symbolic in terms of validity or authenticity but that the two are part of a plurality of systems that constitute the text's meaning: "the literality of the text is a system like any other." /65/

Peggy Rosenthal remarks that "What Barthes is doing, to borrow Thomas Kuhn's language, is offering a new paradigm for literary criticism, a set of terms that divides the area of investigation differently than the current paradigm does." /66/ This is probably claiming too much for Barthes' book, but it *is* a stunning and immensely stimulating study that is worth the difficulty of entry and the continuing eccentricities throughout. It is a major document of structuralist criticism, not a model of a method that one could emulate and yet an invitation to one to experiment with a similar close reading that opens up to an ontology of the narrative sign. *S/Z* is, after all, a grand reaffirmation and correction of Jakobson's declaration in 1958 in "Linguistics and Poetics" that poetry is language concentrating on itself, a preoccupation with the linguistic message for its own sake rather than for its referential value. Barthes dramatizes this view, but whereas Jakobson's treatment of poetry (and Barthes' commentary on "Sarrasine" has the characteristics of poetry analysis as much as of prose criticism) tends to be reductionist, Barthes' is expansive; 200 pages of explication of a thirty-page text witness to a belief in the generative and regenerative power concentrated in the fictive text.

Fredric Jameson has an illuminating passage on *S/Z* in *The Prison-House of Language.* He sees Barthes' emphasis on the double structures (reminiscent of Lévi-Strauss' stress, in *The Savage Mind,* on the double functions of "primitive" tools that represent their actual usage as well as a mythic "history") coming to focus on the Balzacian double story; specifically the interplay of narcissism and castration (the familiar excess and lack from Freudian and Lacanian psychoanalysis) in both narrations which at the end remains in tension is a situation that recalls for Jameson "what Greimas would call the superposition of a teleological and communicational axis: one *isotopie* or narrational level having to do with desire for an object, the other with the emission of a message. The reversal which takes place—in which a message replaces the object and becomes as it were *a* message about a *lost* object—is . . . profoundly emblematic of Structuralist interpretation in general." /67/

R. E. Johnson, "Structuralism and the Reading of Contemporary Fiction"

Johnson believes that even though structuralist critics sometimes make grandiose claims for their approaches, one should learn to use structuralism, for in more modest ways it enables one to appreciate modern literary texts that one might otherwise dismiss. /68/ He depicts the paradoxical nature of literature (for example, it is simultaneously full of meaning and yet always intentionally frustrates full understanding) and of the critical act (the critic's effort is to regain and overcome, at the same time, the author's embodiment of his uniqueness in his text), and presents then eleven questions that a structuralist critic might address to a literary text. Some of the most important are:

1. To what system does the pivotal language belong, i.e., what system
    of stasis or exchange is metaphorically rendered in the dominant
    language? What sort of structural patterns and relationships
    emerge from the repetition and interplay of these terms?

    . . .

3. What sort of structural similarities/antinomies can be discover-
    ed/generated from the linguistic ambivalences?

    . . .

6. How do [*sic*] the inventory of other relationships (linguistic, plot,
    character, etc.) reflect the paradigmatic structure? (How can they
    be *translated* into its terminology, equations, etc.?) How does this
    basic structure and the variations on it explain the otherwise
    inexplicable (referring here not to meaning, as such, but to
    function)?

    . . .

8. How does the basic structure(s) govern the architecture of the
    whole (as opposed to the architecture of the part questioned in
    number 6)? /69/

Johnson then begins an analysis of fiction by the contemporary
American authors William H. Gass, Donald Barthelme, and
Robert Coover. Addressing himself first to Gass' "The Pederson
Kid," he defends Gass against the charge of solipsism by arguing
that his stories both express a reality beyond the language that
conveys them and "mock that reality" by revealing how it consists
of exercises played with linguistic elements. The structural
analysis of the story itself focuses on various interrelated
exchanges linked to covering real or metaphorical distances, the
main one of which is the trade of "a fallen world for a
prelapsarian existence," which is reinforced by the exchanges of
"warmth for cold," the narrator "Jorge for the Pederson Kid,"
"time for space," "the imagined for the real." /70/ By the end of
the story, when all of the exchanges have been carried through and
only Jorge is left in his self-generated imaginative and linguistic
Eden, the achievement and mockery of a solipsistic reality are
complete: "Jorge is, at the end of the story, both the liberated and
the isolated word." "He has attained a degree of transcendence

which is mocked by the fact that there is nothing to transcend."
/71/ What saves Gass' fiction from sheer solipsism, Johnson
seems to say, is that reality is infinitely redundant and such fiction
attains meaning by informing us, through linguistic-narrative
models, of this fact.

The system to which the pivotal language of this story belongs,
then (to return to Johnson's key critical questions asked by the
structuralists), is the imagery of the historical versus the ideal
"Edenic" world which becomes a parable of all human attempts to
fashion meaning (historical relevance) out of a paradisiac stasis in
which only playful repetition is possible. In Johnson's second
explication, that of Barthelme's narratives ("The Catachist,"
Snow White, "Me and Miss Mandible"), he finds that the
dominant system is the redundancy versus the novelty of
language—a version of the system that characterizes Gass' story.
Rather than merely collecting and cleverly juxtaposing odd
fragments of experience for their comic effect, Barthelme
examines the arbitrariness of signs to discover how repetition
creates both similarity and disparity; the same process of language
formation disclosed by the structural linguist is at work as the
dynamics of narration and as the exemplum that reflects on this
dynamics in Barthelme's prose. For example, the bits of movie
magazine gossip that titillate the elementary schoolchildren in
"Me and Miss Mandible" form a paradigm of the aptly combined
arbitrary units that one orchestrates to create a story's meaning,
just as the gossip writers both invent and tailor their rumors to
fashion the game of popular culture "reality."

The opposition in Coover's fiction, finally, is of the same order
as in Gass' and Barthelme's but is singular in that Coover does not
seem to recognize the ironic and paradoxical nature of the
opposition. He wishes, according to Johnson, to overcome the
"unconscious mythic residue in human life" but does not realize
that he must implement the very language he tries to disarm. /72/
That is to say (although Johnson does not) that Coover employs
myth in the name of novelty (to replace outmoded narrative form)
while failing to grasp that this very use of myth entails a necessary

and crucial redundancy and repetition. Coover's structural narrative system is especially fascinating, therefore, because it reveals Coover unwittingly employing it while ostensibly fighting it. Not that Coover is unsophisticated; in his *The Universal Baseball Association,* for example, the gradual merging of the protagonist's table-top baseball game with his historical existence is metaphoric of the view of life as endlessly redundant (the hero's mundane existence) yielding to the effort to make new meaning (the ballgame)—once again the tension between similarity and difference evidenced elementarily in structural linguistics. But, Johnson says, Coover does not see or does not grant the final irony that the fabrication of meaning remains a fabrication, that the game outside of the novel is not transparent to a deeper symbolic meaning but is simply a game. Rather, by suggesting the analogy between himself as all-powerful author and the novel's hero as all-powerful gamester, Coover projects an absolute signification that the structural critic would challenge.

This last argument should be of special interest to theological critics of secular literature, for it declares, as does Matthieu Casalis in his Genesis study, that the structural analyst may not fall back on the "prose of the world" era grounded on an acceptance of the Absolute Signified. /73/ In general, Johnson's brief essay is one of the most lucid and stimulating to appear to date for describing the options and methods for structuralist criticism of modern American fiction. In demonstrating how three authors of our age both use and illustrate structuralist-derived concepts of artistic creation and meaning, he confirms, in an appropriately paradoxical way, how structuralist theory is valuable. More convincingly than many structuralists who engage the texts to expound the theory, Johnson makes the application reverberate with theoretical import.

Günther Schiwy, "Peter Handke's Short Letter, Long Farewell"

The Munich journalist Günther Schiwy, who has been for many years a popularizing interpreter of structuralism, in his book *Strukturalismus und Zeichensysteme* devotes a brief chapter to a structuralist gloss on the young Austrian author Peter Handke's novel *Der kurze Brief zum langen Abschied* (translated as *Short Letter, Long Farewell* in 1974). /74/ Schiwy's discussion merits recognition both because it claims that Handke's novel itself is uniquely structuralist fiction and because, unlike the main effort of the academic critics I have been sketching, who apply structuralist interpretative techniques to a text or bolster a theoretical argument with an occasional reference, Schiwy finds certain structuralist principles *embedded* in the narration that he identifies and enlarges on. He starts with the observation that Handke is really a sort of semiologist, for in his work *I Live in the Ivory Tower* Handke confesses that his formal education was a failure and his life-orientation has taken shape through the system of signs that is literature (by his participating both in the reading and writing of it), also that he has learned to expect of good literature that it will change him and reveal new possibilities of existence to him. It seems also, however, that Handke's novel deals with the difficulties of change. The neurotic (as Handke's heroes always are) narrator and hero has come from Austria to America seeking radical change, above all from a disintegrating marriage, yet he is pursued by his wife, who threatens to kill him. The structuralist element that Schiwy sees operating here is the tension between maintaining and changing a system, specifically a system of personal orientation and habit; one might even designate it as a tension between closed and open systems.

Like Handke himself, his protagonist suffered through an adolescent education that by its many rules and restrictions *systematized* him, but in a unique way: in a rebellion against the proscriptions he nurtured an active fantasy life that revealed to him the countless possibilities of experience beyond the isolation of his boarding school life. These fantasies, in turn, were disciplined by the rigorous order of his formal education and thus, through this dialectic, his system was formed. Schiwy views this evolution of a personal system as analogous to a linguistic code; it contains all of the vital components for patterning one's life, even those crucial experiences that lie in wait for one.

Yet in the narrator's journey to and through America his system is jeopardized, and he must confront the danger. Especially through his American lover's small daughter, who is neurotically compulsive, he finds that a rigid adherence to one's system is the result of an insecure identity and that one must learn to tolerate the systems of others: "The story, the trip that he [Handke] narrates is the way that the hero needs to take to learn patience with his system and with the system of his wife from whom he wishes to separate. It is only because his patience grows and through it the insight that the system of the other must be tolerated that the book has a happy end." /75/

Schiwy remainds us that Handke is also concerned with non-literary texts, with feuilltons, legal texts, radio and television scripts, for instance, and that this interest appears in *Short Letter, Long Farewell* in the form of attention paid to still other sign systems. Schiwy sees a Barthes-like spatially-oriented sign system as very important in the novel, focussing on rooms, architecture, streets, cityscapes and landscapes. Especially for a foreigner, as is the Austrian visitor in America, the new impressions cohere into such systems that both confirm and expand his wonted codes. The narrator observes, for example, that his lover's daughter cannot grasp the signs of nature, indeed doesn't even know that they exist, but accepts in their stead the components of the technologized world as natural. Even beyond that, the child does not distinguish between signs and their referents, a situation which Schiwy sees as a warning for and by structuralists that one can emphasize sign systems to the extent that one loses the sense of a primary reality—a statement that places Schiwy himself outside of structuralism, for what he is wary of is exactly what Barthes and Marin, among others, have described as the normal interpretative and culturizing process: the substitution of a message for the object, the absorbing of the event into one's system of signification.

Schiwy finally calls attention to the role of cinema as a dominant sign system in Handke's novel. The narrator particularly admires the director John Ford, and in fact the novel concludes with a meeting between Ford and the narrator. This attraction to cinema is not surprising, for the world of film is a powerful sign system that tends to obscure its referent, the object world, and Ford's films especially, with their nostalgic evocation of older times, constitute a message in place of a lost object. Thus without probing very deeply into structuralist theory, Schiwy does demonstrate how one major contemporary novelist seems to incorporate a structuralist vision into his art.

Lucien Goldmann, "Genet's Plays"

Influenced by Marxism, the Hungarian critic Georg Lukács, the sociology of knowledge, and to a lesser degree Freud, Rumanian-born Lucien Goldmann offers a kind of structuralism markedly different from the linguistically based methodologies of Jakobson, Lévi-Strauss, Barthes, etc. It is a genetic structuralism that, he claims, as a literary critical method moves a radical step beyond the old sociology of literature approach that sees in the content of the literary text "a *reflection* of the collective consciousness." /76/ According to Goldmann, neither the individual nor collectivity is the subject of the human sciences (including literary study), but rather collectivity is the genuine subject understood as an intricate "network of individual inter-relationships" that must be carefully defined by the critic. /77/ Further, Goldmann says, the relations that obtain between a good literary work and the social context that generated it are homologous with the relations between the work and its structural components.

To clarify this concept, one might say that Goldmann expands and corrects Barthes' individualized homology between language and literature; for Goldmann the correspondence is between social existence and literature and is based on what he calls the categorical structure (the deep structure) beneath the author's fictive world and the real social world. One hopes to discover through studying these correspondences exact structural parallels to the real world that the outmoded context analysis of literary sociology could not reveal. Thus the genetic structuralist recognizes the text not so much as a reflection of collective consciousness but more as a central formative element of consciousness that brings to a focus what the persons who comprise the group consciousness are already tacitly thinking and acting on. Moreover, he need concentrate only on groups whose consciousness is directed toward an enveloping world-wide vision, for only such groups will create great literature.

The main procedural problem for the genetic structuralist critic is that of *découpage,* or delineation of the object to be examined. It is a "methodological circle"—one cannot scrutinize the structures before defining the range of analyzable data that characterize them, yet one cannot know what data to isolate until one has a fairly clear sense of what constitutes the structures—a dilemma that can be overcome by gradually approximating structures and data to each other until they coincide. /78/ If correctly utilized, the method permits both understanding and explication, that is, permits a basic understanding of the object but also an explanation of how it is integrated into a broader social context.

Only two contemporary "schools," Marxism and Freudianism, encourage this double act of fundamental understanding and totalization. Since Freudian psychoanalysis remains attached to the past and to the individual, it is not very viable, and hence Marxism remains as the direction to follow, for it involves the future in its explicatory strategy and it combines the individual and his communal import in a balanced way. But how then can one comprehend the relation of individual and collective cultural (for our purposes literary) creation? Goldmann's hypothesis is that on the individual, psychic level a conflict exists between the "ensemble of aspirations, tendencies, and desires" whose total fulfillment is thwarted by reality, so that, as Freud has shown, one seeks symbolic satisfaction for unconscious repressions, a satisfaction that always consists of possession; on the collective level, however, the conflict between desire and lack of fulfillment is not based on repression in the unconscious (Goldmann does not accept the theory of a collective unconscious), and hence the drive toward satisfaction does not converge on possessing an object but on achieving a solidarity or unity. /79/ The collective urge toward such cohesion in the creative act thus offsets the individual desire for possession that is usually frustrated. Goldmann mentions not only Marx and Lukács as students of the dynamics of collective modification of desire in the face of reality but also Piaget as one who has examined such modification in a non-Freudian manner, on the individual level; since so little has been done to apply Piaget's structuralism to literary study, Goldmann's reference suggests where one might begin in adapting Piaget's research to structural literary analysis.

In the essay "Genet's Plays" Goldmann demonstrates the practice of genetic structuralist literary criticism. /80/ He analyzes the body of Genet's drama (five plays) chronologically to show the author's evolution from a natural (non-conscious and unrepressed) artistic representative of the nonconformist *Lumpenproletariat* to that of the new revolutionary who senses the advent of a classless society beyond oppression and force but also recognizes the immense difficulty of its realization. Goldmann sees Genet's first play, *Deathwatch,* with its prison setting and unsavory characters, as a work that seeks to dramatize the fight for moral recognition in a world of criminals who value everything that society outside has condemned. In Genet's next two plays, *The Maids* and *The Blacks,* the emphasis shifts from the conflict among the underworld characters themselves to a struggle between oppressor and oppressed. Both plays are permeated by the despair of the oppressed losers, yet in *The Blacks* a dawning recognition of a revolutionary reality is already apparent.

The decisive change in Genet's playwright's consciousness comes in his fourth play, *The Balcony,* where a new dynamic dialectic is in evidence. The characters in *The Maids* and *The Blacks* recognize their oppression and try to overcome it in symbolic ways, but in *The Balcony* a false judge, bishop, and lawyer in a brothel—representatives of the ruling class—act out their fantasies while a *real* revolution goes on outside. In other words, Genet comes a step closer to joining the symbolic with the real revolution. Finally, in his fifth play, *The Screens,* Genet breaks through to a paradoxical projection of the new revolutionary human. Against the background of the Algerian revolution, the hero Said, a poor thief and traitor to the revolution, rejects all of the ruling groups from the colonial powers to the successful revolutionaries and even after his death rejects heaven in favor of nothingness. Rather than accepting the existentialist interpretation of Said's actions as a refusal to let others determine his fate for him, Goldmann argues that Said's rejection of the three political orders—the European class society, the leftist revolutionary groups, and the eschatological vision of the future classless paradise—represents Genet's repudiation of all of these to choose instead a still more radical future whose social-political outlines have not yet been shaped but can be projected only through the artistic imagination.

Obviously, Goldmann's model for the categorical structure in his analysis is the Marxist vision, whereby the contours of the socio-economic base and the pattern of the artist's stages of growth correspond to the pattern of the structuralist's deep structure. And because Goldmann has the deep structure in mind, he does not treat the plays in ways that merely illustrate a Marxist perspective. Instead, he expands the dialectic within Marxism to include a consideration of the structuralist-oriented conflict between desire and satisfaction on the individual and collective levels and is thus able to view Genet's drama as projecting a new radical social-political stance that has not yet been articulated in historical form.

Robert Detweiler, "Updike's A Month of Sundays and the Language of the Unconscious"

The French psychoanalyst Jacques Lacan's marriage of linguistics and psychoanalysis, his combining of Saussure and Freud to disclose the language of the unconscious based on structuralist principles has tremendous implications for literary criticism, even if his theory is idiosyncratic and overstated. One can sample his own almost hermetic but still provocative literary criticism in essays such as his "Seminar on 'The Purloined Letter'," in which Edgar Allen Poe story he sees the ratiocinative efforts of constructing a solution to a crime from bits of evidence as a parallel to the discovery of patterns of transformation whereby the psychoanalyst changes the signs of the unconscious (word slips, puns, word associations, dreams) into the language of awareness. /81/ However, Lacan's crabbed and arrogant writing style frustrates summary, and it would be pointless to attempt a sketch of the Poe analysis here. In "The Insistence of the Letter in the Unconscious" Lacan refers to a "kind of tightening up that I like in order to leave the reader no other way out than the way in, which I prefer to the difficult," and indeed, this preference for taxing his readers often seems to present them no way in or out at all. /82/

Hence I will present a short version of an essay of my own that employs Lacanian concepts. /83/ My effort in this essay concerns four pairs of oppositional terms derived from Lacan's psychoanalytical theory that, applied to John Updike's 1975 novel, serve to explicate a text that might appear otherwise to be merely a self-indulgent display of virtuoso craftsmanship. The novel has to do with a midwestern Protestant minister, Reverend Marshfield, who is also the narrator, drafting sermons and composing his daily quota of confessional prose at a southwestern desert spa for wayward clergy, where he has been banished for a therapeutic month for his sexual misadventures among his female parishioners. His writing is full of Freudian slips (which he glosses), puns, and wordgames that suggest an articulation of the "language" of the unconscious as well as a neurotic sensitivity to the polysemous quality of spoken and written language.

Regarding the first pair of terms, language and the unconscious, Lacan argues that what Jakobson in *Fundamentals of Language* called the metonymic and metaphoric poles of language in his study of aphasia are like displacement and condensation in Freudian dream theory, culminating for Lacan in the concepts of desire (a lack resulting from metonymic displacement) and symptom (an abundance caused by metaphoric condensation). The expression of the unconscious through language, then, is caused by the over-determination of meaning inherent in metaphor and the absence of meaning in metonomy, both of which are present in dreams, the discourse of madness, inadvertent expressions, etc.

The second pair of oppositional terms, self and other, Lacan explains by defining the ego as a "paranoid construct" both in competition and identification with an Other, a dilemma that evolves during the childhood "mirror stage" of development when the ego seeks to model itself on the body image or the image of another person and thus becomes separated from its *own* self. /84/ If one does not mature normally beyond this stage, one must discover through psychoanalysis that one need not struggle to become the Other but merely take on the role of I-in-relation-to-others that permits society to function. In structural linguistic terms, one emerges from the undifferentiated state of the signified to the articulated state of the signifier, or from a metonymic (displaced) to a metaphoric (symptomatic) position in the world, or from a condition of unconscious desire through a state of making demands on others to a recognition of the need to comprehend the desire of the Other.

The third pair of terms is comprised of the Imaginary and the Symbolic stages. The Imaginary stage is the one in which the ego imitates the body image and the image of an Other, while in the Symbolic stage one learns to replace such imitation with empathetic projection. Through a metaphoric leap, that is, one "becomes" the Other in order to get a distance on oneself and learn to know oneself. Lacan declares not only that the structure of language and the structure of the unconscious are similar but also that the unconscious is the discourse of the Other, so that one recognizes one's deepest self in the Other.

The fourth pair of terms consists of the penis and the phallus, which Lacan discusses in the context of the Oedipus complex. In the Imaginary stage the penis is the threat of the father to both son and daughter, but in the Symbolic stage the phallus as symbolic object replaces the literal penis and functions as the signifier of desire and as the symbolic exchange object. As signifier of desire it represents metonymic lack—a fear of castration reflecting the original loss of the maternal womb and the inability of language ever to express all that it wishes to. As symbolic exchange object it represents metaphoric fulfillment; like the gift or the name in some "primitive" cultures the phallus in western society is "exchanged" as a promise of faith and love between marriage partners, an expression of manhood between father and son, etc.

In Updike's novel the typographical errors (like Freudian slips of the tongue and pen), puns, and wordgames call attention to Lacan's insistence on the correspondence between the structures of language and the unconscious. One finds in *A Month of Sundays* many examples of linguistic displacement and condensation ("sermon" is mistyped as "semon" and is glossed as hinting at "semen"; "omnipotent" and "impotent") that betray the pastor's problems with religion and sex that are expressed and treated therapeutically through language. /85/ The Lacanian opposition of self and other appears in the novel in the form of the protagonist's failure to mature beyond the defensiveness and isolation of his childish ego state. Although as spiritual counselor, husband, and father, Reverend Marshfield should be available and open to others, he is instead secretive, competitive, and insecure. Like most of Updike's other main characters, he is caught in a fundamental selfishness that makes him a lonely man.

In terms of the third pair of Lacan's concepts, the pastor cannot grow beyond the Imaginary into the Symbolic stage. Even though he claims to have negated the influence of his father and father-in-law (both liberal clergymen) on himself, he continues to live in reaction to them, and even his tenacious Barthian neo-orthodoxy seems to be more the result of a guilt-ridden father-son affiliation than of a healthy theology. He comes closest to a recognition of his deep self through the Other in his relationship with Ms. Prynne the resort supervisor, but even their sexual intimacy that concludes the novel leaves open the question of whether he has indeed gained sufficient distance on himself through her to absorb redemptive self-knowledge or has merely satisfied a visceral drive. At any rate, he never does learn the crucial difference between penis and phallus, in Lacan's terms, and persists in romanticizing women in ways that reinforce an adolescent lust for them rather than learning that erotic relationships, involving the symbolic phallic exchange, are not necessarily physical-sexual.

In this interplay of desire and fulfillment, lack and plentitude, carried by the metonymic and metaphoric functions of language as they relate to the displacing and condensing activities of the unconscious, the significance of Lacanian theory and Updike's narrative art is expressed in ways that attest to the facility of analysis based on structuralist models.

NOTES

/1/   The only essay I have found that uses Piaget as a basis for structuralist literary theory is Fernando Ferrara, "Theory and Model for a Structural Analysis of Fiction," *New Literary History*, 5, No. 2 (Winter, 1974): 245-268. One of the few essays I have found in English that uses Goldmann's method is Sunday O. Anozie, "Genetic Structuralism as a Critical Technique: Notes Toward a Sociology of the African Novel," *The Conch*, 3, No. 1 (March, 1971): 33-44. However, the whole issue of *Alternative: Zeitschrift für Literatur und Diskussion*, 13, No. 71 (April, 1970), is devoted to essays on Goldmann's literary sociology.

/2/   Helga Gallas, "Strukturalismus in der Literaturwissenschaft," in Heinz Ludwig Arnold and Volker Sinemus, eds., *Grundzüge der Literatur- und Sprach- wissenschaft, Vol. I: Literaturwissenschaft* (Munich: Deutscher Taschenbuch Verlag, 1973), offers a somewhat different categorization. She distinguishes among the paradigmatic analyses of Barthes and Lévi-Strauss respectively; the structural analyses of narrative units (Barthes, Todorov); transformational, generative analysis (Kristeva); structural analysis as commentary (Barthes); and genetic-structural analysis (Goldmann). "Paradigmatic" for Gallas means the interpretive substitution of "vertical" or metaphoric patterns for "horizontal" or metonymic patterns, as Lévi-Strauss demonstrates in his Oedipus analysis. Gallas' description of this process sounds much like the reduction of experiential patterns into eidetic typologies after the fashion of Poulet.

/3/   Scholes, *Structuralism in Literature*, cf. Chapter I, n. 28; Fredric Jameson, *The Prison-House of Language: A Critical Account of Structuralism and Russian Formalism* (Princeton: Princeton University Press, 1972); Jonathan Culler, *Structuralist Poetics: Structuralism, Linguistics, and the Study of Literature* (Ithaca: Cornell University Press, 1975).

/4/   Dan O. Via, Jr., *Kerygma and Comedy in the New Testament: A Structuralist Approach to Hermeneutic* (Philadelphia: Fortress Press, 1975); John

Dominic Crossan, *The Dark Interval: Towards a Theology of Story* (Niles, Illinois: Argus Communications, 1975); Daniel Patte, *What Is Structural Exegesis?* (Philadelphia: Fortress Press, 1976); Matthieu Casalis, "The Dry and the Wet: A Semiological Analysis of the Creation and the Flood Myths," forthcoming in *Semiotica;* François Bovon, "French Structuralism and Biblical Exegesis," in *Structural Analysis and Biblical Exegesis: Pittsburgh Theological Monograph Series No. 3,* tr. Alfred M. Johnson, Jr. (Pittsburgh: The Pickwick Press, 1974). Cf. also John Bowker, *The Sense of God* (London: Oxford University Press, 1973); and Robert Polzin, *Biblical Structuralism: Method in the Interpretation of Ancient Texts* (Philadelphia: Fortress Press, forthcoming). Bowker's *The Sense of God* uses both structuralism and phenomenology in an attempt to chart a theology drawing from the social and informational sciences.

/5/   Jakobson and Halle, *Fundamentals of Language.*

/6/   Jakobson, "Linguistics and Poetics," in De George, ed., *The Structuralists from Marx to Lévi-Strauss,* p. 86.

/7/   *Ibid.,* pp. 89, 95.

/8/   *Ibid.,* pp. 85, 95.

/9/   Lévi-Strauss, "The Structural Study of Myth," *American Journal of Folklore,* 78, No. 270 (October-December, 1955): 428-444; "How Myths Die," *New Literary History,* 5, No. 2 (Winter, 1974): 269-281. The *Mythologiques* volumes consist of *The Raw and the Cooked,* tr. John and Doreen Weightman (New York: Harper & Row, 1969); *From Honey to Ashes,* tr. John and Doreen Weightman (New York: Harper & Row, 1973); *L'Origine des manieres de table* (Paris: Plon, 1968); *L'Homme nu* (Paris: Plon, 1971). Roman Jakobson and Claude Lévi-Strauss, "Charles Baudelaire's 'Les Chats,'" tr. Fernande De George, in De George, ed., *The Structuralists, pp.* 124-146.

/10/   Cf. Günther Schiwy, *Strukturalismus und Zeichensysteme* (Munich: Beck, 1973), pp. 48 ff.

/11/   Lévi-Strauss says in "Charles Baudelaire's 'Les Chats'," p. 124, that a single version of a myth cannot be analyzed this way but only "horizontally," on its semantic level, because its style and form are not artistically crystallized.

/12/   Michael Riffaterre, "Describing Poetic Structures: Two Approaches to Baudelaire's 'Les Chats,'" in Jacques Ehrmann, ed., *Structuralism, Yale French Studies,* No. 36-37 (1966): 200-242.

/13/   Scholes, *Structuralism in Literature,* p. 40.

/14/   James A. Boon, *From Symbolism to Structuralism: Lévi-Strauss in a Literary Tradition* (New York: Harper & Row, 1972), pp. 52-53.

/15/   Lévi-Strauss, *The Savage Mind*, p. 19.

/16/   Jakobson and Lévi-Strauss, "Charles Baudelaire's 'Les Chats'," p. 124, italics mine.

/17/   Susan Sontag, Preface to Roland Barthes, *Writing Degree Zero*, tr. Annette Lavers and Colin Smith (Boston: Beacon Press, 1970), xi. Barthes' *Elements of Semiology* is published as the second part of this edition. Barthes' conflict with the French university critics such as Picard is treated by Germaine Bree, "French Criticism: A Battle of Books?", *The Emory University Quarterly*, 22, No. 1 (Spring, 1967): 25-35. For an excellent recent assessment of Barthes' career cf. Michael Wood's review-essay, "Rules of the Game," in *The New York Review of Books*, 23, No. 3 (March 4, 1976): 31-34.

/18/   The whole of *Writing Degree Zero*, for example, is historically oriented.

/19/   Barthes, "The Structuralist Activity;" cf. Chapter I, n. 28.

/20/   Barthes, *On Racine*, tr. Richard Howard (New York: Hill and Wang, 1964). Cf. also Gras, *European Literary Theory*, pp. 21-22.

/21/   Barthes, "To Write: An Intransitive Verb?", De George, ed., *The Structuralists*, pp. 155-167.

/22/   *Ibid.*, pp. 156-157.

/23/   *Ibid.*, p. 157.

/24/   Barthes, "An Introduction to the Structural Analysis of Narrative," tr. Lionel Duisit, *New Literary History*, 6, No. 2 (Winter, 1975): 237-272.

/25/   *Ibid.*, p. 238.

/26/   *Ibid.*, 241.

/27/   *Ibid.*, 243.

/28/   *Ibid.*, 253.

/29/   *Ibid.*, 255.

/30/   *Ibid.*, 257.

/31/   A. J. Greimas, *Sémantique structurale* (Paris: Larousse, 1966). I am indebted to Culler, *Structuralist Poetics*, for much of my information in this summary.

/32/   Culler, *Structuralist Poetics*. pp. 79, 86.

/33/   *Ibid.*, p. 85.

/34/   *Ibid.*, pp. 233-234.

/35/   *Ibid.*, p. 234.

/36/   Tzvetan Todorov, *Littérature et signification* (Paris: Larousse, 1967). Cf. Culler, *Structuralist* Poetics, p. 235.

/37/   Cf. *Ibid.*, and Scholes, *Structuralism in Literature*, p. 111. I am indebted to Scholes for much of my information in this summary.

/38/   Todorov's "Comment lire?" is an essay in his *Poetique de la Prose* (Paris: Seuil, 1971).

/39/   Todorov, *The Fantastic: A Structural Approach to a Literary Genre*, tr. Richard Howard (Ithaca: Cornell University Press, 1975).

/40/   Scholes, *Structuralism in Literature*, p. 158.

/41/   *Ibid.*, p. 159.

/42/   Gérard Genette, *Figures* (Paris; Seuil, 1966); *Figures II* (Paris: Seuil, 1969); *Figures III* (Paris; Seuil, 1972). I am indebted to Scholes' *Structuralism in Literature* for much of my information in this summary.

/43/   Cf. the "Structuralism" issue of *Soundings: An Interdisciplinary Journal*, 58, No. 2 (Summer, 1975) for examples of both emphases.

/44/   Edmund Leach, "Lévi-Strauss in the Garden of Eden: An Examination of Some Recent Developments in the Analysis of Myth, in E. Nelson Hayes and Tanya Hayes, eds., *Claude Lévi-Strauss: The Anthropologist as Hero* (Cambridge: The M.I.T. Press, 1970), pp. 47-60.

/45/   Leach, "Lévi-Strauss in the Garden," p. 59.

/46/   Casalis, "The Dry and the Wet;" cf. n. 4. I am grateful to Professor Casalis for sending me a pre-publication copy of his essay.

/47/   Roland Barthes, "The Struggle with the Angel: Textual Analysis of Genesis 32:23-33," tr. Alfred M. Johnson, Jr., in *Structural Analysis and Biblical Exegesis*, p. 22.

/48/   I have retained the spelling of *actantielle* and *actionnelle* as used by the translator.

/49/   *Ibid.*, p. 27.

/50/   *Ibid.*, p. 29.

/51/   Jean Starobinski, "The Gerasene Demoniac: A Literary Analysis of Mark 5:1-20, tr. Alfred M. Johnson, Jr., in *Structural Analysis and Biblical Exegesis*, pp. 57-84.

/52/   Lawall, *Critics of Consciousness*, p. 177, n. 7.

/53/   Starobinski, "The Gerasene Demoniac," p. 58.

/54/   *Ibid.*, p. 83.

/55/   *Ibid.*, p. 84.

/56/   Louis Marin, *Sémiotique de la Passion: Topiques et figures* (Paris: Aubier Montaigne, 1971). I am indebted to Elaine Beaty for extensive help in the translation and interpretation of Marin's book.

/57/   Marin, *Sémiotique*, p. 14: "et dans la césure du dédoublement symbolique. . . ." My translation.

/58/   *Ibid., p. 16:* "système 'culturel' dans un autre système qui soit à fois en continuité avec le premier et en état de rupture?" My translation.

/59/   Cf. Jeffrey Mehlman, "The 'Floating Signifier': From Lévi-Strauss to Lacan," in Mehlman, ed., *French Freud: Structural Essays in Psychoanalysis, Yale French Studies*, No. 48 (1972): 13.

/60/   Marin, *Sémiotique*, p. 51: "le langage sous la forme du nom propre unique, 'Jésus'—devient corps consummable—c'est-a-dìre chose sacrifiée, lieu sacré contenant et contenu de sacrifice." My translation.

/61/   *Ibid.*, p. 179: "le Fils glorieux dans la glorie du Père." My translation.

/62/   Roland Barthes, *S/Z*, tr. Richard Miller (New York: Farrar, Straus & Giroux, 1974).

/63/   Cf. Barthes' discussion of metalanguage in *Elements of Semiology*, pp. 92-94.

/64/   Barthes, *S/Z*, p. 19.

/65/   *Ibid.*, p. 120.

/66/   Peggy Rosenthal, "Deciphering S/Z," *College English*, 37, No. 2 (October, 1975): 137.

/67/   Jameson, *Prison-House,* pp. 148-149.

/68/   R. E. Johnson, "Structuralism and the Reading of Contemporary Fiction," *Soundings* (Summer, 1975): 281-306.

/69/   *Ibid.,* 283.

/70/   *Ibid.,* 285.

/71/   *Ibid.,* 290.

/72/   *Ibid.,* 298.

/73/   Casalis, "The Dry and the Wet," manuscript p.1.

/74/   Schiwy, *Strukturalismus und Zeichensysteme,* pp. 28-39. Peter Handke, *Short Letter, Long Farewell,* tr. Ralph Mannheim (New York: Farrar, Straus & Giroux, 1974).

/75/   Schiwy, *Strukturalismus,* p. 35: "Die Geschichte, die Reise, die er erzählt, ist der Weg, den der Held braucht, um Geduld mit seinem System und mit dem seiner Frau, von der er sich trennen will, zu bekommen. Nur weil diese Geduld wächst und darin die Einsicht, dass das System des anderen zu tolerieren ist, hat das Buch ein 'Happy-End'." My translation.

/76/   Lucien Goldmann, "Genetic Structuralism and the History of Literature," tr. Catherine and Richard Macksey, in Macksey, ed., *Velocities of Change,* p. 94.

/77/   *Ibid.,* p. 90.

/78/   Cf. *Ibid.,* pp. 95-96.

/79/   *Ibid.,* p. 101.

/80/   I have had access only to a German version of this essay entitled "Genets Bühnenstücke," published in Helga Gallas, ed., *Strukturalismus als interpretatives Verfahren,* pp. 73-104.

/81/   Jacques Lacan, "Seminar on 'The Purloined Letter'," tr. Jeffrey Mehlman, in *French Freud,* pp. 38-72. Cf. also Lacan, *Écrits* (Paris: Seuil, 1966); and Anthony Wilden, *The Language of the Self.*

/82/   Lacan, "The Insistence of the Letter in the Unconscious," in De George, ed., *The Structuralists,* p. 287.

/83/   Robert Detweiler, "Updike's *A Month of Sundays* and the Language of the Unconscious," in Joyce Markle, ed., *Updike* (Port Washington, New York: Kennikat Press, forthcoming).

/84/   Cf. Anthony Wilden, "Libido as Language," *Psychology Today*, 5, No. 12 (May, 1972): 85-86. I have found this essay very helpful in summarizing Lacan.

/85/   John Updike, *A Month of Sundays* (New York: Knopf, 1975), pp. 142, 202.

Chapter IV

Phenomenological
and Structuralist Literary Criticism:
Possibilities of Reconciliation

A. Theories and Practice

Such a study as I have presented thus far should culminate in a comparison of phenomenology and structuralism as literary critical methods and in an accompanying discussion of how they can complement each other. A considerable number of confrontations, challenges, and attempts at mutual accomodation have been taking place, the results of which have already affected the development and rapprochement of both methods. Further, some critics other than myself have attempted to step back from the two methods to discover what the main issues are that separate them and how they might be reconciled. Finally, a few efforts at practical criticism utilizing combinations of both methods have been undertaken and addressed to religious and secular texts. I will review these various events and endeavors and try to show how authentic interrelations can be mediated, concluding with a description of a series of steps that one might implement in applying a combination of the two approaches to actual textual interpretation.

One of the earlier skirmishes occurred between Sartre and Lévi-Strauss when Lévi-Strauss in "History and Dialectic," the final chapter of *The Savage Mind* (1962), attacked Sartre's *Critique of Dialectical Reason*. /1/ Feeling himself misinterpreted and misrepresented by Sartre in that text, Lévi-Strauss used Sartre's vocabulary in a structural anthropological framework to show that his (Sartre's) understanding of dialectical thought overvalues the self, raises the concept of history to a mystical power, and limits the range of human experience. Especially when seen in contrast to the schematizing and totalizing (all-embracing) propensity of the "primitive" mind, Sartre's dialectic appears impoverished to Lévi-Strauss and in need of structuralist correction and expansion. Sartre, of course, responded in kind with the observation that what is significant is not the structures that "determine" man's condition but what one does with those structures, and what man does is to make history, the totalizing *praxis* whereby one may even be able to create new structures—to recreate human existence. /2/

Phenomenologists and structuralists have also addressed each other more or less formally at academic symposia, two of the best-known of which were held during the height of French structuralist popularity in 1966, one at Cerisy-la-Salle in France and the other at The Johns Hopkins University. /3/ At Cerisy-la-Salle phenomenologists and their sympathizers such as Serge Doubrovsky faced structuralists such as Genette, while at Johns Hopkins structuralism represented by major figures such as Barthes, Goldmann, Lacan, and Todorov met phenomenologically-based arguments from critics such as Poulet, Jean Hyppolite, and James Edie. The issues of discussion and dispute were the predictable ones: the relationship of language to reality, the nature of the subject, the problems of origins and history, the coherence of the two methods as versatile and comprehensive critical instruments. What also became apparent, especially at the Johns Hopkins symposium, is that little unity exists within each method among its practitioners. That fragmentation among the structuralists has been accelerated meanwhile by the declarations of several prominent figures that they are not structuralists and indeed never have been at least according to popularizing, often journalistic, definitions of the term. Lacan, Foucault, Derrida, among others, have disavowed a structuralist identity, and it has become fashionable to speak of the "decline," "demise," "end," and "death" of structuralism. /4/

At the same time, however, a definite trend among phenomenologically-oriented critics toward an accomodation of structuralism or even an embracing of it can be observed. Among the first-generation phenomenologists, no less a thinker than Merleau-Ponty came to grips with structuralism and, as Culler points out, seems to have intended in his unfinished *Le visible et l'invisible* "to ground structural linguistics and a structuralist vocabulary of configurations and articulations on a phenomenological ontology." /5/ Barthes himself began as a writer with phenomenological presuppositions, and even his 1963 *Sur Racine,* that so offended the French "university critics," shows evidence of surviving phenomenological reflexes. Hillis Miller, who in his earlier writing combined a Poulet-style criticism of consciousness with American formalism, has in recent years (influenced strongly by Derrida) turned to structuralism, while the Geneva critic Jean Starobinski, as we have seen, sometimes practices structuralist criticism in ways that complement and supplement Barthes' analyses yet without actually abandoning his phenomenological fundamentals. /6/

Derrida has been instrumental not only in Miller's evolution toward structuralism but has been a pivotal figure otherwise in the inter-critical dialogue and is becoming increasingly more influential in American criticism as the philosopher who embodies many of the crucial issues in that dialogue. The reasons why are easy to see; as a Husserl scholar and interpreter of Nietzsche and Heidegger who challenges, from the standpoint of an original linguistic position that at least resembles much of structuralism, the presuppositions of the Western metaphysical tradition, he serves as a focal point for phenomenological and structuralist critics who have also questioned that tradition but less radically than he. Thus in the past five years alone significant literary history and criticism provoked by Derrida has been composed not only by Miller but also by Paul de Man, Geoffrey Hartman, Joseph Riddel, and Edward Said. /7/

Ricoeur has been pivotal in a somewhat different direction. If Derrida has been important to the critics who are excited by the prospect of a total revolution in Western thought, Ricoeur appeals more to those who wish to explore the new without wholly sacrificing the old—and in this respect Derrida and Ricoeur represent what Willis F. Overton has labelled the difference between holistic and elementaristic structuralism, a distinction I will treat later. /8/ Ricoeur has disputed above all the structuralist pronouncement of the death of the subject, and his criticism has been effective and convincing, yet he has come to acknowledge more and more the need for structural analysis at least as an operation that precedes hermeneutical considerations, and in this fashion has been valuable especially to the biblical exegetes and theologians who want to use structuralism as a textual-interpretive tool without being bound by it as an ideology or ontology. /9/ Ricoeur's influence has been strong particularly in the area of New Testament parable studies, and his own parable analysis has been exemplary. /10/

Some of Ricoeur's best writing (such as "The Question of the Subject: The Challenge of Semiology") combines phenomenology, structuralism, and Freudian psychoanalysis, and a stimulating contrast to this approach is offered by M. J. Peters, who uses the same combination in a different way. In his provocative essay on "Psychoanalysis, Structuralism, and Consciousness," Peters uses the three methods to clarify the dynamics and structure of cognition and in the process suggests ways in which phenomenology and structuralism may be related. /11/ For example, he leads one to consider the similarity among intentionality, Freudian cathexis, and the structuralist personification of the object (as explained in Lévi-Strauss' studies of primitive cultures); but especially in speaking to the matter of the connection between consciousness and the unconscious, he shows that the ideal ultimate stage of personality development, the realization and adaptation of unconscious motivations in the name of rational control, can also be interpreted as a pathological condition because it excludes the freedom of aesthetic perception. One implication of this observation is that the phenomenologist, who wishes to interact with his object rather than master it, can temper the excessive categorizing (systematizing) of the structuralist, while the structuralist who maintains the necessary distance of the holistic perspective can help the phenomenologist to avoid a sentimentalization of his intended object. The phenomenologist can teach the structuralist to *experience* the unconscious (not merely study it), while the structuralist can warn the phenomenologist against the dangers of infatuation with consciousness.

Following this general overview of phenomenology/structuralism inter-relations I want to treat in somewhat more detail the work of major phenomenologists and structuralists as each addresses the other method.

Husserl and Jakobson

In "Jakobson and Husserl: A Contribution to the Geneology of Structuralism," Elmar Holenstein presents a meticulous and convincing account of the strong influences of Husserl on Jakobson and the resultant possibilities for extending the effectiveness of phenomenological criticism suggested by Jakobson's linguistic studies. /12/ Holenstein begins by describing direct connections between Husserl and Jakobson, starting with the influence of Husserl's *Logical Investigations* on Jakobson while he was still a student in Moscow, and extending to Husserl's appearance as lecturer, through Jakobson's instigation, before the Prague Linguistic Circle in 1935. Holenstein shows then how Jakobson's linguistic theories were often marked by his readings in Husserl and revealed strong similarities to Husserlian concepts. For example, from Husserl Jakobson derived at least in part his antipsychologistic bias, the strategy of the generative linguistic interplay of sound and meaning (from Husserl's work on expression and signification), the search for essences, his version of the reduction, and the concept of a universal grammar. His indebtedness to Husserl and supersession of him are especially clear in the matter of the investigation of essences and the practicing of the reduction. Regarding essences, Holenstein demonstrates that Husserl's search for the invariant elements of the object (those without which it would no longer be thinkable) that constitute its essence has been incorporated by Jakobson into his own search for universals in linguistics, for the invariants in all linguistic systems that one can identify and organize into general laws. Holenstein even thinks that Jakobsonian terms such as "literaricity" and "poeticity" reveal a Husserlian orientation by calling attention to the essential and universal in the various disciplines rather than to the individual and particular. Further, while Husserl's kind of distillation of essences has not proved very productive, because of its narrowly prescribed and rarified nature, Jakobson's appropriation of it to study phonological entities and the semantic-morphological qualities of a particular linguistic-geographic area affords a model, through its thoroughness and precision, of how the faltering eidetic project might renew itself.

Regarding the reduction, Holenstein says that although Jakobson definitely does not advocate the isolation from the other sciences that characterizes the essentialist phenomenological attitude, and instead practices a carefully stratified methodological pluralism, he nevertheless takes his starting cue from Husserl and follows him a part of the way. Husserl's own antipathy toward traditional psychology had anti-reductionist tendencies, and Jakobson has paralled these, for instance, in his refusal to reduce linguistic signs to their phonic dimensions because, as Husserl has shown, such a reduction excludes an aspect of the sign's meaning. The fact that Jakobson will not go all the way with Husserl's reduction points to a shortcoming of Husserl's phenomenology, its unwillingness to incorporate anything into the epoché that is not the result of perceptual and intuitive experience. Jakobson's use of acoustics in his structural-analytical linguistics shows that physical features can be included in the reductive process without the practitioner succumbing to the methodology of the natural sciences.

In more general terms, Holenstein describes the two stages of Husserl's reduction and how Jakobson follows the first but rejects the second. The first is the phenomenological attitude (or the attitude of the human sciences) in which the object is described in terms of its inherent characteristics rather than according to a method borrowed from the empirical sciences. The second is the operation that considers the object only as it is formed according to the categories of consciousness; Jakobson dispenses with this step, for it would only hinder his research. Yet Jakobson's procedure that substitutes for this second step can be instructive for the phenomenologists. Especially Jakobson's dual expansion of the linguistic subject from the single consciousness to include both intersubjectivity and the unconscious recalls Husserl's own amplification of the transcendental subject and encourages phenomenologists to extend their efforts toward an involvement with community and psyche (efforts which, although Holenstein does not say so, have already been initiated by the sociologists of knowledge).

Heidegger and Structuralism

A second essay that treats the interrelationships of first-generation scholars of both methods is Donald G. Marshall's "The Ontology of the Literary Sign: Notes toward a Heideggerian Revision of Semiology," which contrasts Saussure and Jakobson with Heidegger and, for good measure, draws in the work of the American new critic William Wimsatt as well. /13/ Marshall's study is not so much a combining of structuralist and phenomenological theory to produce a new understanding of literary semiotics as it is a careful re-reading of Heidegger against a background of the inadequacies of Jakobson's (and Wimsatt's) theory in order to reveal how "Heidegger's conception of the literary sign profoundly radicalizes the historical thinking of philological linguistics . . . and helps us grasp the existential (and therefore historical) relation of sign to signified." /14/ He uses C. S. Peirce's distinction of three kinds of signs, the symbol, the icon, and the index, to categorize the positions represented by Saussure and Jakobson, Wimsatt, and Heidegger respectively and to try to demonstrate why Heidegger's is the most fruitful. "Symbol" in this context refers to the familiar Saussurian hypothesis of the purely arbitrary relationship between sign and referent. In reviewing that position, Marshall shows how it translates into Jakobson's definition of the poetic function of language as the emphasis on language for its own sake rather than for discursive communication. In other words, the sign is divorced even of its arbitrary reference in poetry and made self-referential, and hence "poetry is discourse generated out of pure signs." /15/ The poetic sign thus conceived is a model for the structural linguist's understanding of language, because its abstractness and self-sufficiency suggest an autotelic ontology that can be articulated in purely grammatical terms. This is, of course (although Marshall does not make the charge), a positivistic definition of the sign by Saussure and Jakobson.

Somewhat more to Marshall's liking is the iconic understanding of the literary sign evolved by the Russian and American formalists, where the sign's referent is not established in a wholly arbitrary way but is determined by some characteristic of the sign. Thus according to Wimsatt, such inherent traits can be seen in onomatopoeic or autologistic words that simultaneously illustrate what they name, and in less direct but like manner all poetic language creates rules that run counter to those of logical discourse and therefore consists of signs corresponding to internally compatible referents. Whereas for Jakobson the self-referentiality of the poetic word is stressed and poetry in this manner is distinguished from ordinary communication, for the new critics (especially Wimsatt), the poetic sign retains a double sense, a connection with ordinary discourse that produces a fundamental ambiguity and irony leading to more open-ended ontological implications.

Heidegger, however, develops the lexical dimension of the literary sign which emphasizes its components of totality and continuous activity. In line with his analysis of *Dasein,* Heidegger begins his treatment of the literary sign with an attempt to formulate an ontology of it and in the process uncovers an existential rather than arbitrary relationship between the sign and its referent: "The power of the sign to indicate is not something added to its 'mere' existence but is rather its ontological foundation as what it is." /16/ Because the sign is always involved in and emerges from the totality of being and becoming, it cannot exhibit an arbitrary relation to its referent but rather always struggles to reveal its ultimate ontological reference: "The power of a word to disclose a thing rests on the articulation of human existence's Being-in-the-world." /17/ Heidegger's "recollective thinking" that consists in good part of "regioning"—a meditative abiding in linguisticality through which a simultaneous combination of the "namable, the name and the named occur"—- is the way to appropriate this revelatory power of the word and shows itself, of course, as the language of poetry. /18/ An emphasis on this lexical dimension of the literary sign, then, that existentializes the relationship of sign and referent, is a way of proceeding that transcends the unnecessary polarity between philological (including structuralist) and formalist criticism.

Although Marshall's provocative reading of Heidegger (to which my summary does not do justice) tends to caricature Jakobson's position and hence weaken its possibilities for complementing and correcting the "totalizing" tendencies of the Heideggerian literary sign, it does show, at the very least, that structuralists and phenomenologists can—indeed must—engage in dialogue both in terms of their historical assumptions and their basic vocabularies.

Piaget and Phenomenology

Although Jean Piaget has not figured in the development of structuralist textual criticism, he does emerge as more important among the critics considering interconnections of the two methods. Among the Husserlian phenomenologists, first, Aron Gurwitsch has compared Piaget's psychology to phenomenology. In *The Field of Consciousness* (published in 1964 but completed in 1953), as part of his phenomenological investigation of the organization of perceptual experience, Gurwitsch examines Piaget's concept of "schema" ("a crystallization of functional processes and activities dominated by the opposite tendencies towards 'assimilation' and 'accommodation'") and points out that phenomenology does not study perception from any such genetic or developmental perspective but rather in terms of the acts of consciousness that constitute the ability of perception to "objectivate." /19/ He believes, however, that Piaget's analyses are sufficiently significant to "be integrated into phenomenology, that is interpreted in phenomenological terms and allowed for in a phenomenological account of perception." /20/ In *Studies in*

Phenomenology and Psychology (the relevant chapter was first published in 1953), Gurwitsch briefly compares Husserl and Piaget on the difference between generalizing and formalizing abstraction and finds them in virtual agreement. /21/

Although such comparison helps to throw light on the reductive process, it is not central to our literary critical inquiry into possible combinations of phenomenology and structuralism. Edward W. Said in "Notes on the Characterization of a Literary Text," however, begins with an orientation derived from Piaget that also refers to Derrida and Poulet. /22/ Writing out of an obvious acquaintance with phenomenological modes of inquiry, Said studies the evolving careers of certain major writers whose works are composed against the prevailing intellectual mood of their epoch. It is an approach designed by Said to startle the reader out of the Anglo-American habit of identifying the literary text with a more or less immutable and finished book, and to cause him to consider the text instead as always in progress and open to change. Said uses Piaget's concept of the developing subject as a way of characterizing his countermoving authors and at least at the start refers to the Piagetian stages of growth as categories for describing the changes that the artist passes through and that the critic must notice in tracking the relation of the text's dynamics to the era. Said soon abandons Piaget as he progresses in his essay (and, regrettably, does not return to him in his brilliant *Beginnings,* except to repeat the paragraphs of this essay), but he has demonstrated a measure of Piaget's utility for literary criticism and his partial compatibility with phenomenology.

As David Funt shows in his excellent review of Piaget's *Structuralism,* it is misleading to identify Piaget with the linguistically-oriented structuralists, because his premises are in certain key ways directly opposed to theirs. /23/ For example, his version of what Derrida has labelled "decentering," the creation of meaning "from the infinite play of signifiers" (that we have seen functioning in the essays of Barthes, Marin, etc.), is much less radical than that of the linguistically-based structuralists and refers really to the fairly mundane genetic epistemological process. Similarly, as Funt states, Piaget differs from Lévi-

Strauss, arguing that the "primitive" mind, like the child's, is indeed inferior, because it has not yet matured to the stage where it can accomplish the intricate operations that characterize Western logical thought. /24/

Where then is the value of Piagetian thought for mediating between literary critical phenomenology and structuralism? It is certainly in its analogical generative potential, as Said uses it, but Willis F. Overton has displayed a more important function of it in "General Systems, Structure and Development." Writing out of a background of Bertalanffy's systems theory, Overton describes Piaget's theory of cognitive development (genetic epistemology) as a holistic structuralism and (in systems-theoretical terms) an open system, characterized by a belief in the primacy of activity and the effort to define and thus impose stability or "momentary constancy" on the dynamic object. /25/ In this view structure is a "primitive construct" because it is basic to further development, or in philosophical language (mine, not Overton's), it evokes an ontology. This holistic model Overton contrasts to elementaristic structuralism, which is the sort based on an acceptance of a static view of the world, the primacy of substance rather than of activity, and thus is the appropriation of structuralism as a derived method.

This distinction seems important to me because it clarifies a difference in attitude between most of the structuralist critics of secular texts and those of biblical texts who often have come to structuralism from some version of phenomenology. The secular critics seem more willing to embrace a holistic structuralism with its ontological implications, while the biblical structuralists wish to employ it in an elementaristic fashion as a static methodology that can be applied to its interpretive task and then suspended as the critic incorporates the results into another, presumably broader, ontological framework. This is not to say that the phenomenologists who have started to accomodate structuralism work in a static context, for phenomenology in most aspects of its program is energetically dynamic. It does mean, however, that such erstwhile phenomenologists, in hedging their bets, do not permit structuralism the full range of its ontological potential—although structuralism has a way of insinuating its ontology into the criticism of those who intended to accept it originally only as a methodological aid. We shall see, in discussing Merleau-Ponty and Ricoeur, how the camel's nose in the tent invited the presence of the whole beast, and then, in treating Derrida, we shall observe how the presence became intolerable.

Merleau-Ponty and Structuralism

Following his comment that Merleau-Ponty in his last work apparently wished to involve structural linguistics in a phenomenological ontology, Culler remarks, "The suggestion seems to be that the phenomenologist becomes a structuralist if he considers the implications of his theory, and perhaps inversely that the structuralist must become a phenomenologist as he scrutinizes the foundations of his method." /26/ Then, in a new paragraph, he continues, "The prospect is a tantalizing one. One can only regret that Merleau-Ponty did not live to complete his projected work, which would have challenged the accepted view that phenomenology and structuralism are radically opposed, though possibly complementary." /27/ Jameson agrees with this assessment of the trend of Merleau-Ponty's later thought and implies that Barthes, in fact, inherited by default the role of major spokesman for structuralist literary criticism that Merleau-Ponty would have assumed had he lived. More importantly, Jameson reminds us that "There is a sense in which all sensory perception already constitutes a kind of organization into language. It is this more than anything else, no doubt, which explains the sympathy of Merleau-Ponty in his last years for the then emergent Structuralism." /28/

Culler goes on to trace how for Merleau-Ponty phenomenology led to structuralism as a step toward the eventual incorporation of structuralism into a phenomenological ontology. Merleau-Ponty, he says, stressed the intentionality of consciousness and the inherent structured condition of the objects of perception as a way of overcoming the subject-object duality: consciousness as consciousness of something does not structure that something but perceives it as already structured, and thus meaning inhabits the perceptual objects as a result of their innate form. This view not only weakens the dominance of the thinking subject; it reduces the subject to a "système hiérarchisé de structures" which functions as an "intersection" for many *Gestalten*. /29/ But this position does not lead Merleau-Ponty to declare man's superfluousness, as Foucault does. Instead, he redefines the Cartesian *cogito* so that it consists of a *je peux* (I can) rather than *je pense*. /30/ He emphasizes competence, in other words—man's competence, through which the system of language and other systems can function. Man is part of all the systems he deals with (an object) but also the indispensable articulator of the systems (a subject) and hence, as the fusion of subject and object, man and his perceptual environment are comprehended structurally in a way that prepares for a situating of them in a phenomenological ontological framework.

This argument, with its stress on competence, means that man as systemic subject does not create language but employs it skillfully and creatively to confer meaning. Applied to literary criticism, the argument suggests that structuralism be used to analyze literary competence—to show how we are able to understand, interpret, and appreciate a text—and thus be made an aspect of the phenomenology of reading, or of hermeneutics, or of *Rezeptionskritik;* as we have observed, such efforts are already in progress.

Ricoeur and Structuralism

Merleau-Ponty obviously sees structuralism as, in Overton's terms, elementaristic, but Ricoeur is an even more interesting example of a phenomenologist in energetic dialogue with an elementaristically-perceived structuralism. In "Structure, Word, Event" (French original published in 1968), an essay that has provided a rallying point for anti-structuralists, Ricoeur tries to set limits on structural analysis by stating that it can be applied successfully only to closed, "dead" systems; to furnish catalogues of a system's components; to establish these components in oppositional relations; and to provide an "algebra" of the components' organization. /31/ The sum of this set of limitations is the recognition, according to Ricoeur, that structuralism can only create "taxonomies" (the categories and inventories, in this context, of language as *langue*—the dead phonological, lexical, and syntactical levels of language) because it subordinates *parole* to *langue* and does not permit *parole* the opportunity to fulfill its mediating function. Even more, Chomsky's "poststructuralist linguistics" as a generative grammar addressed to the analysis of sentences and sentence origins marks for Ricoeur the beginning of the end of the old static structuralism. /32/

Culler, however, in his *Structuralist Poetics* takes issue with a number of Ricoeur's restricting comments on structuralism. It is not true, he says, that structural linguistics deals only with taxonomies. As Count Trubetzkoj demonstrated in the late 1940s, phonological study of basic units is not comparable to the classifying methods of the natural sciences because, unlike those essentially neutral taxonomical procedures, in phonology one seeks viable linguistic traits and checks the validity of the classes to which they are assigned against the evidence of actual language usage. This method is hardly characteristic of a closed or dead system. Further, Culler argues, it is incorrect to pose generative grammar as a corrective to structural linguistics, for structural linguistics already contains the implications that generative grammar has developed. Finally, Culler denies Ricoeur's declaration that structuralism is concerned only with an abstract formulation of inter-objective relations and not with subject-object relations. Structuralism recognizes the subject through its attention directed toward the speaker: "Linguistics attempts to formalize the set of rules which, for speakers, are constitutive of their language, and in this sense structuralism must take place within phenomenology: its task is to explicate what is phenomenally given in the subject's relation to his cultural objects." /33/

In terms of literary criticism, this task translates into a poetics that examines not the formal properties of the text (as the new critics do) but the circumstances that permit the text to take shape and to communicate with the reader. This poetics, in turn, becomes an examination of competence, of how one is able to respond to the literary text, and how well one responds, and as such it must be placed within the framework of phenomenology, for phenomenology stands ready to check the results of this encounter against "lived experience." /34/ The gist of Culler's argument, as I follow it, is that structuralism is led by its methodology to point beyond itself to an ontological basis that is found in the lived experience of phenomenology. Thus also, according to Culler, Ricoeur is right about structuralism functioning as a pre-interpretive method for phenomenology, but he is right for the wrong reasons, for structuralism is more versatile and open-ended than Ricoeur has seen.

Culler remarks at the end of his essay that "There is . . . a strong hermeneutic strain in phenomenology which is absent from structuralism," but Jameson, on the final page of *The Prison-House of Language,* sees a possibility for "the description of the Structuralist procedure as a genuine *hermeneutics*—although one which would have little to do with the theological overtones which that term has acquired, with Ricoeur, in France, and with Gadamer, in Germany." /35/ Jameson's idea of hermeneutics here is a good deal like Culler's project for using the concept of competence to make structural analysis a part of the phenomenology of reading. It would involve a bracketing of the *object* of structural analysis in order to emphasize the *process* of "transcoding"—the accomodation of the semiotically-recognized tendency of meaning to shift endlessly from one language level to the next or from one language to another and thus to reveal itself as nothing but the infinite play of transposition. /36/ This process, which would also of necessity underscore the role of the transposing subject, would direct one toward a means of discovering "truth," even if that truth turns out to be the incessant shifting of meaning, and in this sense it is both a hermeneutic and an aspect of holistic structuralism.

But Jameson dismisses Ricoeur too rapidly for his theological-ly-toned hermeneutics. "The Question of the Subject: The

Challenge of Semiology" is a typical Ricoeur essay that confronts from the position of hermeneutics the problems posed by structuralism to phenomenology and that confronts them, moreover, without resorting to theological statements. /37/ In the half of the essay that concerns us (the other half has to do with psychoanalysis), Ricoeur describes how structuralism endangers the concept of the Husserlian and post-Husserlian phenomenological subject through the structural linguistic argument that language as an autonomous, closed system of signs has no "outside" and thus has no use for the subject. Ricoeur counters this challenge by distinguishing between semiological and semantic units of language. The semiological order merely makes possible articulation, which is admittedly important, but it does not generate signification; that is the task of the semantic order, whose basic unit (in contrast to the phonemic, lexical, and syntactical units of semiology) is the sentence or utterance. Semiology, in other words, is the foundation of *langue,* but semantics is necessary for the subsistance of *parole.* Thus, while it is true that the question of the subject is irrelevant on the semiological level (where the *I* is simply another grammatical entity), on the semantic level the speaking subject, in the process of giving the sentence an individual identity (its difference) attains central importance. What is an empty sign on the semiological level (the *I* or *you*) is for the phenomenologist working on the semantic level the invitation to "the speaker to posit himself as subject and to oppose to himself another as listener" according to "the extralinguistic presuppositions of the personal pronoun." /38/ Such positing breaks through the closed system of language and reveals that language is not a foundation but a mediation "in which and through which the subject posits himself and the world shows itself." /39/ But this postulating of the *I* must always be understood as part of the language event through which *langue* becomes *parole.*

Turning to the question of the subject in terms of the phenomenological reduction, Ricoeur shows that the structuralist concentration on *langue* to the exclusion of *parole* is drastically opposed to the epoché, through which consciousness infuses its intended objects with meaning. But if one approaches the reduction positively as a new way of interpreting existence by a certain kind of signifying process, then one can regard it (the reduction) as the originating moment of symbolic thinking and thus of the creation of language. Ricoeur is employing here the logic of his final chapter of *The Symbolism of Evil* ("The Symbol Gives Rise to Thought") but reinforces it by answering the possible structuralist objection that the genesis of symbolism requires only difference and not a subject. This view, says Ricoeur, is based on the failure to separate the semiological and semantic orders of language. The reduction indeed functions by determining difference, as does the semiological description of language, but on the level of *parole* or discourse the positive dimension of the reduction emerges as the "*return to the self by way of its other* which makes the transcendent no longer a sign but a kind of signification,"—just as the speaking subject posits itself to fill the empty sign. /40/

In the final section of the essay, then, Ricoeur joins the discussion of the structuralist challenge to that of psychoanalysis to construct a "hermeneutics of the 'I am.'" /41/ He links the Freudian concept of libido to that of symbol in order to speak of a "semantics of desire," which can be interpreted as a combination of the "I am" (the declaration of the desire to be) and the "I speak." Desire in this sense is comprehended as prior to speech, so that "The task of a philosophical anthropology is to show in what ontic structures language occurs." /42/ With this last statement we are returned at last to the relationship of phenomenology to structuralism and the reaffirmation that structuralism, as Ricoeur uses it, must function elementaristically, within the context of phenomenology.

This summary covers difficult material, and since the essay is crucial I should like to sketch it again very briefly in other terms and connect it to Ricoeur's broader hermeneutical project. Ricoeur is arguing, essentially, that the arbitrary connection between sign and referent and the absence of the sign-producing subject are impossibilities, for the signified-signifier liaison cannot occur until the intending speaker establishes a denotative identity between sign and thing; speech is always intentional, always speaks of something, and this "referring-to" provides a symbolic orientation to the whole spoken language act. /43/ The intentionality of the sign-become-symbol cannot operate unimpeded, however, but is challenged by desire, the language of the unconscious that intends in its own way and obscures the language of consciousness. The language of desire carries a regression toward childhood, while the language of consciousness drives toward new insights and syntheses. As Gras states it, "Balancing the regressive archaeology of Freudian psychoanalysis with the progressive teleology of a Hegelian intentionality, Ricoeur emerges with a comprehensive theory of symbolization holding within its parameters the central tension of human existence." /44/ This tension between desire and creativity Ricoeur universalized as the central modern conflict between nature and freedom, and for purposes of literary interpretation it becomes a matter of restoring freedom to nature by restoring art to desire.

In Ricoeur's criticism, a dialectic between a narrator's regressive and progressive tendencies is established, and the resolution occurs through the transformation (not always successful) of desire into new meaning—a dynamic that, much like Poulet's strategy, also describes the author's own creative process. Ricoeur also sees in the symbolic function of spoken language a tension between difference (that which separates the world of signs from the world of things) and reference (that which restores language to the world of things) and argues that this fruitful tension is ruined in written discourse. /45/

Ricoeur's involvement with structuralism has deepened since the writing of *The Conflict of Interpretations* essays; particularly his 1975 monograph on "Biblical Hermeneutics" exhibits his recent attempts to encompass structuralism and also, conveniently for us, allows us to see how he adapts this endeavor to the consideration of biblical texts. /46/ The essay is a contribution to the lively discussion of the nature of New Testament parables among contemporary exegetes that we need not review (although some of it consists of a sophisticated literary criticism that critics of secular texts could find instructive), but two parts of the study are very important for our mediatory concerns. The first is a critique of Louis Marin's "ultra-structuralist approach that combines Greimas, Lévi-Strauss, and Barthes" and that addresses the Parable of the Sower in Matthew 13:1-23. /47/ Marin's analysis parallels the tactic and results of his *Sémiotique de la Passion,* which I have already sketched, so we need not dwell on it except to remark that Marin, proceeding achronically and disregarding form-critical problems, fashions out of the parable a cluster of "articulations" characterized by shifting addressers and addressees that produces "transcodage" or a system of transformations from which interplay meaning emerges, just as Jameson declares it should in his projection of a structuralist hermeneutics at the end of *The Prison-House of Language.*

Ricoeur defines Marin's analysis, in fact, as a "substitutive hermeneutics" proclaiming that the parable, as indeed the Gospels as a whole, is "a communication about communication." /48/ Marin demonstrates this most dramatically in another essay that Ricoeur refers to, where the narrative of the women at Jesus' tomb is interpreted as an instance of a transformation in which the women's desire to have Jesus' body is frustrated and then satisfied symbolically by the substitution of the message, "the Lord is risen." The empty tomb, the frustrated desire, like the empty sign of semiology, is replaced by the modulation to another level of articulation whose foundation is the linguistic process itself. Ricoeur rejects this hermeneutic, of course, calling it "the proclamation of existential meaninglessness," but he sees in it the possibility for the speaking subject to posit itself and transform the text from a system of signs into "discourse" capable of signifying in the semantic sense. /49/

The remainder of this section of "Biblical Hermeneutics" works out Ricoeur's argument from "The Question of the Subject" in narrative-parabolic terms but also adds the claim that Barthes in "The Structural Analysis of Narrative" confirms the thesis that a narrative must transcend itself and become more than the interplay of its codes. Barthes (as we have seen in Chapter III) posits three levels of narrative, of which the third, the level of discourse (Ricoeur calls it the level of narrative communication), stresses how narrator and audience offer and receive the story and is marked by "signs of narrativity." Although these inhabit the narrative (they are part of the structuralist closed system), Ricoeur argues that "they are signs for an *exchange* which envelops the narrative *from the outside*" and in this way both restates his contention that narrative transcends itself and revives the concept of *mimesis* that influences his recent work on metaphor. /50/

Ricoeur's consideration of metaphor, that has resulted in his 1975 *La Métaphor vive,* is represented in "Biblical Hermeneutics" in the third section called "The Metaphorical Process." /51/ It is the other part of his study that is worth examining for its importance to the reconciliation of phenomenology and structuralism. Here Ricoeur repeats, in different language, much of what he expounded in the 1974 essay (which I sketched in Chapter I) on "Metaphor and the Main Problem of Hermeneutics": the correct explication of metaphor acts as a model for interpreting a whole text, explanation must be distinguished from interpretation, metaphor establishes reference through *mimesis* as the equivalent of the phenomenologists' "world disclosure," and hence metaphor offers new patterns of reality. In "The Metaphorical Process," however, he shifts the distinction between explanation and interpretation to another pair of terms that duplicates those used in his earlier arguments to challenge structuralism. He refers to a "rhetoric of the *word*" versus a "semantics of *discourse* or of the sentence" in order to argue that metaphor is not, as the long rhetorical tradition states, merely "an ornament of discourse" but rather, seen from the perspective of semantics (which has the sentence as its minimal unit), provides new information about reality. /52/

This strategy is another way of confronting semiology with semantics, as Ricoeur did in "The Question of the Subject" to demonstrate more explicitly how the empty sign of *langue* is filled by what takes place in *parole*. He shows how metaphor is not really grounded in resemblance, as the rhetorical tradition has it, but in a tension between different interpretations of a sentence statement that operates through absurdity: "Metaphorical interpretation presupposes a literal interpretation which is destroyed. . . . We are forced to give a new meaning to the word, an extension of meaning which allows it to *make* sense where a literal interpretation does not make sense." /53/ What the critics in the rhetorical tradition saw as the principle of resemblance now emerges as a "calculated error" through which "metaphor discloses a relationship of meaning hitherto unnoticed between terms which were prevented from communicating by former classifications." /54/ Thus genuine metaphors are "semantic innovations," are untranslatable, and say "something new about reality." /55/

Following this analysis largely of the rhetorical, i.e., semiological dimensions of metaphor, Ricoeur turns to a more properly semantic analysis and distinguishes between sense (or meaning) and reference in all statements—another way of differentiating between explanation and interpretation, although here he defines sense as the immanent quality, while reference is that to which the sense speaks and which is extra-linguistic. He emphasizes this distinction because it reveals the point at which he must part ways with structuralism. Structuralism, he says, does not recognize the referential aspect of language that gives form to our experience of the world, yet to him this aspect is crucial and central. The hermeneut may not stop where the structuralist does, at the analysis of the sense of a work, that is to say of its immanent meaning, but must go on to disclose the world that the text points to. Metaphor shares in this disclosure because as an untranslatable purveyor of news of reality it projects a new view of experience ahead of the text that the critic tries to incorporate into his field of awareness.

Ricoeur then attacks the central Jakobsonian definition of the poetic function of language, the stress on the message for its own sake rather than for its referentiality. This suspension of the referentiality of ordinary language, Ricoeur says, actually sets the conditions for activation of another kind of reference: of ambiguity, or split reference. Because metaphor puts out of play the literal meaning of its juxtaposed images, it encourages a new kind of meaning tied to a new referent. By engaging the concept of model in relation to scientific language and showing that metaphor is like a model of poetic language that uses a "heuristic fiction" to project and approximate a new view of reality, Ricoeur exhibits the new ambiguous or split reference (that which remains when the literal reference has been suspended) as the Husserlian life-world or the Heideggerian being-in-the-world; the illumination of this life-world is the "fundamental ontological import of poetic language." /56/ This use of metaphor as heuristic fiction to produce new meaning through its reference to the life-world Ricoeur considers the equivalent to the Aristotelian understanding of *mimesis:* "Poetic language does not say literally what things are, but what they are like. It is in this oblique fashion that it says what they are." /57/

Obviously, Ricoeur has undertaken here a reduction of poetic language, or of metaphor, in order to discover the life-world as its referent, along the lines of the strategy he uses in the earlier essay to meet "the challenge of semiology." Once one sees this, it also seems obvious that his break with structuralism is not as clean as he declares, for the question then becomes, if the referent of the metaphor is the life-world, what is the nature and content of that life-world in its myriad forms, and how does one discern that nature and content? Ricoeur has revealed phenomenologically the life-world in the abstract as the referent, but, it seems to me, structural analysis becomes valuable again in disclosing the substance of concrete life-worlds. Or at least one should be willing to take the "detour of semiology" over and over again in examining the individual life-worlds in order to establish sense and explanation before one can turn to reference and interpretation. Thus phenomenology and structuralism for the hermeneutical critic remain intertwined.

It is also worth mentioning that Lévi-Strauss has already accomplished, perhaps in an unaware fashion, what Ricoeur has described explicitly. Lévi-Strauss' explanation of the function of myth, namely, points to Ricoeur's dialectical method that results in his definition of metaphor; the combining of mythic clusters by "primitive" societies to blur the stark oppositions of an intolerable reality and allow persons to live according to more comfortable fictions is an action much like the process Ricoeur describes whereby metaphor finds its ground in the life-world. In both instances resemblance and difference are employed to suspend a certain level of unacceptable, even absurd literalness and introduce instead an ambiguity that mediates a brighter vision. In both instances poetic language creates the world it imitates and intends what is already there but in the intending changes the substance of the already-there. Here too one has evidence of a necessary cooperation of phenomenology and structuralism. Lévi-Strauss has done in concrete semiological terms what Ricoeur has redescribed in a more viable phenomenological-hermeneutical way.

Jacques Derrida, Phenomenology and Structuralism

Derrida has performed the most radical "reduction" of all, the suspension of presence to examine the possibility of a world functioning only in terms of difference. Derrida clearly deserves to be included in my discussion of mediators of phenomenology and structuralism; as a philosopher who has taken both Husserl and Lévi-Strauss, among others, to task for their continued reliance on the (for him) outmoded Western metaphysical tradition, he has become a commanding figure in the current dialogue involving the two methods. /58/ Mindful of Hillis Miller's warning, however, about the pitfalls awaiting the unready who try to deal with Derrida's constantly evolving position, I will make do with a tentative sketch of, for the most part, his earlier work as it affects our mediatory aims. /59/

As I stated briefly at the close of my first chapter, Derrida has fashioned a philosophy based on dissimilarity that has precipitated a crisis in structuralism; it presents just as great a threat to phenomenology. Like Ricoeur, Derrida has confronted Freud to elucidate his own theory; he maintains that even what can be gleaned from the unconscious through dream analysis, dialogue with the insane, wordplay, etc. does not constitute a body of reliable data to tell us what we mean in the opaque language of the unconscious, for such an application of data betrays a false comprehension of language and meaning in relation to presence. /60/ Derrida's philosophy is at odds with the Saussurian semiology that follows the Western tradition in equating the immediacy of spoken language with presence. Western thought according to Derrida, for all of its vaunted rationality that reached its apex in Descartes's proof of the self's existence in the *cogito,* is still basically romantic, for this "self-evidence" is grounded on the assumption that truth and what is immediately accessible to consciousness are identical.

According to this pervasive "metaphysics of presence," what is uttered in the spoken word is closer to truth than the written statement, which is at further remove from the apodicticity of consciousness (and secondary to speech) and a symbol of the spoken word which is itself a symbol of the unexpressed truth of the *cogito.* Further, according to this commonly accepted view, the task of interpretation of the text is to translate the written word back to an approximation of the spoken word as if in the recovered presence of the author speaking one would discover what he *really* meant. This grand faith in presence incarnate in the spoken word, in knowable and available objects of reality, is challenged by Derrida, who argues that not speech but writing—*écriture*—is primary, not because it is the locus of an original meaning but because it consists of the semiotic elements that *project* signification. This is not to say that writing *achieves* signification, rather that it looks forward constantly to the meaning that never arrives, so that the signification is precisely one of deferred meaning and thus a more accurate representation of the conditions of reality. This deferment within writing, which Derrida characterizes by the French neologism *différance* (suggesting both to defer and to differ), stands in opposition to the transparency of the spoken word through which original meaning is thought to shine, implying a certain solidity and thereness to writing that is constituted by its physicality—marks made on paper, pages forming a manuscript. The solid difference of writing lends it subjectivity; unlike speech, it is itself in its own record, independent of the author's constant and repeated instigation. Because it is its record, it also has a history, and because it has a history it can anticipate a future.

In order to deny the influence of "logocentrism"—of the dominant spoken word—Derrida employs the Freudian concept of "trace." We can never, he says, return to an original meaning, can never stand in the presence of pure meaning, because in order to evince meaning, the event must already have taken place; hence all intelligible language is a trace, and "Meaning is in its very structure always a *trace,* an already-happened." /61/ The false premise of absolute presence is shown to be intertwined with the false hypothesis of a pure (i.e., transparent) speech that reveals an original meaning, and in the place of pure speech Derrida places the brokenness and ambiguity of *écriture.* Because written discourse as trace is always exterior to itself, always lapsing immediately into history, a necessary gap opens up between what it is and says. Yet this very distance of the text from itself incites interpretation, which is the attempt to bridge the gap, to make the text say what it means, for in this interpretive act toward which we are compelled again and again and which must always fail is the irresistible impulse to leave a "trace" of ourselves.

In deferment and difference, in the postponement of meaning toward the past and the future and in the inability of the text to be self-identical, to be what it is or say what it means, is also the rationale for Derrida's strategy of decentering, his conscious attempt to make written discourse reflect its inherent unreliability, by a highly disciplined yet intentionally ambiguous style (including a Heideggerian stress on etymologies) that resists the tendency of writing to crystallize into set meanings that reinforce the myth of absolute meaning.

In this manner Derrida undermines even structuralism, or as Funt points out, structuralism itself is decentered, because meaning does not derive from an "original or central signified, but

arises from differentiation, from the infinite play of signifiers."
/62/ Or again, "it is not in a presence that the source of sense is to
be found but in the endlessly strung out discourse in which all
objects come into being and are defined and from which all
unitary sense arises." /63/

It is impossible to say if Derrida is a phenomenologist or a
structuralist. Perhaps he is both or perhaps neither. In a negative
way he has minimized the disparity between phenomenology and
structuralism by revealing how they arise from and perpetuate the
same faulty tradition, but beyond that he presents an inversion of
Ricoeur's views on the relationship between the two methods and
even an extension of those views.

The key to this insight comes from Jeffrey Mehlman, who says
that "Derrida's effort has been to show that the play of difference,
which has generally been viewed as exterior to a (spatial or
temporal) *present,* is, in fact, always already at work *within* that
present as the condition of its possibility." /64/ It would seem that
Derrida's emphasis on difference, which points to the absence of
presence signified by writing, is totally at odds with Ricoeur's
commitment to the primacy of the spoken word, of *parole.* But
Ricoeur's response to Marin's analysis of the narrative of the
women at Jesus's tomb is instructive here. One does not merely
stop with the empty tomb or the empty sign; one fills the void
through a shift to another level of discourse where the subject can
posit itself, transcend narrative, and project through *mimesis* its
life-world. Derrida, I believe, is doing something of the same with
other terminology. He sees as clearly as Ricoeur the transforming
power of metaphor that, by precipitating a "conflict of
interpretations" of a semantic unit (the sentence) destroys literal
meaning (resemblance) and initiates a new view of reality
(difference). But whereas Ricoeur moves beyond the metaphoric
moment, the instant of the collision of matrices, to adjust the
resultant news of reality and his life-world to each other, Derrida
tries to remain constantly at the instant of collision, or
recognition, that produces difference. /65/ The fact that this
difference is always also an absence that negates the very
transforming moment of metaphor does not, I think, prevent the

moment from occurring; it only prevents it from settling into place as part of a metaphysics of presence, or into what Ricoeur calls the "polysemy of the word." /66/

In this sense, then, Derrida's "play of difference," as Mehlman calls it, functions within a "present as the condition of its possibility." This is an inversion of Ricoeur's position regarding metaphor in that where Ricoeur works to relate the metaphoric innovation to an extra-linguistic experience, Derrida probes deeper into metaphor itself. It is an extension of Ricoeur's position in that the metaphor as heuristic fiction is forever denied a union with the reality it evokes and remains poised on the brink of revelation—untranslatable, as Ricoeur says genuine metaphor must be, but more radically untranslatable than he has recognized.

Does one reach then with Derrida a paralysis of discourse in which phenomenology and structuralism are trapped? Precisely the opposite: absence and difference set the conditions for generating meaningful discourse. And if Derrida's philosophy constitutes a crisis for phenomenology and structuralism, it is also an invitation for interpreters of both to imagine themselves and their worlds in relation to their texts more daringly, which is no more than a reaffirmation of the spirit that has marked the origins of both methods.

Mediatory Efforts and Practical Criticism

A few attempts have been made to apply a combination of the two methods to textual analysis. All of the examples that I have found but one are not real fusions of the two, however, but rather subordinate one to the other. Dan O. Via, Jr.'s *Kerygma and Comedy in the New Testament: A Structuralist Approach to Hermeneutic* is a thoughtful attempt at such a methodological fusion. /67/ Via says that he wishes "to work out a genuinely literary-critical hermeneutic for the New Testament based on a synthesis of structuralist, phenomenological, and existential modes of interpretation," and indeed engages competently those three modes to fashion a versatile approach to the Pauline and

Markan material that will no doubt be borrowed by other exegetes. /68/ Yet at the same time Via does not pay a great deal of attention to phenomenological concepts except as they appear through the hermeneutical concern. His emphasis is on the adaptation of structuralism for the analysis of Biblical texts, and as a result the gestures toward merging phenomenology with structuralism remain elementary.

Joseph Riddel's important study of William Carlos Williams in *The Inverted Bell* is another work that joins the two methods, largely through his use of Heidegger and Derrida, yet Riddel's orientation, as Hillis Miller points out, seems finally to be Heideggerian both in terms of the reliance on aletheatic metaphors and the underlying paradigm of a primal dynamic unity behind human fragmentation, which unity poetry seeks to illuminate and recover. /69/ Even more, the Derrida that appears in *The Inverted Bell* is himself more a phenomenologist than a structuralist, and in this sense also the blending of the two methods in applied criticism is not accomplished.

Roger C. Poole in an essay called "Structuralism and Phenomenology: A Literary Approach" undertakes an ambitious analysis of Joyce's *Finnegans Wake* and Woolf's *The Waves* that employs first two "formalizations," one that studies "structure to the exclusion of subjectivity" and a second that treats "subjectivity to the exclusion of structure." /70/ The third formalization that would merge the two is never presented, unfortunately, except through a graph, although Poole sketches what it would do: "We should be able, . . .deploying this third kind of formalization, which includes the range of insights of Spitzer's, Dilthey's, and Barthes' hermeneutics, to compare the various readings within a novel and thus find ourselves comparing different subjective viewpoints (perspectives) of the same fictional world. Through these comparisons we might well glimpse the originating subjectivity of the absent (hidden) author, catch hold of the 'for me' or 'by me' quality of the work." /71/ One has the feeling that this formalization (which has overtones of Riffaterre's "superreader" approach), if carried through, would prove to be a phenomenological-hermeneutical appropriation of structuralism, for Poole is very critical of the shortcomings of structuralism while indulgent of phenomenology. Nevertheless, his fusion of methods should be put to the test.

The critical piece that suggests best how the two methods might be joined is a short subtle essay by Hillis Miller on "The Interpretation of *Lord Jim*." /72/ Miller reveals his background in phenomenologically-oriented criticism, referring to the necessity of the interpreter to "enter into the text" and add "his own thread of interpretation" to it, also to the task of the critic to travel "from one word or image to another within the text in the unending spirals of the hermeneutical circle," and finally to the assertion that "critical interpretation is of the same nature as the self-interpretation within literary texts." /73/ Yet he also brings into play the view, a criticism of Poulet's approach, that one can never arrive through his interpretation at an original source of the text, at the foundation of the sign, or the ground of the self. He treats Conrad's novel as an example of a text that displays in theme and structure "this absence of origin, center, or end," and proceeds to demonstrate through a reading of it that no decisive or final interpretation is possible. /74/ Above all, when the novel is examined in terms of the structuring principles of temporal form, interpersonal relations, and the relations of imaginary and real (principles that Miller has developed in his *The Form of Victorian Fiction*), it reveals a Heideggerian openness of temporality, an unreliable narrator, and in the relations of imaginary to real "an ambiguity arising from the lack of a fixed point of reference" even in what look at first like unequivocal binary oppositions. /75/

One might object that Miller does not involve structuralism sufficiently in his analysis and that it is therefore not a true fusion of methods, yet it is clear from the context of the essay that he has structuralist techniques at hand as part of his interpretative method. If anything, his procedure, like Derrida's, is constructively critical of the presuppositions of both methods in order to make the methods more viable for application. His analysis reminds us of what both phenomenology and structuralism teach us: that difference, no matter how utterly other it may be, is already part of us—that we are, and exist in, a system of disparate elements. The literary critic who works with our two methods confirms the power of that difference but at the same time, in the act of interpretation, experiences the familiarity of his own creation.

B. Steps Toward Reconciliation: Summary and Example

Since this study has traversed an often confusing array of concepts and examples belonging to phenomenology and structuralism as literary critical methods, it may be helpful to conclude with a summary of the main traits of the two modes, stressing those that lead to a reconciliation. Then, out of the summary I will develop a series of steps that one might follow in actually applying a combination of the methods to the interpretation of a text. This strategy should not be construed as an effort to establish a critical formula, one that need only be superimposed on the text in order for a "correct" analysis to emerge. As we have seen, this is just the sort of misappropriation of their approaches that most phenomenologists and structuralists hope to avoid. My comments, rather, should aid in the creation of flexible, adaptable, and open-ended tactics, based on the precepts and practices of the two methods, that can produce a plenitude and depth of interpretation.

This reference to a desired richness of interpretation is a good place to begin my summary, for a number of critics we have discussed from both orientations have emphasized the goal of opening up the text to a wealth of interpretive possibilities. The text for the phenomenologist is seen as a starting point for the exploration of the endless variety of the experience of consciousness that must be grasped, somehow, in the very fullness of its potential, while for the structuralist the text is the nexus of an enormously complicated linguistic and social process that must also be delineated in a way that does not minimize the complexity. This opening-up to a richness of interpretation is achieved by both phenomenologists and structuralists through a kind of paradox. For Merleau-Ponty, for example, the phenomenological reduction is a process of exclusion that liberates consciousness for its *essential* task of experiencing the world's fullness, while for Barthes, structuralist criticism, with its many categories, does not limit the text but aligns it to participation in the world's discourse. These attempts to provide plenitude do not yield breadth at the expense of depth, for the phenomenological and structuralist critics are capable of as intense and exacting an analysis as the formalists. The difference is that the phenomenologist or structuralist does not view his interpretation as definitive or as part of an effort to produce a definitive interpretation. Rather, he suggests that his elucidation is merely one way to engage in the game of interpretation.

To speak of interpretation as a game leads to the second trait evidenced by practitioners of the two methods, their desire to challenge not only the goals of interpretation but also the presuppositions of the interpretive act. They question the assumption that one knows what the context and process of interpretation are, and they are skeptical about the analyst's ability ever to express fully and clearly his findings or even to be fully aware of what he wishes to utter. Thus they shift the emphasis from the text to the "pre-text," from descriptions of the technique of interpretation to questions about the analyst's readiness and ability to interpret. This new self-consciousness regarding the analyst's preparation for interpretation circumvents the tenets of scientific objectivity and raises doubts about the usefulness of the empirical process (based on verification of a theory through experimentation) for the *human* sciences and about the competence of the analyst for employing that process.

Although this skepticism began with Husserl's involvement in an exact science (mathematics), it was intensified by the existentialist strain of phenomenology, mainly as revealed in critics with strong hermeneutical biases from Heidegger to Ricoeur; yet it is also active among the structuralists, even though they have been accused, on occasion, of practicing a hyper-rationalist methodology. Lévi-Strauss' endorsement of a *bricolage* approach to problem-solving, for instance, runs counter to conventional attitudes of empiricism, and Derrida's vast project for recasting Western metaphysics, grounded at least partially on structuralism, is an embodiment of an enduring skeptical moment. To call interpretation a game, therefore, is to grant a certain amount of gratuitousness as necessary for the interpretive act, also to grant the need for freeplay and even capriciousness in hermeneutical attitudes and practices because the analyst remains fundamentally unsure of his premises. The stress on competence that occupied Merleau-Ponty toward the end of his life, as part of a strategy intended to reconcile phenomenology and structuralism, is instructive in this connection; to see man as constantly, creatively organizing and reorganizing the network of systems of which he is a part is to recognize the game-like quality of all interpretation, textual and otherwise: one plays out various possibilities—one interprets—as a way of discovering the bases of one's awareness and the limits of possibility.

A third trait of the two methods, one that expresses further the dissatisfaction with an empirical approach, is the search for an original perspective. One discovers it first in Husserl's *Zurückfragen,* the incessant questioning-back that occurs through the reductions and jettisons all the excess baggage of the descriptive process. One sees it in Poulet's disclosures of the bared creative consciousness of the literary artists he examines, and one sees it in the structuralist stress on the meanings to be extricated from the deep structure of a text, object, or event. Important is the structuralist qualification that the original perspective can never be an absolute perspective, that the questioning-back is endless and reveals finally not a primordial "truth" but rather the possibility of transposing the ultimately-reduced entity into another context, another dimension: everything is infinitely variable. An original perspective, then, is not one that can ever help to constitute the *ab*original perspective, for there is no such thing. It is original only in the sense that it is the individual's *own* perspective, distorted as little as possible by the prior interpretation or interpretive methods of others. What keeps this kind of original perspective from becoming a hermetic element of individual subjectivity is precisely its quality of communicability; something commonly recognizable adheres to the most unique of perspectives and gives it comprehensible expression. Thus the perspective that the phenomenologist and structuralist strive for is the one that offers the most difference while remaining communicable. This intense and variable difference is central because no absolute core of common identity is recognized that could be recovered or reconstructed. Practitioners of the two methods therefore seek to adopt original perspectives that produce original perceptions, perceptions of difference; these in turn do not cohere into a "world view" but contribute instead toward the opposite, toward the recognition that one's view or grasp of the world is never encompassing enough to permit an overview to form.

A fourth trait of the two methods is one that prevents its users from falling prey to vertigo in our relativized "semiological age." Both approaches are vitally linked to language and linguisticality. In the sketch of structuralism we have marked the predominance of the linguistic model. The nature and structure of language as described by Saussure and his successors constitute the semiotic system that provides the paradigm for textual interpretation, for comprehending social structures and customs (Lévi-Strauss, Barthes), the structure of the unconscious (Lacan), for treating neurological problems and mental illness (Jakobson, Lacan), and even for shaping an ontology (Barthes). But we have also observed the phenomenologist focus on language: Heidegger, Sartre, Bultmann, Ingarden, Gadamer, Ricoeur have all, for example, dealt with the centrality of the word and of discourse. Language is so basic to the critical enterprise of both approaches, in fact, that it sometimes functions in a curious metaphoric sense. Structuralists especially refer to the "language" of the unconscious, phenomenologists to the "language" of gesture or the "language" of play.

In circumstances where one examines the experiencing of phenomena rather than the causal universe, or where one grants the loss of the "absolute signified," language itself becomes the surrogate absolute, and the linguisticality of existence becomes central. The phenomenological implications of this are evident in

Ricoeur's theory that "the symbol gives rise to thought": primeval human nature (for Ricoeur consisting of a fundamental brokenness seeking wholeness) strives to express its condition and its hope in utterance, so that the very grammatical and semantic aspects of language embody the original human condition. The structuralist implications are present in Jakobson's theory of metonymy and metaphor: the discovery of basic linguistic units of similarity and difference (phonemes, morphemes, etc.) and their intricate interplay that causes language to function, and the projection of these operations into larger units of discourse (including literary expression) form the model for essentially non-linguistic studies, so that they become "metalinguistic" systems, and reality is thus described in analogical linguistic terms.

Further, the designation of language as a code, favored by the structuralists, suggests the concept of the double function of language endorsed also by the phenomenologists. It is a code in that it acts as a shorthand for expressing the immensely rich and manifold experience of reality that cannot be expressed in its immediate fullness. Implicit in this view is the sense of language as a secondary element in the service of a greater, primary reality. But language as code can also mean that it takes the chaotic, unformed, and primitive stuff of existence and shapes it into rich and meaningful experience. Implicit in this view is the sense of language as the primary, creative reality that gives life to inchoate thereness. This double function is, of course, still another way of stating the metonymic and metaphoric qualities of language. Language as shorthand is metonymic, an extension of the significant already-there. Language as creative force is metaphoric, a conferring of significance upon what is merely there.

How these two qualities of language interact becomes apparent in a consideration of a fifth trait of phenomenology and structuralism as we have studied them; they emphasize not only the text, the written form of discourse, but also the crucial relationship of author, reader, and text to each other in the act of interpreting the text. The text is considered not so much a finished aesthetic object as it is one component of the total act of interpretation, and this act, in turn, contributes to establishing the world of discourse. The text exists not merely to be interpreted; it is itself already an interpretation by the author and awaits another interpretation by the reader. All of this is in keeping with the insistence that one can reach no original perspective; one can only add to the history of interpretation already established. Thus author and reader are placed in new roles.

The phenomenologists especially have emphasized the responsibility of the reader to work through the text in order to expose, as clearly as possible, the author's life-world and thereby to grasp the process of literary creation as one way of coming to consciousness—although this is not the accent of the Ingarden-Dufrenne "school." The structuralists have stressed the reader's task as that of comprehending the text as part of the total system of discourse, as modelled on the analysis of the smaller linguistic units and projecting the possibility of identifying and categorizing ever larger units for analysis; ideally, we should be able to "read" metalinguistic systems (after identifying them as such) such as socio-cultural constructs, as large and complicated texts. Oversimplifying, one could say that the phenomenological interpretive effort is largely metaphoric, insofar as it encourages the reader to use the text as a way of disclosing the author's *creating* consciousness, for this task consists of naming the elements of a system in the process of infinite generation, the system of consciousness, and hence is a task aligned to difference. The structuralist effort is mainly metonymic, insofar as it asks the reader to place the text in the context of the established linguistic system (even though the assertion that such a system exists is a metaphoric statement!), and hence is aligned to sameness. Further, the structuralist tendency to dismiss the subject does not mean that the author is totally ignored in the interpretive act. He is at least implicitly present as the speaker, or voice, or "I," as a rhetorical component of the text which, because of its capacity for disguises, must be taken very seriously by the reader. And in tracking down the "I" of the text the reader finds himself involved in the experience of searching for the elusive original perspective. Just as that perspective always slides toward transposition into another, so also the "I" of the text becomes translatable into endless modulations of consciousness or language.

A sixth characteristic of both methods is the centrality of a reductive step in the interpretive process. We have observed through Holenstein's comparison of Husserl and Jakobson the similarity of and difference between the phenomenological reduction and structuralist coding. Both seek to distill the minimal identifying elements from the object or experience under scrutiny, but whereas the phenomenologist then organizes these elements into a description that necessitates new vocabulary, i.e., new language, the structuralist arranges them according to a pre-established linguistic pattern. Moreover, the structuralist resists the radical step that the phenomenologist takes when he isolates himself from all other interpretive influences. At this point the structuralist is more open to the world, for he does not try to deny its constantly impinging impressions on him but instead tries to translate these systematically into linguistic terms. Yet for this reason also he does not "leave" the world and therefore interprets mainly in a manner metonymic of and contiguous with the world's discourse. Since the phenomenologist brackets the world and attempts to "leave" it temporarily, he breaks contact with it and must re-establish a relationship with it metaphorically.

According to the phenomenologists, the structuralist failure to set aside the world means that interpretation, in the hermeneutical sense of the word, never occurs, only a preliminary and preparatory kind of explanation. The structuralist takes no risks, no imaginative leap, and thus cannot offer interpretive news. According to the structuralists, the phenomenologist in practicing the epoché indulges in an exercise of negation that, if taken to its conclusion, must lead to silence and paralysis, for he abandons the only conceivable framework of thought and discourse: one cannot conceptualize in a vacuum. Both Ricoeur and Derrida have suggested ways past this confrontation. Ricoeur has, in effect, shifted the reductive process to another level, from the semiotic to the semantic, and declared that on this level interpretation (the creation of meaning) occurs through the play of metaphor on the basis of already secured (on the semiotic level) linguistic signs. In other words, the reduction, consisting of a concentration on metaphor to discover difference, does not occur until similarity has already been confirmed through linguistic analysis. Derrida, on the other hand, argues that a truly radical reduction has not yet been undertaken, that as long as one does not forgo the whole metaphysics of presence and attempt to describe reality in terms of absence, both the phenomenological and structuralist projects are self-deceiving. For him, therefore, the epoché is a condition for interpretation that must be total and permanent. As we have noticed, references to absence and to metaphors of absence are typical of both phenomenological and structuralist commentary. Images of silence, empty space, suspended time or timelessness, the void, disappearance, waiting, and death appear frequently and convey the combined sense of negation and anticipation that marks the reductive act.

A seventh trait of phenomenological and structuralist methodology is the stress on exchange, interchange, and transformation. We have seen these operations explained and illustrated largely in the structuralist context: in Jakobson's transposition of his linguistic communications formula into poetics, Lévi-Strauss' elaborate system of societal trades exemplified in the modulations of binary oppositions in "primitive" myths, Barthes' interchange of five voices in *S/Z* that dominates his reading of *Sarrasine,* Marin's ingenious transformation of toponyms in his *Sémiotique de la Passion.* But one can discover a similar process at work among the phenomenologists, although they have not drawn explicit attention to it. Ingarden's identification of four interacting strata that form the structure of the text according to his *The Literary Work of Art* is an example of a phenomenological use of interchange. Sartre's theory of the paradoxical creation of existential meaning from nothingness indicates a radical transformational process; and the attempts of Gadamer and

Ricoeur to break free of the hermeneutic circle involve a daring exchange of perspective that puts the interpreter in the position conventionally occupied by the text and the text in the position of the interpreter: one asks to be interpreted by the text. But the tactic of exchange and transformation in both methods assumes meaning only when one realizes what it tries to effect—namely, the interpreter's experience and communication of otherness. This means an effort of the interpreter to put himself in the place of someone or something else, both without losing his own identity or harming the identity of the entity that he wishes to experience.

In a sense, the whole interpretive project of both methods—as of most interpretive designs—is to know and transmit otherness, for self and world enlarging acts occur only through an encounter with otherness, or in the now familiar term, with difference. What distinguishes phenomenology and structuralism from many other critical methods in this regard is that they seek more rigorously to avoid violating the integrity of that otherness, whatever it may be, in the process of making contact with it. Phenomenologists especially have been careful to protect the self-identity of the phenomena they address, whereas the structuralists, for example through the step of "deconstructing" a text, sometimes impair the intactness of the phenomena while trying to convey their alterity. On the whole, however, neither approach displays an "imperialistic" attitude; neither wishes to absorb or control the entity it studies but rather to present and represent it to the self and the world.

The importance placed on a special kind of transformation constitutes the final trait of the two methods that I will describe. It is the transformation of experience into language, or of an object into a linguistic message. If we consider this stated the first way, as turning experience into language, it does not seem extraordinary, for this is the kind of articulation that we all perform constantly. But formulated the second way, as turning an object into a message, it assumes a startling novelty, for it implies that language possesses a powerful nihilating tendency (obliterating the object by changing it into a message) and projects its own ontology (translating objects into symbols of itself—of language—instead of vice versa). In Barthes' *S/Z* but particularly in Marin's "women at Jesus' tomb" analysis one finds illustrations of this dual transformational capacity. Marin argues that the New Testament sequence, from the women discovering Jesus' body missing from the tomb to the formulation, "the Lord is risen," is a clear case of the desire for a lost object changed into a linguistic message, just as the empty sign of semiology is filled by the self-referential meaning of the linguistic process itself.

Jameson explains this transformational maneuver among the structuralists along psychoanalytical lines: the lost object and the message about it represent lack and desire operative in the human personality and symbolized in the Freudian imagery of castration and narcissism. Such explanation, however, does not satisfy the phenomenologists, who also deal with this transformation but in a different way. Ricoeur, who rejects Marin's analysis of the tomb narrative as anti-hermeneutic, states that what is important in such transformations is the appearance of the speaker (or narrator), who shifts the mere semiotic existence of the experience or object to the semantic level and provides the experience or object with meaning. This kind of shift is illustrated in Brodtkorb's Melville study and Halliburton's Poe analysis. The narrators of *Moby Dick* and "The Fall of the House of Usher" indeed transform lost objects (crew, ship, whale; house, inhabitants) into linguistic messages about the loss, but the resultant emphasis is not on linguistic self-referentiality (i.e., not on the poetic function of language as Jakobson has defined it) but on how the loss conveyed in the message affects the narrator. Whereas for the structuralists the transformation is a confirmation of the linguistic orientation of existence, for the phenomenologists it is merely the start of a self and world transformation that must proceed in a *kerygmatic* way—through language, to be sure, but language that wishes to express not just itself but what has not yet been uttered. For the structuralists, such transformation shows that language embodies an ontology.

For the phenomenologists, it shows that language bodies forth an ontology to be developed.

As this summary has revealed, even where the two methods show similar traits, these are often based on different presuppositions and intend different effects. This circumstance raises the question of how to undertake the final task of suggesting certain practical steps to follow in applying the methods to textual interpretation. Without wishing to infer that serious difficulties do not remain between the two approaches, I propose nevertheless to delineate steps in a way that will reveal how one can alternate and interrelate the methods rather than feeling constrained to choose one over the other or playing one off against the other. It will become clear immediately that most of these steps involve the cultivation of attitudes as much as the adoption of techniques.

1. First, if we accept the aim of both methods to provide a richness of interpretation, we must begin the textual study with an inventory, listing and examining the kinds of analysis that have already been applied to the text (assuming that it is one that has been previously analyzed). We may discover some approaches that claim exclusivity, but we do not discard these, for we are working in a spirit that encourages the mediation of contradictions.

2. Next, once we have completed the inventory of prior approaches to the text at hand, we consider how to engage in the "game" of interpretation, in order to remind ourselves that our task cannot be accomplished in the aura of scientific objectivity. This step also calls attention to the "pre-text," which is to say to the condition that obtains before interpretation begins and which confirms that we are concerned with our ability to comprehend the text and to express adequately what we comprehend. We create rules for the game by deciding which of the approaches from the inventory to incorporate into our analysis—which will

be compatible with our biases, or with the substance of our training, experience, and concerns. This step is not unlike Ricoeur's wager in *The Symbolism of Evil* (a wager is a kind of game): one commits oneself consciously to a particular compatible strategy out of many possibilities, in the faith that a strategy chosen that reflects one's beliefs will confront the problem of the hermeneutic circle and overcome it.

3. In our third step we seek to discover an original perspective that will be, we realize, not *ab*original but an individual expression of the combination of approaches we established in the second step. In other words, in the third step we begin our unique playing of the game according to the rules we have adopted. We do not, however, discover an original perspective and then interpret the text from this vantage point. Rather, in interpreting the text according to our creative play within the rules we shape an original perspective. This perspective is as much the result of interpretation as it is its inspiration.

4. Here we try to understand first, in the structuralist sense, how the text is contiguous with language *per se,* how it reflects in its construction the basic semiological operations. This step is somewhat like the first one, where we sought to relate the text preliminarily to the history of its interpretation, yet here we are trying to relate the text *qua* its linguistic composition to the "history," i.e., the evolved form of linguistic composition itself. Next we seek to grasp the difference of the text, in the phenomenological sense, from the linguistic pattern while granting the necessity of expressing this difference in linguistic form; we ascertain, that is to say, in what ways the text strives to expand the conventions of language or even to transcend the restrictions of language.

5. In this step we put the text "in its place" by reminding ourselves that is is only one component of the interpretive act that involves also the author and us as readers. We proceed in two ways, by trying to delineate the life-world of the author as it can be deduced from the imagery and action of the text, and by seeking to distinguish among the various forms of the "I" represented by author, implied author, narrator, and (other) characters. In both

instances we recognize the subjectivity of the author speaking through the text as object to our own subjectivity, and we respond in the awareness that our depiction of the author's life-world and the relationship among the forms of the "I" also reflects our efforts at self-identification.

6. In accomplishing the previous step we have already begun this one, which consists of engaging in the phenomenological reduction and in structuralist coding. Yet initially describing the author's life-world and the relationship among the forms of the "I" is only a small—if important—part of the procedure of each method that must be expanded and refined. It is true that the reduction and coding must be practiced in order to define the author's life-world and forms of the narrational "I," but such definition is not the primary aim of the reductive and coding processes. The goal of the phenomenological reduction is above all to grasp the essence of the text and simultaneously the essence of the interpretive act, both as ways of better understanding the experience of coming to consciousness. The goal of structuralist coding is to explode the text and the interpretive act into their basic constituent units and reconstruct the relationship among them in order to increase knowledge of the linguisticality of existence. Thus this step consists of carrying the reduction further, either by applying it to more components of the text to clarify the author's life-world and relate it better to our own, or by applying it for the same purpose, to other relevant texts (i.e., by the same author, on the same subject, etc.). This step consists also of developing the coding by identifying more "voices" that speak out of the text, relating them to their particular contexts in the extra-textual world, and then relating them to each other as a metalinguistic commentary *on* the text.

7.The seventh step involves the effort to preserve and convey alterity or otherness through the process of exchange and transformation. This is the core of the interpretive act: how can one transmit the experience of interpreting the text—itself an encounter with otherness—in a way that protects the integrity of the text as object, of one's experience of it, and of the audience to whom one wishes to offer the experience? The structuralist tactic (at least as Derrida may be said to represent it) at this point is to employ decentering, to argue that the text is never identical with its utterance and hence never reveals the full extent of its otherness. As a result, we can convey its otherness only by creating an approximation, a something other that reflects more or less efficiently the only partially comprehended otherness of the text. Or in Barthes' terms, we create a countertext that articulates by indirection the actual text. We plunge deeper into metaphor and re-present our experience of the text in imaginative terms inspired by the metaphors of the text. In a curious way this attempt continues the metonymic emphasis of structuralism, since we remain within the kind of linguisticality that constitutes the text.

The phenomenological strategy advocated by Ricoeur also involves model-building, yet not the creation of a countertext out of metaphor but a rearranging of the metaphors of the text in ways that do not challenge the *sense* of the utterance (the common recognition of sameness that makes communication possible at all) but that provide new *reference,* a reference that transcends the metaphors themselves by projecting an untranslatable otherness beyond language and linguisticality.

8. Our last step, then, is largely volitional. It consists of a final commentary on the text and on the experience of interpreting the text that can go in one of two directions. It can confirm the structuralist assertion that the linguisticality of existence is ultimate and that an ontology can be fashioned from the components already present in the incredibly rich and complex linguistic universe. Or it can express the phenomenological view that such linguisticality points to an experience of consciousness, relived here through the interpretaton of the text, that is beyond words, so that an ontology can be formed only kerygmatically—through language, to be sure, but a language that strives to become transparent to being. Either way, this step transforms the desire for the object into a message. The interpretive act concludes as a confession of how reality shall be joined.

I will clarify these steps further by suggesting how they could be applied to a specific narrative. The text I have selected is Herman Melville's well-known short story "Bartleby the Scrivener," first published in 1853, two years after the appearance of *Moby Dick*. /76/ The tale, subtitled "A Story of Wall Street," consists of a first-person narration by an elderly Manhattan lawyer who hires the mysterious Bartleby to copy legal documents. After an initial period of cooperation, Bartleby unaccountably refuses to continue his work as a scrivener, gradually turns totally recalcitrant and then passive, yet will not resign nor be fired and in fact refuses to leave the law office premises, even spending his nights and weekends there. After many attempts to reason with Bartleby and after many generous offers of assistance, the narrator in desperation moves his business to another location, leaving Bartleby in the abandoned quarters. Bartleby is soon evicted by the new tenant and sent off to prison as a vagrant. The lawyer-narrator visits Bartleby even in prison and tries to aid him, but Bartleby refuses all help and soon dies.

1. An inventory of interpretations of "Bartleby" (of which there have been many) would include at least three general categories: a) "historical" interpretations that attempt to identify Bartleby with some actual person known by Melville. It has even been argued that Henry David Thoreau served Melville as the model for the character of Bartleby; b) biographical and psychological interpretations that identify Bartleby with Melville himself as artist manqué, so that the story symbolizes Melville's refusal to return to writing successful adventure fiction (such as the novels *Typee* and *Omoo*) following the critics' condemnation of his new metaphysical mode displayed in *Moby Dick*. By extension, then, Bartleby-Melville becomes an archetype of the misunderstood American writer *per se* who abides by lofty but unpopular standards; c) existential interpretations that describe Bartleby variously as a symbol of alienated modern humanity, the rootless urban dweller, the victim of an absurd and nihilistic world, a schizoid personality, or (in combination with the narrator), a psychotic father-son relationship.

2. Such a plethora of interpretative possibilities would incite us to rethink the presuppositions of our hermeneutical effort. What are our capacities for understanding the story—and for expressing what we think we understand? What is the intentionality of this particular piece of fiction? Rather than posing as objective analysts, we would commit ourselves to "rules" aligned to our individual kind of preparation for interpretation that permit us to build on our strengths and compensate for our weaknesses. My own tendency would be to engage in a "game" that would take advantage of my training and experience in formalist explication and an interest—but less expertise—in the philosophical ramifications of a literary text. Thus I would begin with an intrinsic analysis of "Bartleby," paying close attention to matters of verbal texture and organizational structure in the hope of discovering ways of transforming my findings into statements of philosophical (more specifically "existential") meaning. I would not ignore historical, psychological, sociological, etc. insights, should they appear, but neither would I search intently for them.

3. The third step would involve a subtle shift of focus that generates another act of self-consciousness. We would seek to play a version of the interpretive game that makes it uniquely our own. In the context of the dense history of interpretation of "Bartleby," we would strive for an analysis that would be different from the manifold others, not merely in order to be different but to assert the right of saying something about Melville's tale that no one else has yet said. This right must be earned; we must indeed have something different to say, moreover something different enough that it is worth saying yet sufficiently plausible that we will be heard. Since we cannot know, however, if our interpretation is either valuably unique or plausible until we have composed it, we take the risk of searching for an original perspective that may produce at last something imitative or foolish. We may, in other words, play the game poorly. My inclination would be to examine the language of "Bartleby," of Melville's verbal style, for clues to the meaning of the protagonist's strange withdrawal. After all, his

refusal to write and then to speak is a problem of utterance—of language—as well as a symptom of the aggressive passivity of his whole being, and one should be able to find the reflexes of his withdrawal in Melville's own syntax and diction.

4. In our fourth step we would continue this concentration on language. First, from the structuralist perspective we would inquire into the strategy by which Melville constructs a pattern of fictive discourse from individual sentences as "little narratives." We might select what seem to be key paragraphs and deconstruct the sentences in them to show how linguistics serves as the basis of poetics. I would, for example, include among others an analysis of the story's initial paragraph, of one in mid-story (beginning with "Revolving all these things") on Bartleby's condition as existential illness, and of the paragraph comprising the coda. /77/ Next, from the phenomenological perspective we would trace the emergence of the poetics of the story from its linguistic foundation. In this emphasis on the evocative power of language we would show how the text projects more than it says, by examining the basic metaphoric qualities of the paragraphs already analyzed structurally.

5. Here we would supplement the syntactic and metaphoric analyses of selected passages with a consideration of the author's and narrator's involvement in the tale. We would study the lawyer's self-reflective statements, in contrast to his descriptions of his behavior with Bartleby, to learn how his "voice" shapes the identity that the author has created to speak to us and to which we respond. At this point we might also draw on historical and biographical-psychological approaches to "Bartleby," although some phenomenologists would reject this tactic as one that interferes with a legitimate disclosure of the author's life-world. We would wish, in any case, to describe the response of our own "I" to the inflections of the author's and narrator's voices. For example, I am intrigued by the lawyer's implicit reason for telling Bartleby's tale. As with Ishmael in *Moby Dick,* it seems to be a compulsion, brought on in this instance by the frustration of a still uncomprehended situation. Bartleby's life and death remain a

mystery to the narrator, suggesting that Melville chose to embody his view of life as enigma in such fictions. Further, the fact that I as reader am attracted to this particular aspect of voice in the story reveals to me my own modern sense of life as enigmatic.

6. The previous step already encourages the reader's understanding, through the interpretive act, of coming to consciousness that is the focus of the sixth step. We would continue this process by returning to a structuralist coding. I would apply a version of Lévi-Strauss' Oedipus analysis to the whole story, first dividing it into its three natural parts (the introduction of the lawyer's other employees, the long central section on Bartleby's withdrawal and its effects, and the final section on the lawyer's separation from Bartleby), locating common elements· in each (comparable to Lévi-Strauss' mythemes), and on the basis of these undertaking a "vertical" reading of the tale. I would agree with Ricoeur, however, that this exercise takes place on the semiological rather than on the semantic level and would therefore attempt next to transfer the structuralist reading into a phenomenological interpretation. Assuming, for example, that the vertical reading would uncover a stress on the binary oppositions of entrapment and escape, aggression and withdrawal, responsibility and neglect (these are not necessarily the pairs that would actually emerge), we would still need to rework them hermeneutically by re-examining them in the context of the reductions. The three pairs reduced eidetically might then reveal the story's essence as consisting of an emphasis on volition (one of the modes of consciousness registered by the phenomenologists) and language, specifically on the imagery of volition, while a second, transcendental reduction might lead to a consideration of how one's own volitional consciousness is animated by the language of poetic will such as this tale incarnates.

7. We could elaborate on the previous step by applying the reductive process to other components of "Bartleby" (for example, to the setting in order to study spatiality in the tale as another mode of consciousness) or to other fiction by Melville (for

example, to narratives treating his famous isolato theme), or we could approach the story from the perspective of other "codes," after the fashion of Barthes in *S/Z*. These would lead us directly to the seventh step, in which we would first decenter the "Bartleby" text by identifying key metaphors and molding them into a countertext that would comment on the original without impairing its fragile identity. For instance, the images of walls (also of doors and screens) that permeate the narrative and that usually connote separation and impenetrability could be reorganized into a commentary emphasizing the otherness of Bartleby, of the narrator's experience with him, and Melville's struggle to convey intact the meaning-laden alterity of his subject. We would, then, as part of this step, adopt the phenomenological scheme of allowing the text to interpret us—essentially an imaginative projection in which we use the "heuristic fiction" to clarify our reality. We might continue here with the metaphor of walls and try to articulate how the isolation and inscrutability that it carries instructs us on our modern sense of loneliness and the enigmatic. We would, in other words, ask how this metaphor as model of Melville's reality aids in a contemporary world disclosure.

8. We could show, finally, how "Bartleby" lends itself to both a concluding structuralist and phenomenological commentary. It effects a special kind of transformation, in the structuralist sense of turning an object into a message, through its emphasis on writing. More precisely, the scrivener's refusal to write, culminating in his death, impels the narrator to write about *him*. In a way, the story illustrates the nihilating force of language, for Bartleby's repudiation of writing—his vocation—and his reluctance even to speak are at last fatal. Particularly the eccentric epilogue, in which the narrator suggests that Bartleby was perhaps led to despair by his rumored earlier position in the Dead Letter Office in Washington, symbolizes the transformation of the desire for a lost object (the dead letter) into a message about the object, here the classical *memento mori:* "Dead letters! does it not sound like dead men?" /78/ In this way life is interpreted by the

metaphor of language and in the framework of a linguistic ontology. This bleak message we might reinterpret phenomenologically, in turn, in a kerygmatic manner. The narrator's final words are an apostrophic lament: "Ah, Bartleby! Ah, humanity!" /79/ They intimate a sorrow and bemusement beyond expression, and in such absence is where human discourse must struggle, paradoxically, to begin.

NOTES

/1/ Lévi-Strauss, *The Savage Mind*, pp. 245-69.

/2/ Sartre, in *L'Arc*, No. 30 (1966): 95.

/3/ The proceedings of the symposium at the Centre Cultural Internatonal de Ceresy-la-Salle are presented in J. Ricardou, ed., *Les Chemins actuels de la critique* (Paris: Plon, 1967). My information on this conference comes from Robert Magliola, "Parisian Structuralism Confronts Phenomenology: The Ongoing Debate," *Language and Style*, 6, No. 4 (Fall, 1973): 237-48. The proceedings of the Johns Hopkins symposium are presented in Richard Macksey and Eugenio Donato, eds., *The Structuralist Controversy: The Languages of Criticism and the Sciences of Man* (Baltimore: The Johns Hopkins University Press, 1970).

/4/ For example, Eugenio Donato in "Structuralism: The Aftermath," *Sub-Stance*, No. 7 (Fall, 1973), says that "today we may rightly question whether the concept of structuralism has any critical validity and whether such a thing as structuralism ever existed"(9).

/5/ Jonathan Culler, "Phenomenology and Structuralism," *The Human Context*, 5, No. 1 (Spring, 1973): 35-36.

/6/ Cf. J. Hillis Miller, "Geneva or Paris? The Recent Work of Georges Poulet."

/7/ Representative works by Derrida that have influenced American critics are *L'Écriture et la différence* (Paris: Seuil, 1967); *De la Grammatologie* (Paris: Minuit, 1967); *Speech and Phenomena and Other Essays on Husserl's Theory of Signs*, tr. David B. Allison (Evanston: Northwestern University Press, 1973). Cf. Paul de Man, "The Rhetoric of Blindness: Jacques Derrida's Reading of Rousseau," in de Man,

Blindness and Insight: Essays in the Rhetoric of Contemporary Criticism (New York: Oxford University Press, 1971); Geoffrey H. Hartman, *The Fate of Reading and Other Essays* (Chicago: University of Chicago Press, 1975); Joseph N. Riddel, *The Inverted Bell;* Edward W. Said, *Beginnings: Intention and Method* (New York: Basic Books, 1975).

/8/   Willis F. Overton, "General Systems, Structure and Development," in Klaus F. Riegel and George C. Rosenwald, eds., *Structure and Transformation: Developmental and Historical Aspects* (New York: Wiley, 1975), pp. 64-67.

/9/   Cf. Paul Ricoeur, Chapter I, "Hermeneutics and Structuralism," in Ihde, ed., *The Conflict of Interpretations.*

/10/   Cf. the *Semeia,* No. 4 (1975), issue on "Paul Ricoeur on Biblical Hermeneutics."

/11/   M. J. Peters, "Psychoanalysis, Structuralism and Consciousness," *The Human Context,* 5, No. 1 (Spring, 1973): 138-55.

/12/   Elmar Holenstein, "Jakobson and Husserl: A Contribution to the Genealogy of Structuralism," *The Human Context,* 7, No. 1 (Spring, 1975): 61-83. This essay is now a section (pp. 13-55) of a valuable book by Holenstein entitled *Linguistik, Semiotik, Hermeneutik: Plädoyers für eine strukturale Phänomenologie* (Frankfurt/Main: Suhrkamp Verlag, 1976). I regret that I did not have access to this text nor to Holenstein's earlier *Roman Jakobsons phänomenologischer Strukturalismus* (Frankfurt/Main: Suhrkamp Verlag, 1975).

/13/   Donald G. Marshall, "The Ontology of the Literary Sign: Notes toward a Heideggerian Revision of Semiology," *Boundary 2,* 4, No. 2 (Winter, 1976): 611-34.

/14/   *Ibid.,* 613.

/15/   *Ibid.,* 615.

/16/   *Ibid.,* 622.

/17/   *Ibid.,* 626.

/18/   *Ibid.,* 630.

/19/   Aron Gurwitsch, *The Field of Consciousness* (Pittsburgh: Duquesne University Press, 1964), pp. 36, 37-40. Gurwitsch is referring to Piaget's thought in his *The Origins of Intelligence in Children* (New York: Norton, 1963).

/20/   *Ibid.,* p. 40.

/21/   Aron Gurwitsch, *Studies in Phenomenology and Psychology* (Evanston: Northwestern University Press, 1966), pp. 386-89.

/22/   Edward W. Said, "Notes on the Characterization of a Literary Text," in Macksey, ed., *Velocities of Change*, pp. 32-35, 38-39.

/23/   David Funt, "Piaget and Structuralism," *Diacritics*, 1, No. 2 (Winter, 1971): 18-19. Cf. Jean Piaget, *Structuralism*, tr. Chaninah Maschler (New York: Basic Books, 1970).

/24/   *Ibid.*

/25/   Overton, "General Systems, Structure and Development," p. 65.

/26/   Culler, "Phenomenology and Structuralism," p. 35.

/27/   *Ibid.* Cf. also James M. Edie, "Was Merleau-Ponty a Structuralist?" *Semiotica*, 4 (1971): 297-323.

/28/   Jameson, *The Prison-House of Language*, p. 151. Richard L. Lanigan, *Speaking and Semiology* (The Hague: Mouton, 1972), p. 193, also calls attention to Merleau-Ponty's incipient involvement in structuralism: "Although Merleau-Ponty relies on the basic structuralist schema of the De Saussure semiology, his theory of existential speaking is a major progression beyond De Saussure by an incorporation of Husserl and an interpretation of the Heideggerian metaphysics."

/29/   Maurice Merleau-Ponty, *Le Visible et l'invisible* (Paris: Gallimard, 1965), p. 277. Culler quotes this passage in "Phenomenology and Structuralism," 38. "Intersection" is my term for Ricoeur's and Culler's *entrecroisement*.

/30/   Cf. Culler, "Phenomenology and Structuralism," 38.

/31/   Paul Ricoeur, "Structure, Word, Event," tr. Robert Sweeney, in *The Conflict of Interpretations*, p. 79. Since my completion of this study Ricoeur has published an important book entitled *Interpretation Theory: Discourse and the Surplus of Meaning* (Fort Worth: The Texas Christian University Press, 1976). I regret that I did not have access to this text, since it contains material that would have influenced my analysis here.

/32/   *Ibid.*, p. 89.

/33/   Culler, *Structuralist Poetics*, pp. 26-27.

/34/   "Lived experience" is my translation of *l'expérience vécue*. Cf. Culler, "Phenomenology and Structuralism," 41.

/35/   Culler, "Phenomenology and Structuralism," 41; Jameson, *Prison-House*, p. 216.

/36/   Cf. Jameson, *Prison-House*, pp. 215-16.

/37/   Paul Ricoeur, "The Question of the Subject: The Challenge of Semiology," tr. Kathleen McLaughlin, in *The Conflict of Interpretations*, pp. 236-66.

/38/   *Ibid.*, p. 256.

/39/   *Ibid.*

/40/   *Ibid.*, p. 259.

/41/   *Ibid.*, p. 262.

/42/   *Ibid.*, p. 266.

/43/   Cf. Gras, *European Literary Theory*, p. 13.

/44/   *Ibid.*, pp. 13-14.

/45/   David Funt, "The Structuralist Debate," *The Hudson Review*, 22, No. 4 (Winter, 1969-70), has a helpful summary of Ricoeur's dialogue with structuralism on 641-42.

/46/   Paul Ricoeur, "Biblical Hermeneutics," *Semeia*, No. 4 (1975): pp. 29-148.

/47/   *Ibid.*, 54.

/48/   *Ibid.*, 61, 62.

/49/   *Ibid.*, 63. Marin's essay is "Les femmes au tombeau. Essai d'analyse structurale d'une texte évangélique," *Langages*, 22 (June, 1971): 39-50.

/50/   *Ibid.*, 72.

/51/   *Ibid.*, 75-106.

/52/   *Ibid.*, 75.

/53/   *Ibid.*, 78.

/54/   *Ibid.*, 79.

/55/   *Ibid.*, 79-80.

/56/   *Ibid.*, 87.

/57/   *Ibid.*, 88. Michel van Esbroeck's *Herméneutique, structuralisme et exégèse, essai de logique kérygmatique* (Paris: Desclée, 1968), an attempt to reconcile Ricoeur's hermeneutics with Lévi-Strauss' structuralism through the material of Henri de Lubac's *Exégèse Médiévale,* should be mentioned. According to Esbroeck, Lubac's exhaustive study of the medieval exegetes shows that their fourfold method—the historical, allegorical, tropological (moral), and anagogical (eschatological) senses—has startling similarities to the problematics of both phenomenology as Ricoeur practices it and Lévi-Strauss' structuralism and can bring the two methods closer together. Esbroeck calls his study an "attempt at kerygmatic logic"; he wishes to maintain the element of personal faith implicit in kerygmatic preaching while simultaneously examining the structure of that faith in the context of the church and the unbelieving community. Ricoeur, he says, confirms the decisive meaning of kerygmatic confession but does not explain it structurally, for it contains a moment of the speaker (the confessor) reaching out toward the meaning of Christ the symbol (seeking to bring *parole* and *langue* together) that cannot be analyzed. Lévi-Strauss, for his part, perceives the confession as structure but does not heed the call to decision; he remains the observer, forever outside the system he examines, deaf personally to the spoken word of faith, and hence the kerygma is no longer genuine kerygma, for it loses its sacrificial dimension. In this hiatus, Esbroeck sees his study, with its appropriation of Lubac, as an expression of faith uttered from the interior of a social-historical framework that speaks to Ricoeur in support of a specific tradition (a *parole*) within the truth of a general symbol system (*langue*) and to Lévi-Strauss as a kind of thought situated structurally within a sociological totality that confirms the validity of the universal structural model. Since Esbroeck's study does not undertake textual analysis, I have not addressed myself to it in my discussion of the two methods.

/58/   Derrida's criticism of Husserl occurs in his *Speech and Phenomena;* his criticism of Lévi-Strauss occurs in *De la Grammatologie.*

/59/   J. Hillis Miller, "Deconstructing the Deconstructers," *Diacritics,* 5, No. 2 (Summer, 1975): 24-31; Culler, *Structuralist Poetics;* Jameson, *The Prison-House of Language;* Funt, "Piaget and Structuralism"; John P. Leavey, Jr., "Undecidables and Old Names: Derrida's Deconstruction and Introduction to Husserl's *The Origin of Geometry"* (doctoral dissertation, Graduate Institute of the Liberal Arts, Emory University, 1976) have been very helpful to me for my discussion of Derrida.

/60/   For this discussion I have used Jacques Derrida, "Freud and the Scene of Writing," tr. Jeffrey Mehlman, in Mehlman, ed., *French Freud:* 73-117. The essay is a section of *L'Écriture et la différence.*

/61/   Jameson, *Prison-House,* p. 175.

/62/   Funt, "Piaget and Structuralism," 18.

/63/   *Ibid.,* 16.

/64/   Mehlman, Introductory Note to "Freud and the Scene of Writing," 73.

/65/   The concept of the collision of matrices comes from Arthur Koestler's *The Act of Creation* (New York: Macmillan, 1964). Cf. Chapter I, "The Logic of Laughter."

/66/   Ricoeur, "Biblical Hermeneutics," 80.

/67/   Cf. Chapter III, n. 4.

/68/   Via, *Kerygma and Comedy in the New Testament,* xi.

/69/   Miller, "Deconstructing the Deconstructers," 28. Riddel has replied to
Miller in "A Miller's Tale," *Diacritics,* 5, No. 3 (Fall, 1975): 56-65. His response is
instructive for those wishing to reconcile phenomenology and structuralism.

/70/   Roger C. Poole, "Structuralism and Phenomenology: A Literary
Approach," *Journal of the British Society for Phenomenology,* 2 (1971): 10.

/71/   *Ibid.,* 15.

/72/   J. Hillis Miller, "The Interpretation of Lord Jim," *Harvard English
Studies,* No. 1: *The Interpretation of Narrative: Theory and Practice,* ed. Morton W.
Bloomfield (Cambridge: Harvard University Press, 1970).

/73/   *Ibid.,* pp. 211-12.

/74/   *Ibid.,* p. 213.

/75/   *Ibid.,* p. 224.

/76/   Herman Melville, "Bartleby the Scrivener", in Jay Leyda, ed., *The
Complete Stories of Herman Melville* (New York: Random House, 1949), pp. 3-47.

/77/   *Ibid.,* pp. 3, 24, 46.

/78/   *Ibid.,* p. 46.

/79/   *Ibid.,* p. 47.

INDEX

219

224